PAOLO PORTOGHESI

Series Editors: Tom Avermaete and Janina Gosseye

The Modern Movement was a broad and multifaceted phenomenon which revolutionized the field of architecture. During the twentieth century, modern architects across political, cultural, and geographic divides radically changed the everyday lives of millions of people. However, our knowledge of the Modern Movement remains largely limited to the names of a few famed designers.

Bloomsbury Studies in Modern Architecture sheds light on those modern architects who have languished in the shadows of their canonical peers. Placing particular emphasis on the way in which these architects defined the relationship between architecture and modernity in their respective political, cultural, and geographic contexts, this series seeks to construct a more nuanced and fine-grained understanding of the Modern Movement, and the global networks that underwrote it.

Previous titles in the series:

Ernesto Nathan Rogers, Maurizio Sabini

Sibyl Moholy-Nagy, Hilde Heynen

Kay Fisker, Martin Søberg

Karl Langer, edited by Deborah van der Plaat and John Macarthur

John Dalton, Elizabeth Musgrave

Ludwig Hilberseimer, Scott Colman

Forthcoming titles in the series:

Esguerra Sáenz Urdaneta Samper, edited by Maarten Goossens, Hernando Vargas Caicedo and Catalina Parra

PAGON, by Espen Johnsen

PAOLO PORTOGHESI

Architecture between history, politics and media

Silvia Micheli and Léa-Catherine Szacka

BLOOMSBURY VISUAL ARTS
LONDON • NEW YORK • OXFORD • NEW DELHI • SYDNEY

BLOOMSBURY VISUAL ARTS
Bloomsbury Publishing Plc, 50 Bedford Square, London, WC1B 3DP, UK
Bloomsbury Publishing Inc, 1385 Broadway, New York, NY 10018, USA
Bloomsbury Publishing Ireland, 29 Earlsfort Terrace, Dublin 2, D02 AY28, Ireland

BLOOMSBURY, BLOOMSBURY VISUAL ARTS and the Diana logo are trademarks of Bloomsbury Publishing Plc

First published in Great Britain 2023
Paperback edition published 2025

Copyright © Silvia Micheli and Léa-Catherine Szacka, 2023

Silvia Micheli and Léa-Catherine Szacka have asserted their right under the Copyright, Designs and Patents Act, 1988, to be identified as Authors of this work.

For legal purposes the Acknowledgements on p. xiv constitute an extension of this copyright page.

Cover design: Eleanor Rose

All rights reserved. No part of this publication may be: i) reproduced or transmitted in any form, electronic or mechanical, including photocopying, recording or by means of any information storage or retrieval system without prior permission in writing from the publishers; or ii) used or reproduced in any way for the training, development or operation of artificial intelligence (AI) technologies, including generative AI technologies. The rights holders expressly reserve this publication from the text and data mining exception as per Article 4(3) of the Digital Single Market Directive (EU) 2019/790.

Bloomsbury Publishing Plc does not have any control over, or responsibility for, any third-party websites referred to or in this book. All internet addresses given in this book were correct at the time of going to press. The author and publisher regret any inconvenience caused if addresses have changed or sites have ceased to exist, but can accept no responsibility for any such changes.

A catalogue record for this book is available from the British Library.

A catalogue record for this book is available from the Library of Congress.
Library of Congress Cataloging-in-Publication Data
Names: Micheli, Silvia, author. | Szacka, Léa-Catherine, author.
Title: Paolo Portoghesi : architecture between history, politics and media / Silvia Micheli and Léa-Catherine Szacka.
Description: London : Bloomsbury Visual Arts, 2023. | Series: Bloomsbury studies in modern architecture | Includes bibliographical references and index. | Contents: The postmodern project—Turn to history—Socialism for freedom—Embracing mass media—Epilogue.
Identifiers: LCCN 2023000459 (print) | LCCN 2023000460 (ebook) | ISBN 9781350117136 (hardback) | ISBN 9781350408616 (paperback) | ISBN 9781350117143 (pdf) | ISBN 9781350117150 (epub) | ISBN 9781350117167
Subjects: LCSH: Portoghesi, Paolo--Criticism and interpretation.
Classification: LCC NA1123.P67 M53 2023 (print) | LCC NA1123.P67 (ebook) | DDC 720.92--dc23/eng/20230222
LC record available at https://lccn.loc.gov/2023000459
LC ebook record available at https://lccn.loc.gov/2023000460

ISBN: HB: 978-1-3501-1713-6
PB: 978-1-3504-0861-6
ePDF: 978-1-3501-1714-3
eBook: 978-1-3501-1715-0

Series: Bloomsbury Studies in Modern Architecture

Typeset by RefineCatch Limited, Bungay, Suffolk

For product safety related questions contact productsafety@bloomsbury.com.

To find out more about our authors and books visit www.bloomsbury.com and sign up for our newsletters.

CONTENTS

List of illustrations vii
Series preface xi
Acknowledgements xiv

INTRODUCTION 1

Italian postmodern architecture revisited 3
State of the art 6
Methodology and sources 9
Structure 11
Setting the scene 13

1 THE POSTMODERN PROJECT 21

Impresario of postmodern architecture 22
Choosing Rossi 28
Mendini and the Banal 34
Ideological duel with Tafuri 37
Beyond Italy 42
Galleria Apollodoro, a centre for Roman culture 48

2 TURN TO HISTORY 55

Architect as historian/historian as architect 57
Neoliberty polemic 61
Instrumental value of the past 63
Technique of lap dissolves 67
Geometria borrominiana 70
Casa Baldi, or the rehabilitation of the curve 76

3 SOCIALISM FOR FREEDOM 89

   Rise and leadership of the PSI 90
   Years of the protests 93
   Craxismo and the end of prohibitionism 100
   Staging the PSI 104
   Control over the lagoon 110
   The Mosque of Rome, between religion and oil 115

4 EMBRACING MASS MEDIA 123

   Mediatization of the building 124
   Ars oratoria 127
   Through the pages of the magazines 129
   Architecture on the dance floor 135
   From movie protagonist to stage set 140
   Casa Papanice framed by the camera 142

EPILOGUE 151

   1992 *Annus horribilis* 154
   Retreat to Calcata 156

CODA 161

   By Maristella Casciato

Notes 165
Bibliography 195
Index: Paolo's world 209

LIST OF ILLUSTRATIONS

Cover image Paolo Portoghesi holding his Hasselblad camera in the Sacra Familia Church, Fratte, Salerno, *c.* mid-1970s, © Paolo Portoghesi Archive

I.1	Paolo Portoghesi, dean of the Faculty of Architecture at the Politecnico di Milano, in 1970	1
I.2	Paolo Portoghesi during a postmodern gathering in Chicago, 1982	5
I.3	Paolo Portoghesi's low-angled shot photograph of the Chapel of the Holy Shroud by Guarino Guarino in Turin	11
I.4	Paolo Portoghesi with his parents at Salzburg Castle, *c.* 1957	14
I.5	Frontispiece of the handmade book *Paolo Portoghesi: Di Francesco Borromini*, written by young Portoghesi in 1946	15
I.6	Paolo Portoghesi's photograph of the hall of the ENPAS Office building, Florence	18
I.7	Paolo Portoghesi's low-angled shot photograph of the ENPAS Office building, Lucca	19
1.1	Cover of issue 652 of *Domus*, July/August 1984, portraying Paolo Portoghesi	21
1.2	Paolo Portoghesi in San Francisco for the opening of the itinerant exhibition *The Presence of the Past* at the Fort Mason, 1982	23
1.3	Paolo Portoghesi presenting the *New Dictionary of Architecture and Urbanism* to the president of the Italian Republic, Giuseppe Saragat, in Rome, 1970	27
1.4	Cover of the architectural magazine *Controspazio*, issue 10, 1970, dedicated to Aldo Rossi	30
1.5	Paolo Portoghesi and Aldo Rossi on a water taxi following the Teatro del Mondo on its way from Fusina to the Bacino di San Marco, Venice, 1979	32
1.6	Entrance to the Arsenale with the gate (Porta) designed by Aldo Rossi for the exhibition *The Presence of the Past*, Venice, 1979	33
1.7	Exhibition *L'oggetto banale* curated by Alessandro Mendini, Paola Navone, Daniela Puppa and Franco Raggi, included in *The Presence of the Past*, Venice Biennale, 1980	36

1.8	Christian Norberg-Schulz visiting Paolo Portoghesi in Calcata	44
1.9	Gathering at the opening of the exhibition *Roma Interrotta*, in front of the Nolli's map at the Mercati Traianei, Rome, 1978	46
1.10	Invitation letter to take part in the organization of the First International Architecture Exhibition of the Venice Biennale sent by Paolo Portoghesi to Charles Jencks, 1979	47
1.11	Paolo Portoghesi and Giovanna Massobrio at the drafting table in their office, 1970s	49
1.12	Gate of the Galleria Apollodoro in Rome, designed by Paolo Portoghesi with Giovanna Massobrio	51
1.13	Gate signage of the Galleria Apollodoro in Rome, designed by Paolo Portoghesi with Giovanna Massobrio	52
1.14	Paolo Portoghesi with Francesco Cossiga, at the exhibition *Aci e Galatea* by Marco Rossati, at the Galleria Apollodoro, Rome, 1988	53
2.1	Photographic portrait of Paolo Portoghesi and Giovanna Massobrio in their residence in the Torrino di via di Porta Pinciana, Rome, 1971	55
2.2	View of the homage to Mario Ridolfi, *The Presence of the Past*, Venice Biennale, 1980	56
2.3	Cover of Paolo Portoghesi's foundational book *Borromini nella cultura europea*, 1964	59
2.4	Paolo Portoghesi introducing the then president of the Italian Republic, Giovanni Gronchi, at the opening of the *Mostra critica delle opere michelangiolesche*, Palazzo delle Esposizioni, Rome, 1964. © Paolo Portoghesi Archive	65
2.5	Example of the lap dissolve technique applied to Sant'Ivo alla Sapienza and Casa Baldi, included in Paolo Portoghesi's book *Le inibizioni dell'architettura moderna*, 1974	68
2.6	Panel G – S. Ivo 1, from the section 'La geometria borrominiana', in *Borromini nella cultura europea*, 1964	74
2.7	Panel H – S. Ivo 1, from the section 'La geometria borrominiana', in *Borromini nella cultura europea*, 1964	74
2.8	Casa Baldi during construction works, Rome, 1960	77
2.9	Casa Baldi, detail of the corner	79
2.10	Geometrical construction of the plan for Casa Andreis in Scandriglia	82
2.11	Geometrical drawing of the plan for Casa Andreis in Scandriglia, by studio Portoghesi-Gigliotti, *c.* mid-1960s	82
2.12	Plan of Casa Andreis in Scandriglia, by studio Portoghesi-Gigliotti, *c.* mid-1960s	83
2.13	View of Casa Bevilacqua, looking onto the maritime landscape	84
2.14	Study plan for the Sacra Familia Church, Fratte, Salerno, *c.* mid-1970s, by studio Portoghesi-Gigliotti	84
2.15	Geometrical drawing of the plan for the Sacra Familia Church, Fratte, Salerno, *c.* mid-1970s, by studio Portoghesi-Gigliotti	85

2.16	Interiors of the Sacra Familia Church, Fratte, Salerno, *c.* mid-1970s	85
3.1	Bettino Craxi, Mario Rigo, Giovanna Massobrio, Pietro Longo and Paolo Portoghesi at the Marco Polo airport of Venice, 1976	89
3.2	Paolo Portoghesi's enrolment card in the PSI party, issued in Rome, 1961	92
3.3	The executive board of the Faculty of Architecture of the Politecnico di Milano, sitting at the table for a meeting, 1971	94
3.4	*La rivoluzione culturale*, booklet produced by the research group led by Paolo Portoghesi at the Politecnico di Milano, academic year 1970–71	96
3.5	Dean Paolo Portoghesi, surrounded by the students of the Politecnico di Milano, 1971	97
3.6	Dean Paolo Portoghesi facing the authorities during a protest at the Politecnico di Milano, with Fredi Drugman, Guido Canella, Federico Oliva and Pierluigi Nicolin, 1971	98
3.7	Paolo Portoghesi at his desk at the Politecnico di Milano in front of the book *Dieci Posters Del Partito Socialista Italiano 1905–1925*, 1971	103
3.8	Giovanna Massobrio, Anna Maria Moncini, Paolo Portoghesi and Bettino Craxi, Como, 1984	104
3.9	45th congress of the PSI, LED pyramid designed by Filippo Panseca, displaying the logo of the PSI, Ansaldo, Milan, 1989	107
3.10	Paolo Portoghesi talking at the 45th congress of the PSI. LED pyramid designed by Filippo Panseca displaying the face of Paolo Portoghesi giving a talk, 1989	108
3.11	The crowning element of Paolo Portoghesi's facade for the *Strada Novissima*, revealing the temporary constructive technology, Venice Biennale, 1980	109
3.12	Paolo Portoghesi's frontal photograph of the gate he designed for the pavilion at the festival of antique in Todi, 1982	110
3.13	Biennale – Architettura_INVITO_(recto-verso). INARCH Istituto Nazionale di Architettura, 23 October 1978	112
3.14	Paolo Portoghesi's photograph of the installation of the second International Architecture Exhibition of the Venice Biennale dedicated to the Islamic culture, 1982	116
3.15	Paolo Portoghesi next to the model of the Mosque of Rome	118
3.16	Paolo Portoghesi's sketch for the Mosque of Rome	119
3.17	Paolo Portoghesi's study for the pillars of the Mosque of Rome, sketch, 1979	121
3.18	Paolo Portoghesi's low-angled shot photograph of the Mosque of Rome, showing the effect of the natural light in the space	122
4.1	Still from the movie *Pizza Triangle*, showing Monica Vitti looking down from the balcony of Casa Papanice, 1970	123

4.2	Aldo Rossi's Teatro del Mondo floating in the lagoon of Venice	125
4.3	Cover of the first issue of the architectural journal *Controspazio*, June 1969	132
4.4	Launch of the architectural journal *Eupalino. Cultura della città e della casa*, at the Italian cultural institute in New York, 1985	134
4.5	Paolo Portoghesi, in his white suit, at the Piper, during the trial with Ricardo Bofill, Rome, 1983	137
4.6	Flyer for the invitation to the trial with Ricardo Bofill at the Piper, 1983	138
4.7	Trial with Ricardo Bofill at the Piper, 1983	138
4.8	Paolo Portoghesi speaking at the *Domus* party at the Piper, Rome, 1980	139
4.9	Exterior view of Casa Papanice, Rome	144
4.10	Interior of Casa Papanice, the lounge, 1970s	146
4.11	Still from the movie *The Pizza Triangle*, 1970, showing Ambleto Di Meo (Hércules Cortès) and Adelaide Ciafrocchi (Monica Vitti) inside Casa Papanice	147
4.12	Still from the movie *The Strange Vice of Mrs. Wardh*, 1971, showing heroine (Edwige Fenech), wife of the diplomat Neil Wardh (Alberto De Mendoza), inside Casa Papanice	147
4.13	Still from the movie *The Red Lady Kills Seven Times*, 1972, showing Martin Hoffmann (Ugo Pagliai) and one of his employees in Casa Papanice	148
E.1	Paolo Portoghesi, with Renato Nicolini, at the opening of the exhibition 'Paolo Portoghesi a via Giulia', Rome, 1986	151
E.2	Paolo Portoghesi with the representatives of the Israeli, Catholic and Islamic communities at the first opening of the itinerant exhibition *Lo spazio sacro nelle tre religioni monoteiste*, Venice, 1993	152
E.3	Paolo Portoghesi with Giovanna Massobrio, Residential complex for ENEL workers, 1981–88, Tarquinia	153
E.4	Residence in Calcata designed by Paolo Portoghesi and Giovanna Massobrio, *c.* late 1970s	157
E.5	Paolo Portoghesi in his house in Calcata, July 2023	159

SERIES PREFACE

The Modern Movement was a broad and multifaceted phenomenon that revolutionized the field of architecture. Throughout the twentieth century, and across political, cultural and climatic divides, modern architecture radically changed the everyday lives of millions of people. Yet, to this day, our knowledge of this sweeping and omnipresent occurrence remains largely limited to the names of a few famed designers.

Despite growing research into the Modern Movement and its various actors, most published works focus on a select list of grandmasters. This narrow view restrains our understanding of what the Modern Movement in architecture was, as it limits our insight into the breadth and complexity of the networks that underwrote it, and undercuts the possibility of a more holistic and fine-grained understanding of its impact on architectural culture and the built environment.

The 'Bloomsbury Studies in Modern Architecture' book series seeks to address this dearth. It sheds light on those who played pivotal roles in propelling the Modern Movement in architecture but who have, nonetheless, languished in the shadows of their better-known (and extensively published) canonical peers. Examining the works and ideas of this 'shadow canon', this series does not aspire to canonize those to whom it offers a platform, but rather to construct a more detailed understanding of the different actors that propelled the Modern Movement across the globe, as well as the relationships that existed between these different actors, and the ways in which they contributed to the proliferation, recalibration, acculturation and transculturation of modern architecture.

Some might think that Paolo Portoghesi is an unusual name to find in a book series that seeks to shed light on the 'shadow canon' of the Modern Movement. Throughout his professional career, Portoghesi wore many hats: architect, educator, historian, political provocateur, impresario, 'institutional man', etc. As a result, anyone interested in the twentieth-century history of architecture has likely heard of Paolo Portoghesi. Yet few fully understand the breadth and depth of his contribution to the Modern Movement and, in particular, its counterpoint: the postmodern project – which is a 'shadow canon' of modern architecture in its own right.

Portoghesi was the first director of the 1980 Venice Architecture Biennale, President of the Venice Biennale for two consecutive terms (between 1983 and 1992) and a respected academic who taught at the Scuola di Perfezionamento per lo Studio e il Restauro dei monumenti and the Faculty of Architecture at La Sapienza in Rome, as well as the Faculty of Architecture of the Politecnico di Milano, where he served as dean between 1968 and 1976. Portoghesi was also the founder and editor of the periodicals *Controspazio* and *Eupalino*, and designer of acclaimed buildings such as the Mosque of Rome (1975–95) and Casa Baldi (1959–61), which Charles Jencks cited as an early example of postmodernism in Italy in his seminal book *The Language of Postmodern Architecture* (1977).

Portoghesi's polyvalence, however, is likely one of the reasons why he is less known than some of his Italian contemporaries, such as Aldo Rossi and Manfredo Tafuri, with whom he collaborated and quarrelled on various occasions. If his relationship with Rossi demonstrates that Portoghesi was more of an impresario of postmodern architecture than a true-blue practitioner, his exchanges with Tafuri reveal that he was more of a practitioner than a historian *pur sang*. Portoghesi occupied a position in-between. He was, in his own words, 'a mediating figure'. As a result, Portoghesi defies easy categorization in the historiography of modern architecture. It is telling that even though Portoghesi established his own architectural practice in 1965, together with Vittorio Gigliotti, he was appointed Professor of History of Architecture at the Politecnico di Milano in 1967, rather than Professor of Architectural Design, a position given to Rossi in 1969. Portoghesi's books on Italy's rich architectural history, such as *Roma barocca* and *Borromini*, likely informed this decision. However, for Portoghesi, such books were part and parcel of his (larger) *progetto* which revolved around the idea of the history of architecture as an essential tool for design. Portoghesi wanted to instrumentalize history to develop a new, postmodern architecture. This approach drew ire from historians, such as Tafuri who not only rejected the operationalization of history, but the idea of postmodern architecture altogether, which he instead called 'hypermodern'.

Tafuri's rejection of postmodern architecture is not unique. For many, postmodernism remains a black page in the history of Italian architecture, and many Italian architects of the period refuse to be labelled as such. But not Portoghesi. He saw himself as a principal heir of the tradition of the baroque in the twentieth century; and in his built projects he effortlessly blended historical sources in a technique that has been compared to cinematographic 'lap dissolves' – an act of moving gradually from one picture to another in a way that one scene appears to dissolve seamlessly into the other.

Portoghesi's embrace of postmodern architecture and postmodernity in general is likely another reason why his work has – thus far – not been given much attention in architectural historiography. Many still consider postmodern architecture a style that uncritically validated popular culture to challenge the canon of high art, be it modernist or traditional. And, for many, Portoghesi is the posterchild of all that was wrong with postmodernism: a shimmery sheen without depth. Portoghesi, for instance, disseminated his ideas on architecture through popular magazines and television – even becoming a character for a docu-fiction on architecture – and posed for glossy magazines such as *Vogue* and *Epoca*. During the 1970s and 1980s, he and his architect wife, Giovanna Massobrio, were one of the most glamorous couples of the Italian jet set, holding opulent parties at their house in Via Gregoriana.

Through magazines such as *Controspazio* and *Eupalino*, through exhibitions such as the *Strada Novissima* (1980), and through debates, book launches and music shows hosted at the Apollodoro Gallery in Rome, which he ran together with Massobrio, Portoghesi turned architecture into events and images. He did so to take a stance against high-brow (and elitist) architectural discourse, and to reach another audience, outside the circle of the initiated, to explore the ways in which architectural thought collided with social reality – to look at architecture from the point of view of those who use and are conditioned by it. His interest in this encounter between architecture and social reality also fuelled his engagement with the Italian Socialist Party (PSI), which Massobrio fostered by befriending the party's charismatic leader Bettino Craxi. Sadly, it was this political affiliation that led to the demise of Portoghesi's postmodern *progetto*. When the PSI became embroiled in a political scandal in 1992, the socio-political project that the party had advanced, and the postmodern architecture that had given shape to its ideas, became tainted. Portoghesi and Massobrio moved to Calcata, in the Roman countryside, and (largely) retreated from public life, as Portoghesi shifted his attention from postmodern to 'geo' architecture and a concern for climate and nature in design.

In this book, Silvia Micheli and Léa-Catherine Szacka examine the unique multivalence of Portoghesi's career through key projects, including buildings such as Casa Baldi and the Mosque of Rome; exhibition designs, such as the Strada Novissima; exchanges with peers such as Aldo Rossi, Manfredo Tafuri, Bruno Zevi and Christian Norberg-Schulz; and publications, such as *Controspazio* and *Eupalino*. In doing so, Micheli and Szacka reveal how the crux of Portoghesi's fascinating career, and of his postmodern *progetto*, was based on a triangulation of a renewed interest in architectural history, an unprecedented use of media, and a kinship between architecture and politics.

TOM AVERMAETE & JANINA GOSSEYE
Series Editors

ACKNOWLEDGEMENTS

The idea of jointly writing a book on Postmodern Italian Architecture through the critical analysis of Paolo Portoghesi's work and life originated in Brussels, during the spring of 2012, when we met for the first time, at the second European Architectural History Network (EAHN) bi-annual conference.[1] Here, our research interests converged. Silvia had just published the book *Italia 60/70. Una stagione dell'architettura*, co-edited with her research group at the Faculty of Architecture at the Politecnico di Milano,[2] while Léa-Catherine was working on her upcoming book dedicated to the first Venice Architecture Biennale, of which Portoghesi had been the director.[3] At the EAHN conference, we both presented our on-going work: Silvia with a paper on Portoghesi and the baroque, which would later become a chapter in the volume *The Baroque in Architectural Culture, 1880–1980*,[4] and Léa-Catherine with an analysis of the *Strada Novissima* as a form of large-scale model and curatorial anomaly. For selecting us as speakers at that conference, and therefore contributing to the genesis of this book, we would like to warmly thank our respective session chairs at the conference, Andrew Leach, as well as Mari Lending and Wallis Miller.

Working in two distant parts of the world – Silvia in Brisbane, Australia, and Léa-Catherine first in Oslo, Norway, and later in Manchester, UK – we entered a long-standing international academic research collaboration. The first step was the publication of a joint paper titled 'Paolo Portoghesi and the Postmodern Project', initially presented at the 2015 international conference 'East West Central: Re-building Europe, 1950–1990' at the ETH Zurich.[5] This paper constitutes the inception of our book, the one that contains the main critical ideas around Italian postmodern architecture, Paolo Portoghesi and his disciplinary agenda. For giving us the prompt to start writing a seminal part of the present book, we would like to thank Akos Moravansky and Torsten Lange. Our gratitude goes to the ATCH research centre at the University of Queensland and its director John Macarthur, for supporting our research, including sponsoring Léa-Catherine on a visiting fellowship to spend time in Brisbane in 2016 to strategize the following steps of the research.[6] The outcome was an essay which explored the triangulation of three key Italian architectural historians – Paolo Portoghesi, Bruno Zevi and Manfredo

Tafuri, written for the architectural journal *AA Files*.[7] For his trust, amazing editorial work and for enthusiastically encouraging the publication of our article, we would like to credit Tom Weaver, at the time editor of the journal.

Our deepest gratitude goes to Paolo Portoghesi (*in memoriam*) and Giovanna Massobrio, for their generous availability to discuss with us parts of our study, in person at their apartment in Rome, at their house in Calcata and on numerous occasions via videoconferences. In particular, Paolo Portoghesi has patiently entertained a long conversation with us, providing, over the years, new insight to his career, life and work practice that have been invaluable as we mapped out the larger research project. Maria Ercadi, archivist at Portoghesi's office, kindly helped us to navigate the archival materials, some of which are published here for the first time. The novelty and accuracy of the body of images would have not been possible without her expert knowledge of and guidance through Portoghesi's personal archive.

Our thanks also go to those architects and scholars who have agreed to share their thoughts with us regarding specific aspects of Portoghesi's work and career, dedicating some of their time to this project: Michele Achilli (*in memoriam*), Guglielmo Bilancioni, Marco Biraghi, Maristella Casciato, Pippo Ciorra, Francesco Dal Co, Vittorio Gregotti (*in memoriam*), Alessandro Mendini (*in memoriam*), Francesco Moschini, Luciano Patetta, Giancarlo Priori, Franco Purini, Franco Raggi, Giovanni Rebecchini and Matteo Vercelloni.

Furthermore, we want to acknowledge the help of Albena Yaneva, Marco Biraghi, John Macarthur, Andrew Leach, Antony Moulis as well as Luca Guido and Maristella Casciato, for reviewing drafts of the different chapters and providing useful feedback. We are also very grateful to Maristella for writing the coda of the book, enriching our endeavor. We would like to thank Francesca Giudetti, who patiently assisted us with the collection of the image permissions.

We express our appreciation for the support of institutions which have opened their archives to us, allowing this research to be underpinned by original first-hand documentation. We wish to acknowledge the Centro Archivi Fondazione MAXXI, Fondazione Bruno Zevi and the Fondo Francesco Moschini Architettura Arte Moderna (FFMAAM) in Rome; the Archivi Storici at the Politecnico di Milano; the Archivio Storico delle Arte Contemporanea at the Venice Biennale's archive (ASAC) and the Getty Research Institute. Frédéric Migayrou, Deputy Director of the Musée National d'Art Moderne, Centre de Création Industrielle (MNAM-CCI) at the Centre Pompidou Paris was one of the first to acquire some of Portoghesi's original drawings. We would like to acknowledge his insightful guidance in personally showing us the materials in the initial stage of this research.

Our gratitude goes to Tom Avermaete and Janina Gosseye, colleagues and editors of the series 'Bloomsbury Studies in Modern Architecture', which this book is part of, for trusting in our line of study. We would also like to thank James Thompson, Alexander Highfield and Rosamunde O'Cleirigh at Bloomsbury

Publishing for their patient assistance in the rather long process of completing the manuscript under the challenging circumstances of the pandemic.

A warm thank you goes to our beloved families, friends and esteemed colleagues, for their support during this exciting research journey in the folds of postmodern history. A big thank you to little Aino, Ilka and Satu, for their understanding during the long writing times and their cheerful intrusions in the numerous intercontinental videoconferences.

In dedication to Paolo

INTRODUCTION

FIGURE I.1 Paolo Portoghesi, dean of the Faculty of Architecture at the Politecnico di Milano, in 1970. Photographic portrait by Giovanna Massobrio. © Paolo Portoghesi Archive.

The figure of the architect is often that of a mediator. Between the client and the builder, between art and science and between the profession and theory, the architect operates at the intersection of different realities and moves across disciplinary epistemes. Yet some architects, because of their exceptional talent, play a crucial role in these acts of negotiation, wearing many hats at once and continuously shifting from one task to another. Architect, intellectual, historian, critic, designer, theoretician, educator, political operator, curator and communicator, Paolo Portoghesi has been a protagonist of postmodern architecture who has spent his life in almost constant motion, oscillating naturally between tasks, individuals and events (Figure I.1).

Often described as elegant, suave and discreet, these very traits have also contributed to Portoghesi's reputation as a formidable negotiator with the ability to conciliate opposites, whether between history and design, while building Casa Baldi; or media and politics, while operating in the Italian Socialist Party (PSI); between students and staff as dean of the Faculty of Architecture at the Politecnico di Milano during the year of student protests; or between East and West, while setting up the second architectural Venice Biennale dedicated to Islamic architecture. As Portoghesi himself observed, with regards to his role at the Politecnico:

> It is true that I was seen as a mediating figure, partly because of my age, partly because I was an outsider, coming from a different city, but also because of my political affiliations. As a Socialist, I was in a reasonable position to mediate between the communists, the far left, and the establishment.[1]

Working between two experimental lines of design research put forward by architects Aldo Rossi and Alessandro Mendini, as well as between Bruno Zevi and Manfredo Tafuri, two imposing historians who polarized the Italian architectural debate, Portoghesi played the unique role of representing the commonalities and divergences of Italian architects and scholars to find new strategies of understanding and intervention.[2] He travelled as a means to pursue this agenda, relentlessly moving between Rome, Milan and Venice. At the same time, his connections all over Italy enabled him to set up a strategic network of which no other Italian architect could boast.

Because of his protean nature, Portoghesi intrinsically defies any conventional analytical classification. During the 1970s and 1980s, his dynamism was uncommon, far from the stereotypical view of the architect glued to the drafting table, or the historian holed up in his *studiolo* examining rare documents. In this context his unparalleled cross-disciplinary agility was looked upon with suspicion, and his flair for media was considered somewhat heretical. A controversial figure, his initiatives and cultural directions were either praised or attacked, welcomed or rejected. He was the 'Scully of the Italian Baroque' in the eyes of American architectural historian Richard Pommer;[3] a 'master of fashions' for Tafuri;[4] a 'guru of post-modern', with as many visceral admirers as enemies, for journalist Oreste Pivetta;[5] a 'cultural organiser of regime architecture' at the time of the PSI, as remembered by architect and *Lotus* director Pierluigi Nicolin.[6] The list of labels could easily go on, only adding to the disparate takes on his profile. Such idiosyncratic reactions can be ascribed to the complexity of Portoghesi's shifting operative attitude, which transcended the compartmentalized organization of the discipline of architecture in Italy at that time. And yet it is precisely this polyvalence and adaptability that have distinguished Portoghesi as a unique exponent of postmodern architecture in the second half of the twentieth century. Therefore it is Portoghesi himself as mediator who becomes the common thread throughout the pages of this book, helping to hold together all his facets; unravel the intricacies of his profile; capture his core nature and reposition his life and work in the broader context of postmodern architecture.

Italian postmodern architecture revisited

The main ambition of this book is to address the emergence and development of Italian postmodern architectural culture through a critical analysis of the work of one of its most passionate advocates, Paolo Portoghesi. Casting light on Portoghesi in relation to postmodern culture allows an examination of the dynamics that shaped architectural production from the 1960s to the 1980s, a still under-studied period often dismissed as a 'dark page' in the history of Italian architecture. The patchy history of (Italian) postmodern culture is here analysed and framed through its reliance on three major cultural pillars, which the case of Portoghesi helps to elucidate: history – specifically, architectural history – as an instrumental means for design; politics, relating to the national move towards the ideology of the Italian Socialist Party; and media, with television, cinema, events and magazines being embraced as *de facto* vehicles for the construction and dissemination of architectural ideas. Taken together, these three pillars can be considered representative of an attitude towards design 'as a whole'. Elsewhere in Western culture the three vertices of what can be called a 'postmodern triangle' – centrality of history for the discipline; involvement with neoliberalist policies; mediatization of architecture – appear to have operated separately and in shifting order of importance. This book shows that in Italy they were mediated and synthetized through one particular figure: Paolo Portoghesi, the historian, the political operator and the communicator. Such a combination would have been improbable anywhere other than Rome: cradle of history, political centre of Italy and Hollywood on the Tiber.[7]

While Portoghesi is best known for his role as the first director of the 1980 Venice Architecture Biennale and for his international reputation as an expert of baroque architecture, these two aspects of his profile seem to have limited the overall comprehension of his vast field of action in relation to the construction of postmodern architecture. To appreciate the relevance of Portoghesi's specific contribution, and untangle his polyhedric operative way, it became evident that it was necessary to work at the interstices of the many roles he covered, bringing them together to reassess his highly integrated profile. Thus, for the first time, this book sets out to shed light on the work of Portoghesi in the making of what we have called his 'postmodern project' – his personal take on the above-mentioned 'postmodern triangle'. This endeavour was foundational for the changes in direction that Italian architecture experienced between the 1960s and the 1990s – changes that eventually affected the postmodern discourse globally.

Our research scrutinizes Portoghesi's career and life holistically, considering, beyond his memorable *Strada Novissima* and scholarly studies, interpretative categories that are often overlooked or considered 'minor' for the disciplinary discourse. Such matters include: the management of politics in the sphere of academic education; party-political alliances; the agency of institutions in forging cultural initiatives; the use of popular venues for the dissemination of architectural culture, such as TV, discothèques and magazines; and the ability of cinema to broadcast the postmodern design aesthetic. Exposing these overlooked facets, we add a layer of complexity to the analysis of postmodern design culture, drawing attention to Portoghesi's radical disciplinary revision, creative deregulation and interdisciplinary experimentation. In this respect, our study uses new and alternative sources, adding fresh knowledge to the discipline by going beyond the traditional framing of the postmodern architect as a 'designer' and 'theoretician'.

By broadening the interpretative categories and their interrelationships, Portoghesi's role as 'cultural operator' reveals a series of new strategies, fundamental for the comprehension of the period under scrutiny. This triangulation of factors (historical, political and mediatic) explains the timeframe of our research. Portoghesi's work and life are explored from 1956, the year of publication of his seminal book on the seventeenth-century mathematician and baroque architect Guarino Guarini,[8] to 1992, coinciding with the conclusion of his second mandate as president of the Venice Biennale as well as the start of the fall of the Italian Socialist Party, when it was crushed by the Tangentopoli (Bribeville) scandal. By focusing on this time span, our book reassesses the roaring years of Portoghesi's cultural activity, the period when he became a 'centre of power' in the making of Italian postmodern architectural culture and its international connections.

Portoghesi operated at the very edge between modern and postmodern culture, attempting to resolve that schism between modern architecture and history, a matter which is now openly questioned.[9] More than anyone else, he recognized that the connections between modern and postmodern architecture were as strong as their differences.[10] This book therefore marks an important place in a series that aims to 'create a more comprehensive history of the Modern Movement' by uncovering 'work of "forgotten" architects ... to demonstrate their critical importance in architectural history'.[11] It is our belief that the history of the Modern

FIGURE I.2 Paolo Portoghesi during a postmodern gathering in Chicago, 1982. From left to right: Thomas H. Beeby, Stanley Tigerman, Paolo Portoghesi, Arata Isozaki and Emilio Ambasz. © Paolo Portoghesi Archive.

Movement should also include the history of its demise and critique. In other words, to better grasp an action, one needs to understand its opposite reaction: 'Action and reaction are, as in Hegel's traditional dialectics, thesis and antithesis, with the difference that they are only valuable as long as they are equivalent and postpone their synthesis or merger.'[12] In this sense postmodern architecture was not just a reaction against the Modern Movement, it was, as recalled by Charles Jencks, a 'variety of departures' yet still a derivation from Modernism;[13] the former could not exist without the latter. Adding a layer of complexity to the debate, yet somehow contradicting, Fredric Jameson argues that we should grasp postmodernism as a new cultural logic in its own right, as something more than a mere reaction.[14]

This book also reflects on the process that led Portoghesi to become one of the main supporters of postmodern architecture in the international scene. From Philip Johnson to Charles Jencks, from Emilio Ambasz to Heinrich Klotz, the history of postmodern architecture can be read through its constellation of 'centres of power', an assemblage that is still awaiting a clear contextual analysis (Figure I.2). The Italian case, with Portoghesi at its fulcrum, represents a profitable beginning. However, this book does not attempt to reassess the phenomenon of

Postmodernism as a general category. Rather, it contributes to the ongoing conversation by examining a specific cultural perspective, such as Italy can offer. We argue that through his work, on the edges of history, politics and media, Portoghesi deployed an effective critique of modern architecture and in turn managed – with other important figures of his time including Aldo Rossi, Alessandro Mendini, Robert A. M. Stern, Robert Venturi and Denise Scott Brown – to contribute to shape the contours of what is now commonly called postmodern architecture.

Shifting the discussion on Postmodernism from a stylistic approach to a methodological one is another key objective of this volume. Eva Branscome, in her reflections on the figure of Hans Hollein and on Austrian postmodern architecture in general, has wondered if what happened in Austria between the end of the 1950s and the mid-1980s could be described in any sense as 'postmodernist'.[15] The same question could be applied to Italy, with many Italian architects of the 1960s and 1970s refusing that definition, since in their opinion it referred to the notion of style. Portoghesi provides an exceptional opportunity to re-discuss the ways in which (Italian) postmodern architecture can be framed. Indeed, during this time there was an urgent need to move on from modern architecture to a new phase. The notion of postmodernity was useful for Portoghesi, who by working at the convergence of two architectural epochs voiced the different design and theoretical approaches of an entire generation of Italian architects, making them part of the international discussion. In this respect, the word Postmodernism – referring to the notion of style (*ism*) – hardly appears in this book. Instead, the expression 'postmodern architecture' is used to refer to methodological positions distinctive of the Italian case, which itself plays the role of protagonist in the timeframe considered.[16]

State of the art

Considering the vast and rich production of Italian architecture between the 1960s and early 1990s, a dedicated research output is limited, and complete assessments of the era are still pending. However, a few Italian publications have put forward overarching accounts of the period under scrutiny. These include *Il dibattito architettonico in Italia 1945–1975*, published as early as 1977;[17] Tafuri's *History of Italian Architecture 1944–85* and *Architettura italiana 1944–1994*.[18] Jean Louis Cohen's study, *La coupure entre architects et intellectuels, ou les enseignements de l'italophilie*,[19] also provides insight into the theory and practice of architecture in 1970s Italy through a close examination of the intellectual exchanges between France and Italy via the trajectories of Ernesto Nathan Rogers, Aldo Rossi, Vittorio Gregotti and Manfredo Tafuri, among others. But even while offering comprehensive critical narratives of the period in question, these books were written in the heat of the moment. For instance, in Tafuri's *History of Italian Architecture*, which provides an attentive account of postwar architectural culture, some of the interpretations from the 1960s onwards seem driven by personal relationships.

More recently, two publications examining the second half of the twentieth century at the Politecnico di Milano offer more contemporary scrutiny. The first, *Italia 60/70: Una stagione dell'architettura*,[20] sheds light on the development of Italian architecture after the heroic postwar period, detecting new creative forces and theoretical contributions. The second, *Storia dell'architettura italiana 1985-2015*,[21] follows Tafuri's book on Italian architecture and concentrates on the era of Silvio Berlusconi to give a critical history of the last three decades articulated against the social, political and economic national context. As the years in the titles of both books suggest, the examination of postmodern culture is focused, respectively, on its inception (the former volume) and on its epilogue (the latter). In this sense, these accounts are useful stepping stones towards the research of this book. Another historian, Valerio Paolo Mosco, has put forward his interpretation of the most recent decades of Italian architecture with *Architettura italiana: Dal postmoderno ad oggi*, published in 2017,[22] which acknowledges, for the first time, the word postmodern in the title of a book dedicated to Italian architecture. However, the narrative begins in 1978, with the exhibition *Roma Interrotta*. In addition to the disconnect created by this gap in the narrative of the history of postmodern architecture is the isolating barrier of language: with the exception of Tafuri's book, which itself has long been out of print (and Cohen's book, published in French), all of the above-mentioned sources are available only in Italian.

Taking a broader perspective, Diane Ghirardo's *Italy: Modern Architectures in History*, published in 2013,[23] is a wide-ranging account of Italian architecture and cities over a span of 150 years, from national unification to the present. As observed by Mark Jarzombek, Ghirardo 'gives a grand view and a powerful foundation from which we can work'.[24] One year before the publication of her book, the Centre Pompidou in Paris organized a large exhibition dedicated to *La Tendenza: Italian Architecture 1965-1985* showing a selection of more than 250 drawings, models, photographs, paintings and films, as well as rich documentation that had never previously been exhibited in France. The eponymous catalogue of the show included an essay by curator and collector Frédéric Migayrou, which aimed to reposition and analyse the historicization of this period of Italian architecture (1965-85) in a novel way, by showing how a new critical discourse had sought to redefine the logic of the architectural project.[25] Looking further afield, *Italy/Australia: Postmodern Architecture in Translation* (2018) is one of the first attempts to chart the impact of Italian postmodern culture abroad.[26]

What transpires from these publications is the reticence to use the term postmodern and its derivatives to refer to Italian architecture of the second part of the twentieth century. On the contrary, the use of the 'postmodern' category is second nature in English language literature and historiography. This division between the two cultural perspectives goes well beyond a mere linguistic distinction or terminological disquisition; it reveals deep-rooted ideological inhibitions by Italian architects and critics to accept the postmodern category as a critical lens for reading 1960s–80s Italian architectural culture. Our book, however, aims to fill the gap of this conceptual distance, by making these two historiographical points of view interact.

If the period in which Portoghesi was operating has gone relatively understudied thus far, there has been even less engagement by Anglo-American scholarship with the work of Portoghesi during these decades. Several publications edited by Portoghesi's collaborators and colleagues have documented his design production. These include the very first book on his work: *Alla ricerca dell'architettura perduta* (1975), by the Norwegian historian and critic Christian Norberg-Schulz, Portoghesi's dear friend and colleague. Two concise monographs followed: one by Giancarlo Priori in 1985,[27] and a second by Mario Pisani for Electa, published in 1992.[28] The most complete monograph to date, edited by Giovanna Massobrio, Maria Ercadi and Stefania Tuzi and released in 2001,[29] is a first attempt to present the multifaceted profile of Portoghesi both as a historian and designer. It also includes a thorough bibliography of publications both on and by its subject and is enriched by previously unpublished photos. Recent volumes edited by Francesca Gottardo (2008)[30] and Petra Bernitsa (2012) have appeared in English too.[31] All the above-mentioned publications constitute a comprehensive account of Portoghesi's design production and a detailed insight into the personal archive of the architect. However, these authors have all, in different capacities, been close collaborators and pupils of Portoghesi. Such positioning reveals the control exercised – directly or indirectly – by the architect over the dissemination of his design and scholarly output. In this respect, while these titles remain indispensable bibliographical sources, our book increases the critical distance from the architect (temporal, spatial and personal) in order to undertake a historical analysis and theorization of his oeuvre.

More recently, a new wave of interest in Portoghesi has coincided with the publication of materials that seek to reframe his work by casting light on specific aspects of his architectural process. The recent monograph by French scholar Benjamin Chavardès, *L'Italie post-moderne: Paolo Portoghesi, architecte, théoricien, historien* (2022), based on his doctoral thesis at the University of Montpellier, offers a detailed disciplinary account of Portoghesi's work, with amongst others, a focus on the School of Rome.[32] Nicolò Ornaghi and Guido Tesio have conducted an interview with Portoghesi concentrating on the crucial year 1966, when Portoghesi published *Roma barocca* and was called to serve at the Politecnico di

Milano.[33] Ornaghi and Guido Zorzi, even though mentioning Portoghesi only tangentially, have published an interview with artist Filippo Panseca, raising interest in the relationship between architecture and the Socialist Party, a dynamic in which Portoghesi participated.[34] Another interview by Italian scholars Manuel Orazi and Marco Vanucci drew attention to Portoghesi's interest in geometry, the study of systems and field theory.[35] Following that publication, Vanucci has also dedicated an article to the construction of the drawings by Portoghesi.[36] Offering their own original interpretative ways into the work of Portoghesi, the coexistence of these contributions provides food for thought in the revaluation of our titular figure in the twentieth century.

Methodology and sources

The study underpinning the writing of this book was conducted using a variety of investigative methods and with access to a range of first- and second-hand sources. First, the book has relied on a vast bibliography of works, both focusing on and written by Portoghesi, as well as publications regarding Italian architecture of the second half of the twentieth century.

A few publications written or edited by Portoghesi have proved essential documents for our interpretations. The city of Rome was a subject to which Portoghesi has continually returned during his life, whether through writing (he dedicated numerous books and articles to his beloved hometown) or the design of significant public and private projects. His romance with the Italian capital is poetically described in detail in his autobiography *Roma/amoR: Memoria, racconto, speranza*, whose title finds inspiration in the palindromic nature of the city's name – where *amor* means love, indeed.[37] This personal account has been a rich source of information, providing the architect's personal considerations on specific events and themes key to his oeuvre and life. Likewise, Portoghesi's 1974 book *Le inibizioni dell'architettura moderna* has provided theoretical material that clarifies his approach to design.

Beyond his own writing, the projects and professional output of Portoghesi have provided fertile material for other writers, including the Roman architectural historian Francesco Moschini, whose book *Paolo Portoghesi: Progetti e disegni/Projects and drawings 1949–1979* puts forward an excursus of his subject's work. Organized by analogical combinations of drawings and photographs, the book presents the projects of Portoghesi in the wake of their precedents to disclose the sources to which the architect turned for inspiration.[38] Published in 1979 and written in both Italian and English, the volume introduced Portoghesi to a wider Italian and international public as he stepped into his role as president of the first Venice Architecture Biennale. We have considered Moschini's book as an invaluable document of Portoghesi's historical approach to source blending, which was foundational to the definition of his design method. The Festschrift, arranged for Portoghesi's sixtieth birthday, edited by Mario Pisani, has been a great source of original documentation as well.[39] To articulate Portoghesi's cultural context and milieu, newspaper articles have proved essential first-hand documents, charting the many political and media events that intersected his professional trajectory and saw him operating outside the strict boundaries of the discipline.[40] Finally, documentation held at the archive of the Politecnico di Milano was key to reconstructing the outline of Portoghesi's deanship during the student protests.

Throughout the research for this book, we have enjoyed a series of conversations with Paolo Portoghesi himself, as well as with architects and critics who knew him during the period considered, including Michele Achilli, Guglielmo Bilancioni, Maristella Casciato, Pippo Ciorra, Francesco Dal Co, Vittorio Gregotti (*in memoriam*), Giovanna Massobrio, Alessandro Mendini (*in memoriam*), Francesco Moschini, Luciano Patetta, Giancarlo Priori, Franco Purini, Franco Raggi and Giovanni Rebecchini. These discussions have clarified the contours of the cultural background under investigation. On the one hand, the conversations with Portoghesi have provided new critical insights while allowing us to fact-check key moments in his professional journey and to discover unpublished materials. On the other hand, the dialogues with those figures operating within and around Portoghesi's milieu have greatly helped to fine-tune the critical interpretation that cuts through the book.

Portoghesi's private archive, still partly with the architect and partly donated to the MAXXI in Rome, offered an important visual way into his life and work. Most of the photographs used in this book were taken by Portoghesi himself and come from his private archive. This was a deliberate decision, in order to introduce an approach to communication dear to the architect and still little discussed in the analysis of his oeuvre.[41] As shown on the cover image of this book, Portoghesi was also a photographer, and his low-angled shots (Figure I.3) were 'not Alinari', as rightly put by Richard Pommer.[42] However, from an architectural point of view, they provide way more information about the projects than professional photographs, underlying their spatial dimension, context and treatment of light.

The examination of drawings held in the collections of the Centre Pompidou in Paris and at the MAXXI and Fondo Francesco Moschini Architettura Arte Moderna in Rome also gave excellent insight into Portoghesi's design process.[43] Perhaps more than anyone of his time, Portoghesi understood the significance of how ideas are disseminated; indeed, postmodern culture is intrinsically linked to media. The analysis of images, videos and film has therefore played its own part in the research of this book, providing information about the production of postmodern culture as well as the interpretation of institutional and political dynamics. For this task, we have relied on visual materials and image analysis from

FIGURE I.3 Paolo Portoghesi's low-angled shot photograph of the Chapel of the Holy Shroud by Guarino Guarino in Turin. © Paolo Portoghesi Archive.

Portoghesi's own archive,[44] as well as the archives of Getty Images, which contain a selection of photographs showing the architect's integral position within private, political, academic and scholarly circles. For his years at the Biennale, we have relied on the Archivio Storico delle Arte Contemporanea, at the Venice Biennale's archive in Marghera (ASAC).

Structure

This book does not offer a monographic account of Portoghesi's work, organized in a traditional chronological order. Instead, its structure, comprising four chapters and an epilogue, is articulated to reflect the ways in which Portoghesi deployed his 'postmodern project'. Hence, chapters act as analytical transects that cut through his wide-ranging work between 1956 and 1992. Each chapter opens with a visual analysis of a historical photograph in order to give the reader a sense of the spirit of the time. These images have been chosen for their documentary value and act as 'temporal windows' that open onto the context in which Portoghesi was operating. The chapters then delve into a critical analysis of Portoghesi's works, his activities and agency in postmodern culture, and conclude with an analysis of a specific project designed by Portoghesi which, more than anything else, exemplifies the argument of the chapter. Only a few seminal buildings have been selected to support the main arguments, leaving the analysis of Portoghesi's extensive design work to other monographs.

Despite the centrality of the 1980 Venice Architecture Biennale to Portoghesi's career, *The Presence of the Past* is not singled out in its own distinct chapter, as one might perhaps expect. Instead, this project-event is explored throughout the book to support a variety of arguments and to explain specific facts, dynamics and decisions in Portoghesi's professional trajectory. Beyond the literature that already exists on the topic,[45] the main motivation for this 'sacrifice' is that if it is thanks to the Biennale that Portoghesi's ideas went global, it is also true that its undiscussed success in turning architecture into popular culture and promoting the postmodern language trapped Portoghesi in that very moment, somewhat hindering further critical interpretations of the rest of his work. By scattering *The Presence of the Past* over the four chapters, interpretative room has been generated to put forward an alternative and polycentric analysis of Portoghesi's postmodern project.

Chapter 1 outlines Portoghesi's role as impresario of Italian postmodern architecture and clarifies the notion of his 'postmodern project'. This expression, employed as the chapter's title, has been used to critically analyse Portoghesi's agenda based on the disciplinary reform of modern architecture and its transition to the postmodern phase. Portoghesi's professional network and fields of action are explored through a series of main case studies, while his role is repositioned within the international postmodern discourse, his career set against those of other protagonists. The chapter ends with an analysis of the Galleria Apollodoro in Rome, an epicentre for postmodern culture.

While the first chapter has the task of introducing Portoghesi's overall agenda and the collaboration that allowed it to succeed, the following three chapters correspond to the three main interpretative pillars that ground Portoghesi's postmodern project: history, politics and media. In this sense, Chapter 2, 'Turn to History', discusses the programmatic role of history in Portoghesi's postmodern project and how his pathway through the study of the baroque richly informed his design production. It explores the mechanisms used by Portoghesi to challenge the orthodoxy of the Modern Movement by fostering a cultural turn to history, a move that was crucial to Portoghesi's activities as a designer. All of these considerations are brought to bear in a reflective analysis of Casa Baldi, the house-manifesto that best shows the translation of baroque design principles into a masterful piece of twentieth-century architecture.

Complementing this exploration of Portoghesi's historical interests, the third chapter, 'Socialism for Freedom', analyses the political implications of postmodern architecture in the 1970s and 1980s, examining Portoghesi through his involvement in the Italian Socialist Party. The historian Mary McLeod has observed that linking architecture and politics presents certain difficulties, as neither field can be reduced to the other.[46] Yet, an understanding of Portoghesi's postmodern project is deeply ingrained into the ideals promoted by the then Italian Socialist Party leader Bettino Craxi. This chapter analyses how postmodern architecture intersected with politics in different ways, staging politics while enhancing the rhetoric of the party, as well as through institutional roles, looking in particular at the Mosque of Rome.

If politics played an integral part in the formation of Portoghesi's postmodern project, the media had its own role in shaping his work. The final chapter, 'Embracing Mass Media', disentangles mass media – and media more generally – to show Portoghesi not simply using this new mode of communication but appropriating its forms, language and mechanisms for the dissemination of architectural content. Whether playing a character in a docu-fiction on architecture (*Utopia, Utopia*, 1969), posing for glossy magazines such as *Vogue* and *Epoca*, or promoting socialist ideas in TV shows, Portoghesi became a savvy operator within this world. The chapter additionally considers Italian films that have captured some of the architect's most famous houses as part of their sets, with a focus on Casa Papanice.

The book ends with an epilogue set in 1992, a year considered the *annus horribilis* for Italian architectural culture, and Italy altogether. It was in 1992 that the nationwide Mani Pulite (Clean Hands) inquest took off, exposing a vast network of corruption and bribery at all political, municipal and corporate levels, including the Italian construction industry. This memorable date coincided with the conclusion of Portoghesi's second mandate as president of the Venice Biennale and also marked the quick dissolution of the Italian Socialist Party. As these events unfolded, Portoghesi and his wife Giovanna Massobrio progressively relocated to their retreat in Calcata, nestled in the Roman countryside. For them, Calcata represented the ultimate project, where all their ideals converged, uncompromised, in a place where they could continue their personal journey.

Setting the scene

Paolo Portoghesi was born in Rome on 2 November 1931. His mother, Bianca, was from Piedmont and had trained in chemistry, while his father, Virgilio, was a Roman engineer who would later work on construction projects including Portoghesi's first built single-family house, Casa Baldi (Figure I.4). Virgilio passed

FIGURE I.4 Paolo Portoghesi with his parents at Salzburg Castle, c. 1957. © Paolo Portoghesi Archive.

on his passion for culture and history to his young son, and these interests as well as their professional relationship, as engineer and architect, allowed them to share in the collective heritage of the city of Rome.[47] The Portoghesi household was a typical, close-knit Italian family, and as the youngest of three children (including brother Franco and sister Lucia), Portoghesi found himself tasked with mediating between the opposing sensibilities of his parents.[48] As he has recalled: 'My mother was a woman who based everything on the will and not infrequently disagreed with my father, who in turn was very accommodating.'[49] His childhood home was in via Monterone, in the heart of the eternal city, a stone's throw from the Pantheon and the church of Sant'Ivo alla Sapienza, built by Francesco Borromini – a masterpiece of baroque architecture.[50] 'The notion of space, of architecture and of the city,' Portoghesi would later recall, 'has taken shape in me during the years of childhood.'[51] Such monuments inspired the imagination of young Paolo:

Walking for a long time in a light way, next to the walls of the houses, on the edges of the staircases, we wait for a voice. The journey's itinerary appears described in the city like a waving spiral, in the darkest days, as a pinwheel with intricate tentacles (often returning to the same place!). Or again, like a rock hard net or a despairing parabola. Then, all of a sudden, we discover somebody next to us, we recognise him. More often we see somebody going away who was by us, and only now we know him.[52]

These lines are from *Paolo Portoghesi: Di Francesco Borromini*,[53] a handmade book self-published by the sixteen-year-old Portoghesi in a limited edition of only five copies and sold to classmates and friends (Figure I.5). The volume's typewritten prose is informed by a clear yet naive poetic tone inspired by the cryptic style of the Italian Hermetic poets, a small group of intellectuals that flourished under fascism and which included Giuseppe Ungaretti, Leonardo Sinisgalli, Salvatore Quasimodo and Mario Luzi. In addition, Portoghesi physically pasted in photos cut from five identical copies of the 1942 *EUR Civiltà* exhibition magazine to run alongside his text. With this youthful artisanal publication, he already understood the power of media in sharing his ideas. However it was not until four years later

FIGURE I.5 Frontispiece of the handmade book *Paolo Portoghesi: Di Francesco Borromini*, written in only five copies by young Portoghesi in 1946. © Paolo Portoghesi Archive.

that Portoghesi visited the dome of Borromini's Sant'Ivo alla Sapienza and climbed over the metal cage that crowns the church. The experience made a strong impact on the twenty-year-old. As Portoghesi would write more than two decades later: 'So different from all the other things I knew, it had been for years, in childhood, the physical representation of architecture, the personification of this activity, this craft of building.'[54]

The years of Portoghesi's youth, absorbed by his *flânerie* in the historical mazes of Rome, coincided with the direct experience of fascism and the aftermath of the Second World War. Rome at this time was silent and solitary, and many parts of the historic city centre had been deserted. And yet in 1946 the paternal house in via della Chiesa Nuova 14, also in the centre of Rome, was full of activity. The second floor of the building was turned into the headquarters of the Comunità del Porcellino (Community of the Little Pig), a gathering of Catholic intellectuals, including Giuseppe Dossetti, an official in the Christian Democratic Party; Giorgio La Pira, an academic, politician and future mayor of Florence in the 1950s; Amintore Fanfani, member of Parliament and Minister of Employment and one of the highest-ranking representatives of the Christian Democrats. These members and others were all elected to the Constituent Assembly in 1946–47, leading to the approval of the Italian Constitution,[55] a document that set the foundational principles underpinning the Italian Republic which is still in effect today. The Community of the Little Pig was hosted by Portoghesi's aunts, Pia and Laura. Known as the 'Portoghesi sisters', they prepared food for the meetings, acting as the glue that held the group together. Paolo, then a fifteen-year-old boy, personally witnessed the discussion, construction and promulgation of the Italian Constitution – one of the most intense civic and political moments of postwar Italian history. The experience served as his initiation into politics, *tout-court*.

> In my grandparents' house, I met other young people who dealt with politics ... in whom I perceived, through the conversations I had at the table between one dish and another, a seriousness and a commitment that opened my sensitivity to the great theme of politics understood as a civic vocation.[56]

In this early experience, politics, initially observed with detachment by the young Portoghesi, became determinant of his adolescence and foundational for his career.

It was during this time (in 1946, precisely) that Portoghesi developed his passion for cinema when he began attending film sessions hosted by the Circolo Romano del Cinema at the Cinema Barberini.[57] The Circolo Romano del Cinema, then the most vital cinema club in Rome boasting illustrious founding members, held a great didactic significance for the young boy: alternating contemporary and historic films, it prepared the architect's sensitivity for cinema. Inspired by the work of Italian film critic Umberto Barbaro, Portoghesi began analysing films, reconstructing sequences and trying to determine how the editing was carried out. 'I had the keys to a technical understanding of the language of cinema, and this has remained my way of relating to the art of cinema,' he later commented.[58]

Portoghesi went on to study at the Facoltà di Architettura della Sapienza – Università di Roma (Sapienza University in Rome), the very first school of architecture in Italy,[59] graduating in 1957. When he enrolled, he was aware of the argument pursued by architect Luigi Moretti that baroque architecture had anticipated the idea of freedom from tradition. Long fascinated by the baroque, Portoghesi opted to recover this inheritance,[60] publishing articles on the subject while still a student and intuiting that aspects of modern architecture could be read and understood through the investigation of the baroque architectural experience. As Portoghesi remembers, his experience at the university was a traumatic time when, immediately after the war, the architectural paradigm of functionalism was strengthened by badly digested examples of modern architecture.

> I considered the faculty with contempt: the professors did not teach . . . everyone created his own little school based on personal preferences for this or that 'style'. The impression was that of having entered a ghost vessel adrift. . . . Only the choice of Muratori as professor of composition represented an attempt to seek continuity for the traditionalist tendency . . . the arrival of Zevi, Quaroni and Piccinato opened the way to a hypothesis of renewal, shipwrecked a few years later in the climate of '68.[61]

The nascent architect reacted to this environment by citing the reasons for a more complex and curious culture capable of merging memory and experimentation, artifice and nature.[62] What immediately followed was the pursuit of these ideas through publications and buildings. In 1953, Portoghesi, aged twenty-two and still a student, published his first essay on Borromini in the magazine *Civiltà delle macchine,* founded in the same year by Leonardo Sinisgalli and Giorgio Castelfranco with the aim of creating a dialogue between humanistic culture, technical knowledge and art.[63] His second essay, 'L'opera di Borromini per l'altare della chiesa di S. Paolo a Bologna',[64] was published the following year, coinciding with his first architectural project for the Town Hall of Civitacastellana in Viterbo. Soon after, in 1956, Portoghesi published his first book, *Guarino Guarini, 1624–1683*, a critical account of the life and oeuvre of the Piedmontese baroque architect. While researching and writing the volume, Portoghesi was also working as an architect, designing a residential area at Valchetta, near Rome in

FIGURE I.6 Paolo Portoghesi's photograph of the hall of the ENPAS Office building, Florence. © Paolo Portoghesi Archive.

1955. More architectural work followed; between 1957 and 1964, Portoghesi designed buildings for the state employee health and social security agency, Ente Nazionale Previdenza e Assistenza ai dipendenti Statali (ENPAS), in Pistoia, Lucca, Florence and Cesenatica (Figures I.6 and I.7).[65] All of these projects led to the design of Casa Baldi (1958–61).

Ultimately in the life of Portoghesi, these varied initial experiences proved formative, both in the context of his career and the cultivation of his persona. What began as a youthful flair for history while walking in the streets of Rome would eventually flourish into serious scholarship. A passion for politics first kindled within the family home would later translate into leadership positions at major institutions. An early awareness and interest in media, initially explored in high school through self-publishing and through the discovery of cinema, would

FIGURE I.7 Paolo Portoghesi's low-angled shot photograph of the ENPAS Office building, Lucca. © Paolo Portoghesi Archive.

culminate in his presidency of the Venice Biennale, a role and venue that communicated not only architecture to the world but also the possibilities for its exhibition. If the triangulation of these dimensions was not intentional from the outset, this combination of experiences played out over decades as Portoghesi's career advanced and his programme gained a clarity that led him to choreograph his postmodern project.

1 THE POSTMODERN PROJECT

FIGURE 1.1 Cover of issue 652 of *Domus*, July/August 1984, portraying Paolo Portoghesi. © Archivio Domus – © Editoriale Domus S.p.A.

During the first half of the 1980s, the Italian magazine *Domus*, then edited by Milan-based architect Alessandro Mendini, released a number of flashy and colourful covers featuring some of the icons of postmodern architecture.[1] Among these noteworthy subjects was the architect Paolo Portoghesi, posing on the cover of issue 652, published in 1984, wearing a crisp white suit and red tie (red being the colour of the Socialist Party, of which he was a long-time member). Leaning on a Thonet Art Nouveau chair, a piece of furniture belonging to the historical period of which he is a renowned expert, Portoghesi strikes a cabaret-style pose, as if he were the emcee of a nightclub rather than the president of the Venice Biennale, one of the world's leading cultural institutions.[2] The theatricality of the scene is enhanced by the backdrop: a miniature, white-framed stage and glittering blue curtain (Figure 1.1).

In this image, Portoghesi's presentation matches Mendini's ambition to highlight the ascendancy of Postmodernism. Indeed, the aim of *Domus* to pursue the idea of authorship by treating the cover of each issue as a 'face', coincided with the theme of the facade at the core of the 1980 *Strada Novissima* conceived by Portoghesi – the face/facade being a key point of discussion of postmodern culture.[3] The cover image of issue 652 was carefully curated to synthesize the ways in which Portoghesi was forging his idea of postmodern architecture: not simply via architectural design or theory, whose representations are absent from his portrait, but through the strategic interaction of historical knowledge, political symbolism and mediatic communication.

Impresario of postmodern architecture

At the heart of Portoghesi's work is the question of historic continuity in architecture, a problem that, as Chapter 2 shows, he has always tackled simultaneously and synergically, as both a historian and a designer. Never relying on a singular period but, rather, the full body of history, Portoghesi claimed the centrality of the role of the past in disciplinary discussions in order to reinstitute freedom in the contemporary design process. To achieve this objective Portoghesi deployed what we have called his postmodern project – that is, a life-long strategy, personally and progressively constructed, to bring about a structural disciplinary shift, transitioning Italian architectural culture out of the constricting orthodoxy of the Modern Movement into a postmodern phase open to new possibilities.[4] Building on the masterful work of Ernesto Nathan Rogers and Bruno Zevi, for example, but also on the design methods of postwar architects including Mario Ridolfi, Ignazio Gardella and Gabetti & Isola, Portoghesi was able to push experimentation in design methodology and architectural language, ultimately directing the vessel of Italian architecture into a more international phase. The zenith of this undertaking coincided with his directorship of the first Venice Architecture Biennale in 1980, an event that should not be seen as the inception but the celebration of Italian postmodern architectural culture. Unlike most of the protagonists of the Italian architectural scene of his

FIGURE 1.2 Paolo Portoghesi in San Francisco for the opening of the itinerant exhibition *The Presence of the Past* at the Fort Mason, 1982. From right to left: Alessandra Latour, Paolo Portoghesi, Giovanna Massobrio, Roberto Pirzio-Biroli, Robert A. M. Stern and others. © Paolo Portoghesi Archive.

generation, Portoghesi was one of the first to understand the need to open the country to the international debate and engage in a discussion about different ways of pursuing a methodological and linguistic reform (Figure 1.2).

While Portoghesi's project was involved in the debates on history, memory and typology that were already taking place in schools in Rome, Venice and Milan, he strategically welcomed the tendencies and sensibilities that were flourishing elsewhere at the time – especially in the United States and in England – and blended these other voices into Italian culture.

For Portoghesi to achieve such an ambitious objective, conceived with a clarity of intention that not many other architects could boast, it was necessary to work with different tools, across disciplines and at the centre of a wide academic, institutional and political network. His involvement with neoliberal policies and skills as a communicator enabled his postmodern project to operate across multiple channels simultaneously, and his ability to hold together and manage the interaction of such different realms – namely architecture, politics and media – that elsewhere in Western culture would have existed separately and in shifting orders of importance, was a unique yet crucial ability.

It was quite early in his career that Portoghesi established a centre of power made up of cultural alliances that he formed in order to foster his design agenda.[5]

These cultural and ideological coalitions – carried out between Rome, Venice and Milan, as well as further afield, between Italy, England, the United States and the Middle East, and with differing frequencies and intensity – were meant to maximize the reach of his postmodern project. What might have resembled a heterogeneous bestiary was seamlessly held together by Portoghesi. Even professional enmities and infamous fall-outs – those with Bruno Zevi and Manfredo Tafuri, for example – were significant opportunities for Portoghesi to sharpen his approach and adjust his cultural trajectory.

Writing in his editorial for *Domus* 652, Alessandro Mendini defined Portoghesi as the 'official manager of Postmodernist architecture'.[6] Indeed, his ability to manage such a major cast of players while continuously stirring situations towards his cultural advantage, spoke to the sharpness and strength of his project – a project that he deployed over four decades of substantial transformation. While recollecting the history of Postmodernism, Charles Jencks identified Portoghesi – architect, historian of the baroque and member of the venerable Accademia di San Luca – as 'well-placed to become the impresario of the nascent postmodern movement'.[7] More than anyone else, Portoghesi was able to catalyse Italian postmodern tendencies, some significantly distant from others, as shown in his book dedicated to the young generation of Italian architects *I nuovi architetti italiani* (1985).[8] This comprehensive grasp of the Italian scene went hand-in-hand with an attempt to connect it to an international dimension. Although not necessarily seeking wide international standing for himself, Portoghesi used his intellectual and institutional status to deprovincialize Italian design and join it with the global scene.[9] In turn, those architectural ideas, principles and polemics, once understood as peculiar to Italian culture, through Portoghesi achieved a new international valence. Thus, operating as impresario – organizer of a company of architectural players – he was responsible not only for theorizing and fostering an idea of postmodernity in relation to architecture, but also for many of the key moments (as well as the crossroads, new trajectories and schools of thought) in its ultimate realization.

Like Philip Johnson in the United States and Charles Jencks in the UK, Paolo Portoghesi, through his public exposure, was the Italian architect to take the lead in triggering and guiding the transition from the exhausted condition in which modern architecture had found itself, to what he saw as a more vital postmodern phase. In other words, and following Mary McLeod's line, the support Portoghesi offered to postmodern architects might be compared to that of Vincent Scully, who gave credibility in the 1970s and 1980s to Louis Kahn, Robert Venturi and the Grays, helping validate the rise of postmodern architecture in the United States.[10] On the one hand, organizing exhibitions, publications, institutional events and educational programmes, Portoghesi generated the conditions for a cultural change of direction in the discipline. On the other hand, he strategically promoted specific lines of research deeply rooted in design methods that proved crucial to the development of postmodern architecture. When asked by Mendini if, in his multiform role as a politician, historian, teacher, architect, coordinator of culture and magazines, he sometimes felt the nostalgia for a single prevalent vocation, Portoghesi replied: 'My deep vocation is to design and build, but in the face of the architect's professional crisis I have chosen to fight the battle to change architecture with all possible weapons.'[11]

Though he was aware of the risks and ambiguity that came with the use of the word 'postmodern', for Portoghesi, its very ambivalence was 'liberating'.[12] Even if there were doubts about how it might be defined, 'postmodern' alone seemed capable of breaking the oppressive spell of modernism, and that in itself was useful.[13] While the origin and history of the word 'postmodern' are by now well known,[14] its reception in Italy was problematic because of its stylistic focus. Indeed, in Italy, postmodern architecture coincided with a period of methodological experimentation which was the real contribution to the shift from modern to postmodern architectural culture.

Acknowledging Italy's problematic relationship with the expression, the art critic and philosopher Gillo Dorfles posited that 'postmodern' signalled much more than 'what could only appear as the elucubrations of fashion, whims of a mercantile game or some advertising slogans'.[15] From the beginning of its circulation, Portoghesi embraced the notion of postmodernity as a 'cultural dominant',[16] avoiding the stylistic label (postmodern*ism*) altogether and sticking to the original meaning of term – that is, the departure from modern:

> Of the word 'postmodern', I would use what comes from its etymology. I would attempt to group provisionally under this term those experiences that tend to move away from the perspective of the modern, especially how it has crystallised in the 1950s and 1960s. It is a word that was born from the anger to distinguish from something that was shapeless, that, as said by Aragonne, had such vanishing characteristics to give the impression to his enemies of combating with shadows.[17]

With postmodernity forgoing the modernist impulse toward unity and the reconstitution of the ephemeral and fragmentary within the eternal and inalterable space of art,[18] Portoghesi, to a certain extent, was appropriating Jean-François Lyotard's notion of 'the breaking up of the Grand Narratives'.[19] Lyotard's critique of modernity challenges the presumption and orientation of modern political philosophy according to which knowledge and society are justified in terms of a set of unifying metatheories. For Lyotard, the totalizing perspective of these metanarratives was superseded by a postmodern acceptance of difference and variety. Portoghesi, however, may have shared intellectual affinities with the French philosopher, but he did not completely adhere to his ideas: 'I think that Lyotard's diagnosis – that the central systems were dead – was elegant, but not entirely true (if one thinks, for example, at the religious revival that was going on at that time).'[20]

From the 1960s onwards, Italian cities became active laboratories of original and independent theoretical and design hypotheses, acting as interconnected focal points. First in Venice and then in Rome, Bruno Zevi elaborated an operative approach to history to generate new tools for design. In the Milan of *Casabella-continuità*, Aldo Rossi and Giorgio Grassi theorized a typological approach to history, pursued through the rhetorical figure of the analogy. Rossi's obsession with repetition and his technique of juxtaposing primary volumes resulted in the abstraction of the architectural project and the return of personal and collective memory into the process of design. During the 1980s, the avant-garde group Studio Alchimia, led by Mendini, and the Memphis-Milano, founded by Ettore Sottsass, fostered a heterodox approach to design with the use of irony, ambiguity and hedonistic forms retrieved from the everyday life. In Venice, Saverio Muratori, a pioneer of typo-morphological investigations, had condemned modern urban planning and its lost relations with the historical city. This quick survey, which includes only a few of the many research lines reflecting on new forms of design hypotheses, reveals how the Italian profession was taking action according to different principles and within different theoretical scenarios. If the Italian response to modernity was collective – and the need to find new theoretical premises was agreed upon – the forms that this revision took were independent and gave shape to a rich mosaic of approaches with divergences and contradictions that were not viewed as obstacles but welcomed.[21]

One of the recurrent lines of inquiry and discussion revolved around the concept of *progetto*. In 1960s and 1970s Italy, the word *progetto* meant much more than a set of architectural drawings for a specific project.[22] It was actually understood in its deeper sense, namely, a 'projection' into the future, a long-lasting plan motivated by an intention or a construction of a scenario to be carried out on ideological and political premises. Despite the common understanding of the ideological and intellectual foundations of any *progetto*, its programme was carried out in personal and original terms by different architects. Zevi, for example, deployed his *progetto* to foster democratic ideals through operative criticism, a method to design history in relation to the future.[23] By contrast, Tafuri, drawing on the ideas of Walter Benjamin and ultimately Friedrich Nietzsche,[24] viewed history itself as a *progetto* that was 'surely not architectural'.[25] This attitude was reflected in his *Progetto e utopia*, published in 1973, whose title makes reference to the art historian Giulio Carlo Argan's 1965 book, *Progetto e destino*. Furthermore, in his introduction to *La sfera e il labirinto* (1987), titled 'The historical project', Tafuri writes of 'history as a "project of crisis" ... [where] there is no guarantee as to the absolute validity of such a project, no "solution" in it'.[26]

Another personal take on the notion of *progetto* comes from Aldo Rossi, who aimed to 'write projects, story, film, painting ... [as] a projection of reality'.[27] Distinct from both Zevi and Tafuri, Rossi's *progetto* included 'something that is unexpected and unpredictable'.[28] In the wake of this tradition, Pier Vittorio Aureli, one of the most passionate interpreters of Italian architectural theories of the 1960s and 1970s, has put forward the notion of the 'city as a project' – that is, the result of the relationship between urban history, architecture and politics.[29] Based on these interpretations, design as well as the theory and history of architecture cannot be understood as autonomous from political ideologies; they are instead intertwined and contain broader cultural, social and political dynamics and reverberations, or to paraphrase the title of Antonio Monestiroli's book, they are linked to the architecture of reality.[30]

As for Portoghesi, his *progetto* revolved around the idea of the history of architecture as an essential tool for liberating the discipline from the orthodoxy of the Modern Movement, admitting a pluralism of proposals and approaches. As observed by architectural historian Luciano Patetta, who worked closely with Portoghesi during his Milanese years, 'the maestro was brilliant, for his ability to look at all of history with no prejudice, manipulating it with total control'.[31]

FIGURE 1.3 Paolo Portoghesi presenting the *New Dictionary of Architecture and Urbanism* to the president of the Italian Republic, Giuseppe Saragat, in Rome, 1970. © Archivio Storico della Presidenza della Repubblica, Archivio fotografico, Saragat.

One of the first occasions on which Portoghesi found himself 'at the centre' of Italian architectural culture came in the mid-1960s, when he was asked to edit the *Dizionario enciclopedico di architettura e urbanistica*. The project meant taking part in 'a theoretical re-foundation of the architectural discipline which, after having become aware of the expansion of its domains and its civil commitment, now requires a recognition of its specificity'.[32] By accepting this editorial role, Portoghesi sought to provide architects and urbanists with an annotated vocabulary for working in a renewed disciplinary context. The six-volume edition, published in 1968, was intended to set the conditions for a national debate: 'Ideas, men and things are purposely intertwined to represent the "universe of discourse" of architecture in its richness and complexity – that field of notions and tensions where the architect must make their choices'.[33] Entries to the dictionary were written by internationally renowned architects, historians, philosophers, urbanists and intellectuals, including Arnaldo Bruschi, Christian Norberg-Schulz, Enrico Guidoni, Franco Borsi, Giulio Carlo Argan, Italo Insolera, Ludovico Quaroni, Renato Nicolini, Manfredo Tafuri, Sandro Benedetti, Rosario Assunto, Umberto Eco and Werner Oechslin. The involvement of so many disciplinary experts attests to Portoghesi's desire to cross-pollinate the discipline of architecture with other fields of interest, opening it up to a plurality of points of view and possible connections.

In early 1970, the dictionary was formally presented to the president of the Italian Republic, Giuseppe Saragat, at the Quirinale Palace in Rome, in the presence of Francesco Malgeri, head of the Roman Publishing Institute, as well as members of its board, and Professor of Archaeology Massimo Pallottino. In this moment of institutional recognition and nationwide refoundation for the discipline,[34] Portoghesi stood both as a representative of Italian architecture at the crossroads of culture and politics and as a man engaging an extensive network of scholars from different disciplines, schools and circles (Figure 1.3). The dictionary was a testing ground that had allowed Portoghesi to put himself forward as the linchpin of Italian architecture in the postmodern period while, with the support of state and cultural institutions, giving legitimacy to his postmodern project.

Choosing Rossi

In the Festschrift published for Portoghesi's sixtieth birthday, Aldo Rossi provided a personal account of his colleague, whom he described as a brave and balanced 'superior' with a sense of civic responsibility, an elder presence and a guide in different – and sometimes difficult – institutional situations. The tone of the letter is full of respect for a man who played a fundamental role in the construction of Rossi as a national, and later international, 'hero' of postmodern architectural culture.[35] Both men belonged to the same generation: they were born in the same year and shared many common interests, from theatre and cinema to Russian literature.[36] Yet Rossi, introverted and ill-tempered, was initially seen as a reclusive master of uncompromising thinking, while Portoghesi's outgoing and charming personality was at the opposite end of the spectrum. Even with their differences, the two architects came to appreciate each other reciprocally, with Rossi leveraging the institutional power of Portoghesi to boost his career, and Portoghesi instrumentalizing Rossi's work to deploy his postmodern project in a highly poetic way while strengthening his argument for contemporary design's return to history. This pairing played a fundamental role in the trajectory of Portoghesi's postmodern project during the late 1970s and 1980s.

The two first met in Milan in the 1950s, through a mutual friend, the architect Guido Canella. As Portoghesi remembers, 'I asked if [Canella] would introduce me to the editorial staff of *Casabella-continuità*, and he said that the best way to meet them was to go to Samantha's, a discotheque in the centre of Milan, where they all used to hang out.'[37] On cue, the two men encountered each other that very evening, first exchanging pleasantries over the dance floor before retiring to a quieter corner table to talk more. From that moment on, the two architects were linked by a profound intellectual affinity and friendship. Later, they became colleagues at the Politecnico di Milano, when Portoghesi was dean of the Faculty of Architecture and Rossi was appointed as Professor of Architectural Design in 1969. Between 1969 and 1976, Rossi's built and unbuilt work consistently featured in *Controspazio*, the magazine founded and directed by Portoghesi.[38] During this period Rossi was still very much seen as a 'Milanese matter'. However, to Portoghesi, who in 1970 dedicated the tenth issue of the journal to Rossi's work (Figure 1.4), he was 'an architect who could disseminate new ideas, because he was the first to propose a really alternative architecture'.[39]

But beyond Portoghesi's admiration for Rossi's unique architectural language, it was a series of shared ideas and principles that linked the two men and helped them propel one another's career. Portoghesi admired Rossi's analysis of urban morphology and typology, his poetic of historical fragments recomposed in new terms eventuating in original formal results, and his compelling theory of the analogous city.[40] While the thorough record of Rossi's projects in the pages of *Controspazio* helped his career to move beyond the limits of Milan, his relationship with the magazine was not unidirectional. In response to an article on his work written by the Milanese editor and architectural historian Ezio Bonfanti,[41] Rossi acknowledged that the interpretation had helped him 'clarify what I do in a singular way: above all, the distinction you [Bonfanti] make between compensation and addition ... the description and analysis of the additive process'.[42] Hence, Rossi stated that Bonfanti's enunciations 'step into the very matter of compositive process and are for me elements of clarity, which I intend to adopt and on which I want to work'.[43] These extracts show that through *Controspazio*, Portoghesi engaged in a disciplinary dialogue with his friend and colleague that would eventuate in the recognition of an 'Architettura di Tendenza' – a new tendency. Portoghesi's confidence in Rossi's design potential as

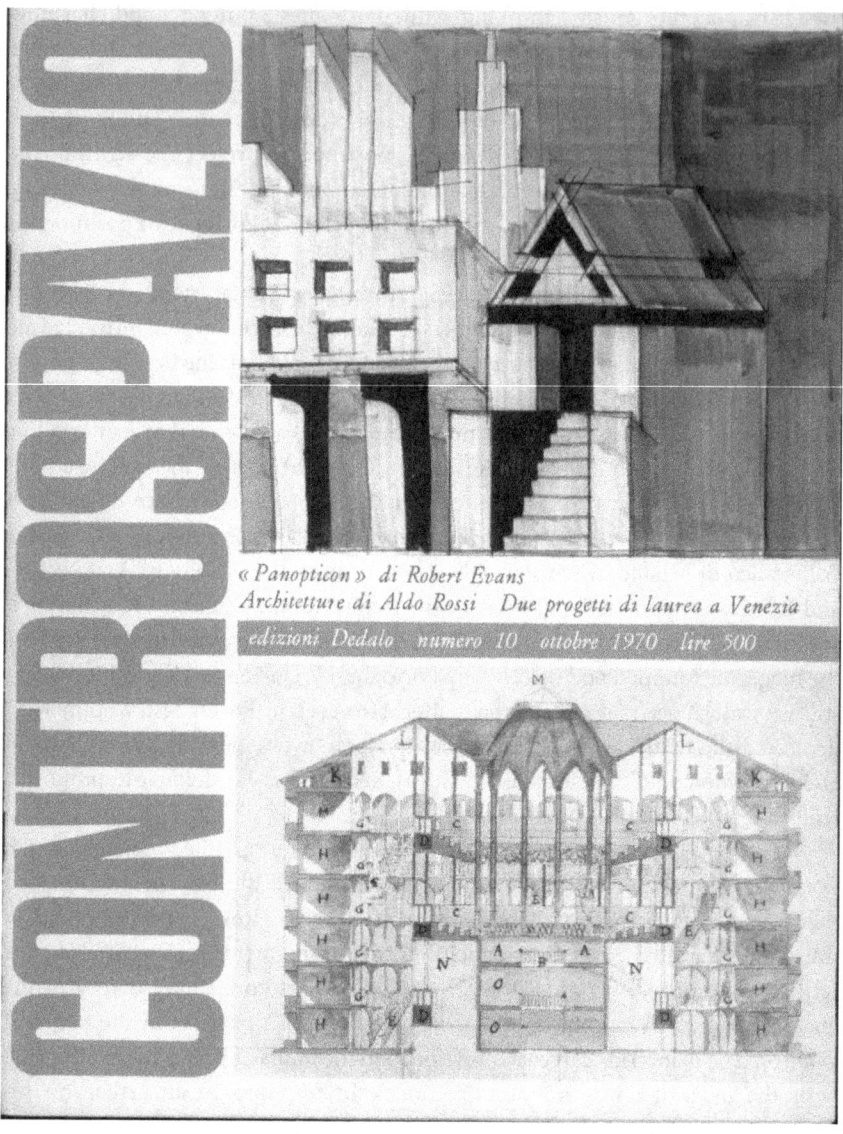

FIGURE 1.4 Cover of the architectural magazine *Controspazio*, issue 10, 1970, dedicated to Aldo Rossi.

transmitted from the pages of his journal was not enough to boost his aura and turn him into a 'case'[44] or even a 'phenomenon'[45] of international stature.[46]

Rossi's work was propelled through different routes throughout the 1970s. Part of a pedagogical diaspora caused by the suspension of eight professors from the Faculty of Architecture at the Politecnico di Milano, Rossi began commuting to

Switzerland, where he was offered a visiting professorship at the ETH Zurich, between 1972 and 1974. From there, he generated ties with the 'German School', establishing connections with, among others, Oswald Mathias Ungers. In the United States, Rossi's projects had been a subject of attention at the Institute of Architecture and Urban Studies (IAUS) in New York, where he landed thanks to his relationships with the Università Iuav di Venezia (IUAV). It was Peter Eisenman, director of the IAUS, who, in 1976, promoted the English translation of an essay by Rafael Moneo on Rossi's architecture in the institute's journal *Oppositions*.[47] In this context Rossi began publishing books with MIT Press: *A Scientific Autobiography* was released in 1981 (in English, even before the Italian edition), and the translation of *The Architecture of the City* was published the following year. While these editorial projects, with Eisenman's support, granted the Milanese architect world-wide visibility, they had the effect of pigeonholing Rossi within the realm of theory.[48]

Portoghesi, however, foresaw that pushing Rossi not just as a theoretician but as a designer too would launch his architecture even further. One simply had to generate occasions to build. Early in his career Rossi had worked with Guido Canella, who had involved the young architect in the Segrate master plan, offering him the opportunity to design the townhall's plaza and fountain (1965–67). Similarly, Carlo Aymonino had invited Rossi to contribute to the Monte Amiata project in Milan with the Gallaratese residential building (1968–73). Recognizing the success of these projects, Portoghesi considered strategic venues where Rossi's architecture could be showcased 'in reality'. This 'take' on Rossi marked a substantial shift from those of Tafuri and Scully, for instance, who wrote profusely about the architect but never promoted his architecture in more pragmatic terms.

One way to give Rossi building opportunities was through architectural competitions. Together with Aymonino, Portoghesi was part of the competition jury for the San Cataldo Cemetery in Modena (1971),[49] which awarded Rossi first prize.[50] In 1984 Portoghesi and Aymonino (as well as Gino Valle) sat on another competition jury, this time for the reconstruction of the Carlo Felice Theatre in Genoa for which the entry by Ignazio Gardella, Fabio Reinhart and Rossi won first prize. Yet, it was the Venice Architecture Biennale that presented the real opportunity to involve Rossi in a spectacular display – one that eventuated in his international success: the Teatro del Mondo (1979–80). It was 1979 when Portoghesi and Maurizio Scaparro, director of the Biennale's theatre department, imagined building a temporary structure that referenced the sixteenth-century models of the *theatrum mundi* while floating in the Bacino di San Marco. The project was the outcome of a unique cultural period of the Biennale and of the exceptional collaboration between the theatre and architecture sectors. The new stage would form part of the exhibition *Venezia e lo Spazio Scenico* (*Venice and the Scenic Space*) as a setting for shows and performances.[51] It would also be used by Scaparro for the first edition of the Venetian Carnival (an event revived in 1980

FIGURE 1.5 Paolo Portoghesi and Aldo Rossi (in the middle), on a water taxi following the Teatro del Mondo on its way from Fusina to the Bacino di San Marco, Venice, 1979. © Antonio Martinelli.

after years of interruption) to host a small theatre season. Following this, it would become the now well-known 'floating fragment' of *The Presence of the Past* exhibition (Figure 1.5).[52]

From Portoghesi's perspective, Rossi was ideally suited to carry out such a singular project. The architect's design poetic, informed by the intent to establish a bond with the history of the city, aligned with the ambitions of this latter-day *theatrum mundi*. And, in practical terms, 'Rossi's architecture worked perfectly!'[53] With a passion for theatre, both as an art and a typology, as well as a fondness for small-scale timber architectures (such as beach cabins, kiosks and confessionals), Rossi accepted the invitation on one condition: the temporary building had to be twenty metres in height. The bold request surprised the two directors who had imagined a more modest structure, but it was motivated by the need for the new theatre to establish a dialogue with its immediate urban context, busy with illustrious Venetian monuments. Torn between the eagerness to indulge Rossi's proposal and the responsibility of managing the project on behalf of the Venetian institution, Portoghesi and Scaparro took the risk and gave Rossi the green light. The episode marked an exceptional moment of intellectual freedom in the history of the Biennale,[54] and Italian culture in general. Despite its ephemeral nature and short existence, Rossi's theatrical machine became a living fantasy that for decades has reverberated across international architecture culture (see Chapter 4).

Despite this major contribution, Rossi did not feature among the twenty architects involved in the design of the facades for the famous *Strada Novissima*. But according to Portoghesi the decision not to join the *Strada* was 'typical of Aldo'.[55] Still, in his role as director, Portoghesi managed to find privileged ways for his colleague to participate, further boosting the overall cultural agenda of the 1980 Biennale:

> The fraternal friendship with Aldo Rossi was also of great help to me in the development of the First International Exhibition ... precisely because I felt the urgency in Aldo to overcome an ideological orientation to devote himself to architecture with full confidence in his poetic strength. This made it possible to fight a battle together for an architecture of research and imagination.[56]

The imaginations of Portoghesi and Rossi were boundless. While working on the Teatro commission Rossi was asked to design the gate to the Corderie dell'Arsenale (1980, also known as Porta), the main entrance to *The Presence of the Past* exhibition (Figure 1.6). Like the Teatro, the Porta was a temporary structure made of timber

FIGURE 1.6 Entrance to the Arsenale with the gate (Porta) designed by Aldo Rossi for the exhibition *The Presence of the Past*, Venice, 1979. Photograph by Paolo Portoghesi. © Paolo Portoghesi Archive.

and steel and offered a typological interpretation of the urban structures that once animated Venice. Mounted between two pre-existing constructions and spanning the Campo della Tana, the Porta was a cheerful greeting for visitors as well as a hint towards the ephemeral display of the *Strada Novissima*.[57] At the same time, the Porta allowed Rossi to erect his 'frontage' without being directly involved in the assemblage of the *Strada*. Moreover, this intervention was not simply a 'facade' – a *capriccio*, like the twenty frontages inside – but a temporary urban element, set within the city of Venice, with its own function of signalling and volumetrically articulating the exhibition's entrance.[58] Unlike the facades of the *Strada Novissima*, but similar to the Teatro, the Porta was designed to become a fragment of the city.

Following the success of the First International Architecture Exhibition of the Venice Biennale, when Portoghesi became president in 1983, he appointed Rossi as the director of the third and fourth editions (1985 and 1986) of the International Exhibition of Architecture. In so doing, Portoghesi ensured that he had a successor who could pursue the project of disciplinary renewal focused on the centrality of history in the design process. Portoghesi should therefore be credited as a key advocate who actively consecrated the work of Rossi in the international context.[59] For Rossi this act of munificence led to numerous commissions in Europe, the United States and Japan, where he could communicate his architectural ideas beyond the idiosyncrasies of Italian culture. Paradoxically, as Rossi's reputation was growing abroad, he lost the competition for the renovation of the Palazzo del Cinema at the Lido of Venice. But by this point he was far from a 'Milanese matter'; Aldo Rossi was a global matter on the postmodern scene – a truth that was confirmed in 1991 when he was awarded the Pritzker Prize. In turn, Portoghesi's postmodern project, as embodied by Rossi's buildings, had become an international point of discussion.

Mendini and the Banal

While Rossi was working on the Teatro for the Biennale in Venice, he also appeared on the cover of *Domus*, then directed by Alessandro Mendini. From this very first issue, and running through the early 1980s, Mendini, leader of the radical avant-garde Studio Alchimia, turned the most internationally recognized Italian design magazine *Domus* into a caravanserai for postmodern culture, bringing about a shift in national and international thinking in the broad field of design. Described by the journalist Barbara Radice as 'a catalyst of situations and supplier of doubts and energies, a sophisticated intellectual',[60] Mendini was well aware of the magazine's reputation and reach, built over decades under the direction of Gio Ponti, and he used the journal as an international showcase for new ways of conceiving architectural and industrial design.

Thus, in the 1980s Portoghesi and Mendini were operating in parallel, from two of the most influential Italian cultural venues, respectively the Biennale in Venice and *Domus* in Milan, to foster postmodern thinking with the shared goal of framing and internationally broadcasting new operative modes based on the free use of historical material. The two cultural operators, as they were, met in the late 1960s, when Portoghesi became dean of the Faculty of Architecture at the Politecnico di Milano. As the years passed, they shared the sense that they were fighting for the same thing: 'There was a sort of human sympathy because Mendini had always had a great sense of humour,' recalled Portoghesi. 'At the same time, he was both a very serious character and a thoughtful person.'[61] In essence, Portoghesi's and Mendini's common ground and practices reveal an alignment of ideas and method: a similar way of using history as a repertoire deprived of any hierarchization between elements and periods.

In perfect harmony with Portoghesi's attitude, Mendini introduced the hypothesis of the postmodern not as a linguistic trend, but as a working method that could be applied to every design and architectural project. In so doing, Mendini distanced himself – as well as his large group of collaborators – from any stylistic take on postmodern architecture. History was a central issue of disciplinary discourse, but unlike the stylistic approach of the United States, Mendini prized the experimentation of design methods that interpreted historical material instead of reproposing it formally. As articulated in the manifesto published by Studio Alchimia, 'memory and tradition were important, but the new design was autonomous from any rhetorical concession'.[62] Similar to Portoghesi's, Mendini's method used history as a horizontal 'repository' of inspiration to be examined 'in a sensitive and not scientific way',[63] an individual and romantic approach to the way historical references were used.[64] Yet, where Portoghesi's 'historical storage' was philologically put together, refined and scientifically explored, Mendini's was full of ordinary objects, buildings and urban rituals, considered with an everyday approach. As discussed at the beginning of this chapter, the facade was an element that found its way into the work of both men. In 1980, the facade became the site for testing the possibilities of postmodern architecture, with Portoghesi inviting international designers to conceive bi-dimensional building facades for the *Strada Novissima*, and Mendini addressing the theme through a new series of *Domus* covers that acted as the proscenium to the magazine. In both cases, the idea of the facade emphasized the ongoing shift from an architecture of space to an architecture of image.

But the metaphor of the facade was not the only tie between the two men. In 1980, Portoghesi invited Mendini to take part in the first International Architecture Exhibition of the Venice Biennale with an exhibition called *L'oggetto banale* (The Banal Object), co-curated with Paola Navone, Daniela Puppa and Franco Raggi (Figure 1.7). With this invitation, one can see Portoghesi's skills as impresario, embracing a similar intellectual premise with different formal output

FIGURE 1.7 Exhibition *L'oggetto banale* curated by Alessandro Mendini, Paola Navone, Daniela Puppa and Franco Raggi, included in *The Presence of the Past*, Venice Biennale, 1980. © Santi Caleca.

in the wake of a common cultural postmodern mission – what Mendini called the 'project's revolution'. The installation *The Banal Object*, which included thirty everyday objects, from a Bialetti coffeemaker to a stiletto heel, each subjected to a surface 'treatment' of re-design through colour and small decorative modules,[65] offered Mendini's version of postmodern design. The display struck an alliance with Portoghesi which has yet to be recognized: Mendini's theory of the banal overlapped with Portoghesi's approach to postmodern architecture, especially in the motivation to overcome the incommunicability of Modernism, which had for so long focused on abstraction and alienated those who did not have the vocabulary to understand it:

> The art had gone in the opposite direction to that of the people. Mendini and I felt this in the same way. I am thinking of the interest in kitsch; when he made the 'Proust' Armchair, he undoubtedly strayed far from my quest to join the modern with the ancient, but at the same time he proclaimed the fundamental flaw of modern culture.[66]

The Banal Object, made of re-styled ordinary objects, focused on the potential of industrial design as a field of linguistic and conceptual experimentation. The exhibition also included a large painting by Arduino Cantafora entitled

La città banale. For Mendini, the notion of 'Banal' informed a bottom-up method that could replace a more elitist intellectual approach: 'One can hypothesize a banal design methodology, a neo-banal design and architecture culturally self-known. A possible, trump card to play in a moment when all the "postmodern" design methods mark the time.'[67] Eight years after the landmark exhibition *Italy: The New Domestic Landscape*, curated by Emilio Ambasz at the Museum of Modern Art in New York (1972), which contributed to the launch of Italian design culture worldwide, Portoghesi's decision to involve Mendini and Alchimia in the Biennale was driven by his awareness of the increasing centrality and agency of industrial design in the production and dissemination of Italian design culture abroad.[68]

Much of Mendini's approach was, in fact, elemental. From the pieces that formed the *Banal Objects* exhibition to the stories and images that shaped each issue of *Domus*, the venues Mendini occupied presented a postmodern vision through a series of parts. As he stated in his seminal essay 'Per un'architettura banale', published in 1979: 'We need a fragmentary and particular vision of the project, and we need to believe that actions and very elemental objects can be instrumental for the project's revolution and to disentangle the reactionary stronghold of the disciplines.'[69] For both Portoghesi and Mendini, the most experimental design outcomes occurred at the intersections of different disciplines. According to Mendini, a fragmented or object-based approach would create the most opportunities for individual disciplines to finally engage with one another. In his role as art director of Alessi, the Milanese homeware and kitchen utensil company, Mendini would once again put this approach into practice. Between 1979 and 1983 Alessi ran the 'Tea & Coffee Piazza' project, in which eleven Italian and international architects, including Paolo Portoghesi, were invited to design a tea and coffee table service. Nine of the designers who participated in the 'Tea & Coffee Piazza' project – namely Michael Graves, Hans Hollein, Charles Jencks, Aldo Rossi, Stanley Tigerman and Robert Venturi – also participated in different capacities in the First International Exhibition of Architecture of the Biennale in 1980. If for Alessi these creative offerings became niche products of high-end design, globally distributed through museum shops and retail outlets (such as Max Protetch Gallery in New York[70]), for Mendini, and Portoghesi too, this was yet one more place to put forward experimental methods, forms and typologies that could nourish the debate on postmodern design on a broad scale.

Ideological duel with Tafuri

One of the most fruitful intellectual exchanges that allowed Portoghesi to refine his postmodern project took place during the 1960s and 1970s with Manfredo Tafuri. While memories, recollections and anecdotes of infamous clashes, arguments and personal resentments between the two have followed one another

– feeding a disciplinary drama 'Italian-style' – their encounters and interactions released dynamic and innovative forces in architectural history, giving rise to the formation of two schools of thought that have distinctively directed the making of architectural thinking in postmodern Italy and beyond.

Born three years apart in Rome, both Portoghesi and Tafuri experienced the brutalities of the Second World War. Each has recollected the emptiness of the capital city, which resulted in an isolating youth and education.[71] As teenagers, they found consolation in culture, taking solitary walks in their shared eternal city and eagerly reading the works of Rimbaud and Leopardi (Portoghesi) and Jean-Paul Sartre and Martin Heidegger (Tafuri). Their careers started within the same cultural and educational system, in the Faculty of Architecture at La Sapienza, and both complained about the quality of teaching and the fact that their professors were never around.[72] Their first recorded encounter took place in 1959, in Vicenzo Fasolo's history of architecture class, where Portoghesi was a course tutor and Tafuri a final year student. Tafuri's term paper – on scenography – had hugely impressed his instructors, and years later, in an effort to dilute Tafuri's savage attack on the scenographic aspects of postmodern architecture at the 1980 *Strada Novissima*, Portoghesi would recall the critic's early affection for the subject. Like Portoghesi, Tafuri embarked on his own academic career immediately after graduating, initially working as Ludovico Quaroni's teaching assistant. During this time he considered becoming an urban planner, but Portoghesi talked him out of such a path and furthered Tafuri's nascent academicism by helping him collect and edit his essays on mannerism – some written for *Casabella-continuità* – into a single volume. This collection eventuated in *L'architettura del Manierismo nel Cinquecento europeo*,[73] appearing in 1966. The same year, Portoghesi published *Roma barocca*,[74] a book understood as an instrument for architects. Of that crucial moment, Portoghesi recalled:

> Manfredo had positively reviewed my books *Roma barocca* and *Borromini*, and following my recommendation, he had gone to Carpegna to rummage in the Spada archive with excellent results. I advised him to leave Quaroni, for whom he had become an assistant, and above all to ditch urban planning for the history of architecture which was, in my opinion, his real vocation. When he objected that he had not yet written a real book, I replied that putting together what he had already done would easily achieve what was needed to become an academic. Together we approached Aldo Quinti, editor of the publisher Officina, and it was decided that a book on Mannerism would be part of the series directed by me.[75]

From 1962 to 1967, Portoghesi taught Italian literature at La Sapienza. He had just completed his first residential building – the wilfully neo-baroque Casa Baldi – and continued to juggle design commissions with his academic work, developing research on Francesco Borromini that he had first pursued as an undergraduate. Tafuri was also involved in practice through his participation in Architetti e Urbanisti Associati (AUA) where he upheld the role of 'controlling critic'.[76] Also during these years, both Portoghesi and Tafuri were registered with the same political party, the Italian Socialist Party (PSI), although Tafuri would soon move to the Italian Socialist Proletariat Unity Party (PSIUP).[77]

This parallel journey was interrupted 'one tragic night'. Tafuri recalled: 'I was miserable because I had to decide between practice and history. I remember I was sweating, walking around ... had the fever. At the end, in the morning I had decided ... I knew at that moment that it should be history.'[78] Triggered by a personal crisis, this stance generated the first ideological split between the two historians who, up to this point, had enjoyed a comparable path. Where now Tafuri saw a sheer division, Portoghesi reinforced his belief in a synergic interaction of history and design, where history was seen as instrumental to design.

In 1966 Bruno Zevi sought to promote Portoghesi and Tafuri, the two most promising historians in Rome – and probably in Italy – to tenure positions as history of architecture professors. To everyone's surprise, the obvious candidate for the role, Leonardo Benevolo, author of *Storia dell'architettura moderna* (1960), among others, had been side-lined. Both Portoghesi and Tafuri were offered the title – Portoghesi at the Politecnico di Milano and Tafuri at the IUAV in Venice. Following their appointments, the two young professors were invited by Zevi to co-author with him a book on the history of architecture. For Zevi this was a significant move to orient the future of the discipline and to establish a framework that could potentially triangulate Italy's three principal architectural centres: Zevi operating from the Sapienza in Rome, Portoghesi from the Politecnico di Milano, and Tafuri from IUAV in Venice.[79] Things did not go as planned, as a letter from Zevi to Portoghesi reveals:

> By writing a letter to you and Tafuri, of which I keep a copy ... I proposed a common action plan. I didn't care much about Tafuri. Instead, the fact that you did not respond to that fraternal proposal is still inexplicable to me. I wanted to strengthen our actions, while ensuring the autonomy of each of us. I wanted these actions to be parallel and convergent. Even in the educational system.[80]

Although Portoghesi has since rectified this statement, saying he welcomed the proposal,[81] he confirmed that Tafuri, unable to agree with the operative criticism fostered by Zevi and embraced by Portoghesi, declined the invitation to collaborate. Tafuri had ditched the historical analysis of individual monuments considered as architectural objects in favour of a more systemic approach, where the building is the result of multiple processes. He never delved into the geometrical verifications that Portoghesi used to undertake in his studies of baroque architecture (see Chapter 2). As pointed out by James Ackerman, Tafuri instead showed how architectural history was woven into the social, economic and political fabric of the time being examined.[82]

Portoghesi, meanwhile, was condemned by Tafuri for approaching the past and present through his agenda as a practitioner.[83] The direct attack, forever remembered as the infamous *quarrel*, came in 1969 with the publication of Tafuri's article, 'Per una critica dell'ideologia architettonica', which appeared in the political journal *Contropiano: Materiali marxisti*.[84] Adopting a strident, somewhat apocalyptic tone, the piece offered a gloomy reflection on the state of architecture and its apparent subjugation to a new power.

> There is no 'salvation' to be found within it ... either by wandering restlessly through 'labyrinths' of images so polyvalent that they remain mute, nor by shutting oneself up in the sullen silence of geometries content with their perfection. Therefore, there can be no proposals of architectural 'anti-spaces': any search for an alternative within the structures determining the mystification of planning is an obvious contradiction in terms.[85]

Portoghesi recognized that the 'polyvalent' images and 'geometries content with their perfection' were references to his own eclecticism and studies on baroque geometry. His response materialized in a new platform that revelled precisely in the 'anti-spaces' that Tafuri had derided: in 1969, together with Ezio Bonfanti, Portoghesi founded the architectural journal *Controspazio* (Counter-space), mischievously appropriating Tafuri's put-down as the very banner under which his group would operate. In his first editorial as director, Portoghesi wrote:

> Rather than undergoing a conversion on the basis of some contrived syllogism – and putting aside a debate that Marxist culture has been rehashing for some forty years now – we must prevail over a nihilistic attitude that threatens to become another 'cultural fashion' and reclaim our right to an active and justifiable role within revolutionary design.[86]

It was not until the sixth issue, also released in 1969, that Portoghesi directly addressed his rival's thesis, countering Tafuri's pessimism with the comment that his 'text does not define the degree of autonomy and the scientific value of the architectural discipline, nor does it specify whether it is to be understood as an art in the traditional sense, or as a particular moment of human labour'.[87] This was a summing up that Portoghesi saw as 'vital', not so much for resolving the debate (which he acknowledged was impossible to do), but in retroactively defining his own position.[88]

In truth, the coexistence of *Contropiano* and *Controspazio*, with their opposing interpretations of the role of architecture, was 'vital for both'. As Portoghesi has remarked, 'It was a constant reciprocal reminder not to be apodictic in the conclusion of the debate, not to exaggerate the trust in the project as well as not to reduce the political action to pure thought and practical action.'[89] Through their animated ideological duel, carried out in the pages of their respective journals, the two historians managed to entertain a fertile dialogue for the Italian architectural community. But the 'old and tested friendship', which Portoghesi has described as an 'idyll', collapsed with Tafuri's reaction to the First International Architecture Exhibition of the Venice Biennale.[90] As Portoghesi wrote:

> Initially, I offered [Tafuri] the opportunity to organise an exhibition on the Bauhaus, but soon my role as director of the new architecture sector of the Biennale, after the launch of the Teatro del Mondo and the announcement of the *Strada Novissima*, appeared to him as an undue interference in the Venetian architectural culture that was becoming his kingdom.[91]

Tafuri ignored the broader event in which the Teatro was embedded, remaining silent on Portoghesi's and Scaparro's crucial role in the commission of the temporary building and the historical premises underpinning it. For Tafuri, the floating theatre was merely a 'poetic and fleeting appearance', while for Portoghesi the little building – the perfect synthesis of past and contemporary architecture – was 'an homage to the genius loci'.[92] Despite the 'uncertain programmes of the Biennale', and being 'in Venice, city of promises not kept with the sacred masters of contemporary architecture', Tafuri wrote, 'Rossi's object turns a disoriented situation into a raison d'être'.[93]

Their relationship quickly deteriorated over the course of the Biennale. The attacks only continued. In 1986 Tafuri published his *Storia dell'architettura italiana 1944–85*, which, in addition to putting his historical approach to paper, makes various criticisms of Portoghesi. The first addresses Portoghesi's plan to break free from the inhibitions of the Modern Movement. While Casa Baldi was presented as a building that 'foreshadowed a "manner" proud of its own involutions', the 1964 exhibition on Michelangelo in Rome curated with Bruno Zevi (see Chapter 2) was where '"normative criticism" may have reached its low point'.[94] The chapter devoted to the 1985 Venice Architecture Biennale curated by Rossi, targeted Portoghesi and his responsibility as president. The exhibition, which displayed the results of architecture competitions for different sites in Venice was, according to Tafuri, 'not worthy of its signatory, Aldo Rossi', and was 'certainly congruent with the cultural strategies of the commission's president, Paolo Portoghesi'.[95] For Tafuri, there was no doubt that Portoghesi was responsible for turning what was meant to be a festival of architecture into 'a kind of banquet around a city treated like a cadaver'.[96] It was not the curatorial operation per se by which Tafuri seemed to be mostly affronted, but the way the city had been treated – offended and insulted. In perhaps his most overarching critique, Tafuri even rejected the expression 'postmodern architecture', preferring to use 'hypermodern' instead,[97] but the term never had the same staying power within international circles.

The antagonism between Portoghesi and Tafuri was not confined to academic or philosophical issues. The two men, along with Bruno Zevi and their growing entourage of acolytes, also adopted increasingly inimical political affiliations, even though all nominally remained on the Italian Left. In Rome, Zevi identified with the Partito Radicale, a group with markedly libertarian social and economic policies.[98] In Milan, Portoghesi remained loyal to the socialist PSI, in particular to Bettino Craxi, leader of the party from 1976, who broke the traditional duality in Italian politics between the dominant Christian Democrats and the communist opposition (see Chapter 3). By contrast, Tafuri was a member of the Communist Party and turned the IUAV into a kind of Marxist fortress whose sights were permanently targeted on Italy's devolving bourgeoisie.[99] Tafuri eventually became an orthodox Marxist, using this position to examine the phenomena of architectural history with the greatest rigour and dedication and in turn producing an innovative methodology; if Marxist culture had created a historiography with a general character, in the field of architecture it had had only a few opportunities to make an impact, and Tafuri offered himself as a guide at an international level, especially in the American context. For the architect and theorist Peter Eisenman, Tafuri was a kind of prophet of an 'international Marxism' – not in political terms, but rather in an intellectual and abstract sense. Portoghesi, by contrast, instrumentalized history as functional to architectural design.[100] He was interested in understanding the reflective and critical process required of creative architects: that is, the methods taken to achieve a form.

Towards the end of his life, Tafuri cut ties with his old friend. Nonetheless, if it is true that the relationship progressively deteriorated over time, their decades-long dialogue resulted in one of the most intellectually fecund exchanges about architecture in postmodern Italy and beyond.

Beyond Italy

If the ideological duel like the one that occurred between Portoghesi and Tafuri was quite unique for its intensity and political stance, other intellectual discussions, operative axes and personal relationships animated postmodern architectural culture around the world. For example, during this period, French architects were becoming aware of new discourses on urbanity and history, which in turn ignited a fascination with Italian architectural culture – a form of *Italophilie*, to borrow from Jean-Louis Cohen.[101] In 1975, *L'Architecture d'Aujourd'hui* invited a delegation of professors from IUAV in Venice (including Tafuri, Francesco Dal Co, Aymonino, Giorgio Ciucci and Marco De Michelis) to contribute to its special issue, 'Italie 75', focusing on Italian contemporary architecture and theories.[102] Meanwhile, across the Atlantic, Americans rediscovered Italy, through publications such as Robert Venturi's *Complexity and Contradictions in Architecture* (1966), and thanks to prolonged stays at the American Academy in Rome.[103]

In 1972, Portoghesi was asked to contribute to the catalogue of New York's Museum of Modern Art (MoMA)'s exhibition *Italy: The New Domestic Landscape*. Recent scholarship on the exhibition argues how the show greatly supported the launch of Italian design culture worldwide.[104] The culmination of a twenty-year national discussion on social, ideological and disciplinary problems,[105] it was the first event to promote Italian design culture on a global scale, triggering a wave of international interest with no precedent in Italy's history. For the next two decades, during which Portoghesi operated as the impresario of Italian postmodern architecture, Italian design dominated the international scene, with Milan and its design fair becoming the creative epicentre for industrial design. Ultimately the MoMA show prompted a response to what could be termed 'the international call': no longer content to be represented by other international institutions, the Italian architectural community set out to erase the national boundaries that once determined the shape and transmission of its architectural debate, and in so doing afforded itself a new kind of agency in its global promotion. Thus, when understood in the context of the First International Architecture Exhibition of the Venice Biennale in 1980, the climax of this decades-long process, Paolo Portoghesi's *Strada Novissima* was the channel through which Italy spoke to the world.[106]

The efforts by Italy's architectural circles to de-provincialize the pedagogy and profession were taking place at a time when the country was itself opening up to the world, as the PSI sought to fortify bilateral relationships with the United States. As a member of the PSI, and a representative of Italian architectural culture, Portoghesi understood that in order to strengthen his postmodern project an international dialogue was urgently needed. This happened in two ways. On the one hand, Portoghesi developed personal relationships with representatives of international postmodern culture, specifically Christian Norberg-Schulz in Norway and Charles Jencks in the UK; on the other, he operated at an institutional level to bring Italy into the broader disciplinary conversation that was becoming ever-more global.

The Norwegian architectural historian Christian Norberg-Schulz was an influential figure of this milieu,[107] playing a fundamental role in Portoghesi's definition of his postmodern project. Between 1945 and 1949, Norberg Schulz studied at ETH Zurich where he was a pupil of, among others, Siegfried Giedion. Later he became a central figure of the architectural phenomenology movement and one to introduce the work of German philosopher Martin Heidegger to the discipline. By doing so, Norberg-Schulz offered a particular take on architecture after modernism and a reading dominated by the idea that architectural history was grasped more truthfully in images than in words. Norberg-Schulz's photo[historio]graphy – sometimes viewed as an anti-historical method – was influenced by Giedion and based on the idea of the importance of truthful experiences and a sense of place.[108]

Portoghesi first met Norberg-Schulz around 1959 in his studio in Rome, when the Norwegian travelled to Italy to work on an article on Casa Baldi.[109] The two men shared an interest in the history and theory of architecture, as well as a fascination with baroque.[110] Finding 'a common friend in [Rainer Maria] Rilke',[111] they often turned to poetry – another mutual passion – in their approach to architectural history.[112] Finally, Norberg-Schulz and Porthoghesi had a similar interest in nature as the ultimate origin of any architecture (Figure 1.8). Norberg-Schulz who had built a polyvalent career as an architect, architectural theorist, historian, editor, professor, also had an important impact on Portoghesi's career, stimulating his new friend – who at that time was mostly a historian – to also pursue his work as an architect and encouraging him in his first architectural projects.[113] Over the years and a life-long friendship that lasted until Norberg-Schulz's death in 2000, the Norwegian repeatedly visited his friend in Italy.[114] Norberg-Schulz supported Portoghesi's career in many ways. For example, when editor-in-chief from 1963 to 1978 of the Norwegian architectural magazine *Byggekunst*, Norberg-Schulz published Portoghesi's projects. Moreover, he also assisted Portoghesi's historical projects, amongst other by providing some of the photographs for *Roma barocca*.

FIGURE 1.8 Christian Norberg-Schulz (on the right) visiting Paolo Portoghesi (in the middle, next to Giovanna Massobrio) in Calcata. © Paolo Portoghesi Archive.

In spring 1978, Portoghesi, together with Vittorio Gigliotti and in collaboration with a team of architects including Norberg-Schulz, took part in the seminal exhibition *Roma Interrotta* – an important international meeting point for Postmodernism that preceded the *Strada Novissima* by two years.[115] Organized by the Roman architect Piero Sartogo with Graziella Lonardi Buontempo and her cultural association Incontri Internazionali d'Arte (IIA), the exhibition centred on a speculative redrawing of Nolli's 1748 map of Rome. Twelve international figures of postmodern architecture were invited to participate.[116] Based on fierce criticism of Roman urban development during the nineteenth and twentieth centuries, the interventions on Nolli's map tended towards the reading of the antique in its essential structures. The operation was equally meant to stimulate the architects' imaginations, while also leading to the production of a unique collection of marketable drawings. Most importantly, the exhibition fostered international exchanges between a carefully selected group of American and European – mostly Italian – architects (a few French and English architects made it into the mix). Each architect was allocated one of Nolli's twelve plates. These individual sheets formed the basis for the project: the architects were asked to work from Nolli's existing city, making 'interventions' (additions or subtractions) on their Nolli plate.

Portoghesi and Norberg-Schulz were assigned the area between the Quirinale and the Esquiline (which corresponds to the plate in the middle of the second row of the Nolli map), for which Portoghesi proposed going back many centuries, prior to the Nolli plan. His idea was to hypothetically reconstruct the original physical environment of the area – before the floods, collapses, backfill and alternating events of the historic city altered its characteristics by reducing its height differences and flattening the original physiognomy of the land.[117] The result was a bright and colourful drawing suggesting analogies between the physical and urban environments – the Treia ravine compared to the Piazza Fontana di Trevi, or the conflux of two ravines near Calcata compared to an upward foreshortening of an intersection along via della Renella. It suggested a critical relationship of continuity between the historical city and its present counterpart, as if the area chosen for intervention could suddenly get rid of the sediments produced by humans and nature and return to a time of the first settlements.

A photo taken at the opening of *Roma Interrotta* shows Portoghesi with his wife Giovanna Massobrio and other protagonists (including Lonardi Buontempo and journalist Alberto Moravia) in front of the Nolli map (Figure 1.9). What is striking about this scene (as in many other images included in this book and spread across the chapters) is the central position of Portoghesi as he proudly holds up the catalogue of *Roma Interrotta* with both hands. All gazes are turned on Portoghesi as the man tasked with placing Italian architecture at the centre of the international scene.

It was, however, ultimately the Venice Biennale that enabled Portoghesi to implement his international 'postmodern alliance' strategy. When embarking on

FIGURE 1.9 Gathering at the opening of the exhibition *Roma Interrotta*, in front of the Nolli map at the Mercati Traianei, Rome, 1978. From left to right: Mario Praz, Alberto Moravia, Paolo Portoghesi, Giovanna Massobrio and Graziella Lonardi Buontempo. © Centro Archivi Fondazione MAXXI.

the task of organizing the first International Architecture Exhibition of the Biennale, Portoghesi carefully put together an international advisory board of figures including Charles Jencks and Norberg-Schulz, as well as the American contingent, made up of Robert A. M. Stern and historians Vincent Scully and Kenneth Frampton (the latter eventually resigned from the board due to ideological incompatibilities).[118] These specialists were meant to give legitimacy and a global outlook to Portoghesi's exhibition, and their participation was viewed as a cultural blessing from both Europe and the United States. Through his strategic alliance with Stern, Scully and Frampton, Portoghesi wanted to ensure the coverage of the American contemporary scene but, most importantly, he wanted to make sure that Robert Venturi and Denise Scott Brown would be on board for his exhibition.

Equally fundamental was the participation of Charles Jencks. In a letter addressed to the Anglo-American critic on 20 March, 1979 (Figure 1.10), following their first meeting in London, Portoghesi invited Jencks to 'become a member of the experts committee', making his intentions clear: 'The title of the exhibition is "the Post-Modern Architecture" and your participation seems to me not only natural but also necessary.'[119] Between the mid- and late 1970s, Jencks had promoted the term 'postmodern' to designate the variety of responses to the demise of the Modern

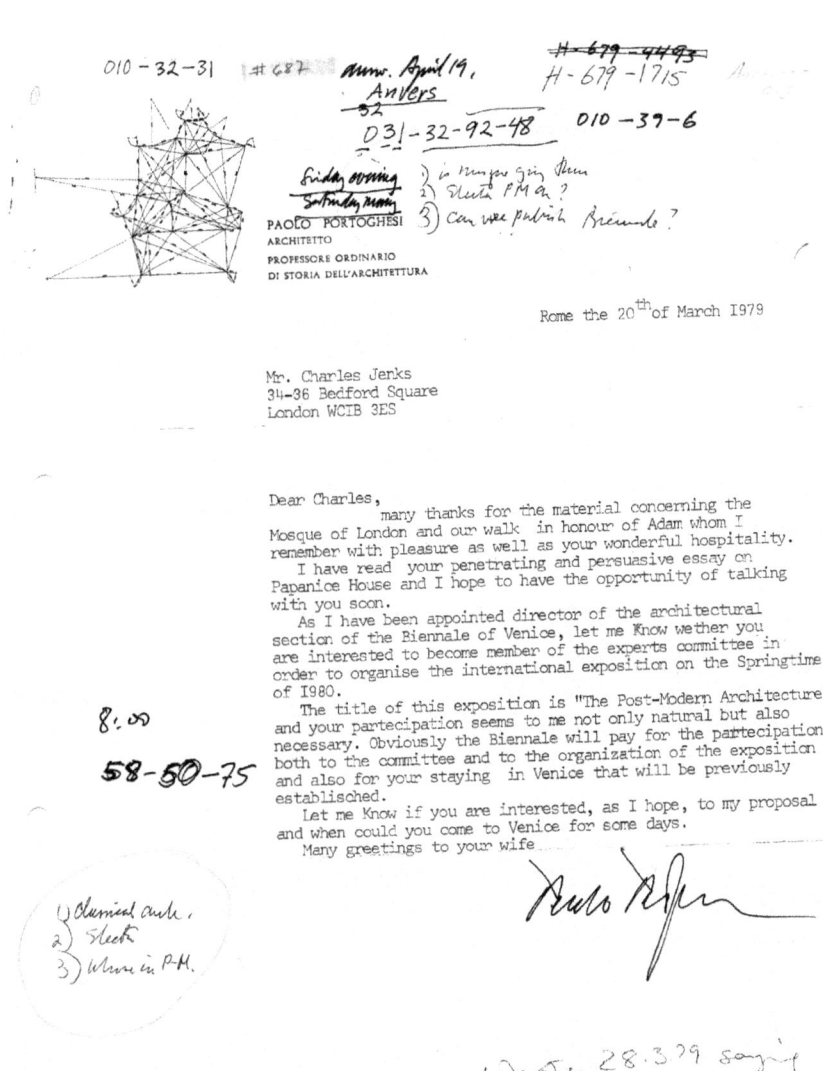

FIGURE 1.10 Invitation letter to take part in the organization of the First International Architecture Exhibition of the Venice Biennale sent by Paolo Portoghesi to Charles Jencks, 1979. © Jencks Foundation.

Movement. Jencks used the world for the first time in 1975, in his article 'The Rise of Post-Modern Architecture', a richly illustrated, twelve-page text published in the *Architectural Association Quarterly*,[120] which opens with the following line, 'The title is evasive of course. If I knew how to call it, I wouldn't use the negative prefix "post"'. Two years later, encouraged by Andreas Papadakis, publisher of London-based Academy Editions, he released *The Language of Post-Modern Architecture* (1977), a book that played a crucial role in further defining the term.[121] In the second edition, published one year later, Jencks included a photo of Portoghesi's Casa Baldi, writing, 'One of the most convincing historicist buildings of the fifties was Paolo Portoghesi's Casa Baldi, an essay in free-form curves definitely reminiscent of the Borromini he was studying, yet also unmistakably influenced by Le Corbusier'.[122] The international echo Jencks gave to Casa Baldi was crucial to Portoghesi's decision to invite him to join the organization of the Biennale. As Portoghesi later recalled, 'The fact that he [Jencks] had indicated Casa Baldi as a foreshadowing of what happened, then had a weight on my choice'.[123]

Galleria Apollodoro, a centre for Roman culture

From the early 1970s onwards, Portoghesi's personal life and career benefited from the strategic assistance and unconditional support of his second wife, Giovanna Massobrio (Figure 1.11). Beyond their love for one another, the couple formed a successful professional partnership that leveraged Portoghesi's institutional roles, media exposure and design opportunities. Theorizing coupling in architecture, Beatriz Colomina has observed that 'collaboration is the secret life of architects, the domestic life of architecture. Nowhere this is more emblematic than architects who live and work together, with couples for whom there is complete identification between home life and office life'.[124] This was precisely the case for Portoghesi and Massobrio, who successfully intertwined their professional and private lives, shaping a distinctive lifestyle based on the ideal of beauty and guided by architecture and design principles.

The pair met at the Politecnico di Milano, where Massobrio, originally from Liguria, was studying architecture and Portoghesi was dean. After graduation in 1970, Massobrio collaborated with established Milan-based practices, including Sergio Crotti and Cesare Battisti, and worked as a tutor for Vittoriano Viganò's courses at the Politecnico. One day, in 1970, instead of entering the room where Viganò was teaching, Massobrio went into the room next door, where Portoghesi was delivering a lecture. She was immediately struck by the professor's charisma, eloquence and charm. Soon after, Massobrio was asked by Viganò to interview some of the Faculty of Architecture during the process of designing a new building. Portoghesi, being the dean, was naturally one of her subjects: 'I had never met such

FIGURE 1.11 Paolo Portoghesi and Giovanna Massobrio at the drafting table in their office, 1970s. © Paolo Portoghesi Archive.

a beautiful woman,' remembers Portoghesi, 'two wide-open blue eyes, pointed like two magnets, with strong and thin features, a little sharp, with very long hands and a light body with a Pre-Raphaelite elegance, combined to a full opened approach towards the cult of beautiful and intriguing things. It was difficult to resist.'[125] The experience for both was a *coup de foudre*. Soon after, in 1971, the couple wanted to move into the BBPR-designed Torre Velasca, one of the Milanese buildings they most admired for its historical and contemporary expression, but their plan never transpired. Instead, one day, while walking through the Metro in Duomo, they heard an announcement on the radio that eight members of the board of the Faculty of Architecture, including dean Portoghesi, had been suspended. The unexpected news prompted a move to Rome, where in 1978 the couple were eventually married, in a civil ceremony officiated by the mayor, Giulio Carlo Argan, a friend and colleague of Portoghesi.

An architect herself, Massobrio assisted Portoghesi in some of his design projects, including the International Airport of Khartoum (1973–82); Casa Corrias (1972–2000); the project for the Royal Palace for King Hussein of Jordan, Amman (1973) and their house in Calcata, discussed in the Epilogue of this book.[126] She also attended public events with Portoghesi, from political congresses to cultural happenings. Given Portoghesi's mediatic exposure through his institutional roles at the Venice Biennale from 1980 and 1992, the pair constantly went to parties and events, becoming one of the most glamorous couples of the Italian jet set. From the Fendi Party in Rome at Palazzo Venezia with aristocratic representatives as well as American buyers, to the Armani Party in Venice during the film festival, Massobrio comfortably appeared in society, networking on her husband's behalf.[127] Yet, Massobrio was much more than a wife accompanying her husband at public happenings and exclusive parties. According to Portoghesi, she was an essential moderator of his 'introverted character'.[128] Indeed, she fostered the involvement of Portoghesi in the circles of the PSI by befriending its leader Bettino Craxi during his long stays in Rome.

Their shared interests were not limited to their social world. Portoghesi's passion for Art Nouveau, bentwood and Thonet was embraced by Massobrio, who was a collector of art and furniture, and the couple made weekly expeditions to second-hand markets in Rome, like the one at Porta Portese, to track down exemplary pieces. Together they wrote a series of visual atlases on the history of taste that reintroduced Art Nouveau and Liberty – a period that had long been disregarded by Italian design culture.[129] The aim was to recover the union of arts, including design, architecture and furniture, and its relationship with nature. For this suite of publications, Massobrio took a key role, bridging her Liberty imaginary towards the design of a new cultural space in the heart of the capital.

Operating, much like her husband, across media and platforms, in 1985 Massobrio decided to focus on the specific cultural life of Rome, opening the Galleria Apollodoro (known as the Apollodoro) in Piazza Mignanelli, a prime location behind the Fontana di Trevi and just next to the Spanish Steps. Designed by Portoghesi with Massobrio, the gallery – whose name was an homage to Apollodorus of Damascus, the architect of the Traiano's Forum of which only a column and the markets have survived – was a tribute to Roman culture. The space was characterized by its peculiar entrance gate, a false-perspective gallery reminiscent of Bramante's inventive design for the altar of Santa Maria in San Satiro, and Borromini's gallery at Palazzo Spada (Figure 1.12).

Above the door, a signboard in Art Nouveau style indicated the name of the gallery (Figure 1.13). Internally, the space (approximately 100 square metres) was covered with a cupola of coloured glass, recreating the feeling of a winter garden of Liberty influence.

With its mix of historical influences, the gallery represented Portoghesi and Massobrio's 'universe' and common passions, a cultural space full of objects and pieces of art.[130] From the moment it opened, the gallery offered an oasis for architectural and design research, until then traditionally confined to academia. The diverse audience of artists, architects and intellectuals who all socialized there provided an opportunity for interdisciplinary connections to flourish. At the same

FIGURE 1.12 Gate of the Galleria Apollodoro in Rome, designed by Paolo Portoghesi with Giovanna Massobrio. Photo taken by Paolo Portoghesi showing the false perspective door open on the urban space. © Paolo Portoghesi Archive.

FIGURE 1.13 Gate signage of the Galleria Apollodoro in Rome, designed by Paolo Portoghesi with Giovanna Massobrio. Photograph taken by Paolo Portoghesi during construction work, 1985. © Paolo Portoghesi Archive.

time, the gallery focused on making unique pieces using ancient and modern techniques, recalling the Wiener Werkstätte of Josef Hoffmann or William Morris's commercial initiatives.[131] A memorable exhibition (1986–87) dedicated to the studiolo of Francesco I dei Medici[132] is documented in an edited catalogue with contributions by Portoghesi, Giulio Carlo Argan and Maurizio Calvesi, among others.[133] Alongside its luxurious publications, the gallery also commissioned famous international designers to create objects to exhibit and sell.[134] This range of work and events soon made Apollodoro the venue for society gatherings, as a film of the gallery's opening reveals. Mingling with artists and architects are also congressmen, like Giuliano Amato; actors and actresses, including Monica Vitti; and the Roman socialite Marina Ripa di Meana.[135] This eclectic group suggests the influence of not just the gallery, but of Portoghesi and Massobrio as they sought to expand the worlds of art and architecture, transforming what would have ordinarily been an academic or cultural assemblage of the usual suspects into a worldly and elegant society gathering. Apollodoro was ultimately a stage for Portoghesi and Massobrio to pursue and make indivisible their lives and artistic agendas from the social world they cultivated (Figure 1.14).

For Portoghesi specifically, Apollodoro provided the space to perform his role of impresario of postmodern architecture right in the heart of Rome, his hometown. Operating from Italy, he had proposed a *progetto* with roots in his country, but which had gained an international reach. Amongst the first to expose Italian architects to the most experimental Anglo-American tendencies, Portoghesi was perhaps also one of the first to really take them into account. This sense of possibility for cultural exchange can be glimpsed in Vincent Scully's essay for *The Presence of the Past* exhibition catalogue: 'The present selection is enormously rich and various and, it seems to me, shows a greater concordance of objectives and methods between Europeans and Americans than might at first sight be apparent.'[136] Portoghesi's clever mix of influences, languages and ideas had successfully elicited a general consensus that constituted the heart of his postmodern project – emphasizing his agency in the global scene.

FIGURE 1.14 Paolo Portoghesi with the then president of the Italian Republic, Francesco Cossiga, at the exhibition *Aci e Galatea* by postmodern artist Marco Rossati, at the Galleria Apollodoro, Rome, 1988. © Paolo Portoghesi Archive.

2 TURN TO HISTORY

FIGURE 2.1 Photographic portrait of Paolo Portoghesi and Giovanna Massobrio in their residence in the Torrino di via di Porta Pinciana, Rome, 1971. © Paolo Portoghesi Archive.

A photograph from 1971 shows Paolo Portoghesi and Giovanna Massobrio in their forty-square-metre attic apartment at via di Porta Pinciana 6 in Rome – the so-called Torrino di via Pinciana (Figure 2.1).[1] The couple, newly living together, blend in with their surroundings in an interior comprising a no. 21 Thonet rocking chair designed in the late 1800s, a masterpiece of craftsmanship for its elaborated curves; William Morris print wallpaper; and a framed portrait of Francesco Borromini.[2] In the centre of the photograph, although somewhat blurred, is the panorama over the Villa Medici gardens and, beyond, an impressive view of Rome.

Situated at the crossroads of different historical epochs, the interiors of the Torrino di via Pinciana had become an amalgamation of personal repertoires and references. It was not by coincidence that Portoghesi had chosen to live in the Torrino. This small building was originally conceived as an office and was designed between 1935 and 1936 by Mario Ridolfi, a representative of the Roman fringe of postwar Italian architects. The group, which also included Ludovico Quaroni, Giovanni Michelucci, Franco Albini and Franca Helg, as well as Ignazio Gardella, worked its way out of the orthodoxy of the Modern Movement by engaging in an unbiased confrontation with local culture and history.[3]

Portoghesi was profoundly inspired by Ridolfi, describing him as 'the poet of fixtures and railings, who had translated into a vernacular full of ancient flavours and sanguine substance the teaching of Mies van der Rohe: "God is in the detail".[4] Proposing a type of research that, in the wake of modern design, was nevertheless attentive to the lessons of the tradition, Ridolfi offered a poetic in which the two dimensions were put together with courage.[5] During Portoghesi's university studies in Rome, Ridolfi was the architect from whom the young student learned the most, albeit indirectly.[6] His foundational programme, based on the recovery of expressiveness in architecture, revealed ways in which both baroque and modern forms and principles were compatible,[7] as convincingly illustrated by the abstract curvilinear brick facade of the post office in Piazza Bologna (1933) in Rome.

FIGURE 2.2 View of the homage to Mario Ridolfi, *The Presence of the Past*, Venice Biennale, 1980. © Paolo Portoghesi Archive.

Portoghesi selected Ridolfi as one of three architects, including Ignazio Gardella and Philip Johnson, to feature in the 'homages' section of the 1980 *The Presence of the Past* exhibition at the Venice Architecture Biennale (Figure 2.2). Although overshadowed by the instant success of the *Strada Novissima*, this historical section complemented the exhibition by presenting the work of three living 'masters' whom Portoghesi and the exhibition advisory board considered to be among the precursors of postmodern architecture.[8] The trio of monographic shows was intended as a series of manifestos on the recovery of history in the architectural design process, a line of research that the postmodern condition had made possible.[9] All three architects were born at the beginning of the twentieth century and were recognized for their creative recovery of the historical inheritance of architecture, their questioning of the orthodoxy of the International Style and their advocacy for historical continuity.[10]

Architect as historian/historian as architect

Portoghesi's *The Presence of the Past*, with its three homages and the *Strada Novissima*, was an opportunity to promote, share and celebrate with an international audience the distinctive method based on the recovery of history in the design process that was so central to the Italian disciplinary debate. With their personal takes on a historical approach to design, Ridolfi, Gardella and Johnson perfectly fit and enhanced Portoghesi's agenda of repositioning architectural history at the centre of disciplinary discussion.

The Presence of the Past was just one of the mechanisms used by Portoghesi to challenge the orthodoxy of the Modern Movement, fostering a cultural turn to history – crucial to his activity as a designer and historian – and to the postmodern discourse in a broader sense. More than a stylistic strategy, this turn to history had a strong methodological approach, and over the years Portoghesi articulated a solid line of research where the past and the concept of memory became relevant to the present moment. Oscillating between his profiles of historian and practitioner – aspects of his persona that seamlessly merged – Portoghesi deployed this method specifically through his studies on baroque architecture and the legacy of Borromini, considered the most experimental of Italian baroque architects.

The attention paid by practitioners to architectural history was a common denominator among Italian architects operating in the second half of the twentieth century – an approach that made Italian architecture unique within the international scene. From Luigi Moretti's *Spazio* in the 1930s to Ernesto Nathan Rogers' *Casabella-continuità*, as well as Bruno Zevi's *Metron* and *L'architettura: Cronache e storia* in the postwar period and, from the late 1960s, Portoghesi's *Controspazio*, Italian architectural journals programmatically and consistently promoted a line of research that saw history and design as inseparable components of the same architectural method. As a consequence – in Italy more than anywhere else – architects undertook historical studies during their training to acquire their own critical positions in relation to modernity. From this, they made individual attempts to depart from the belief that modernity was antagonistic to architectural history altogether.[11]

While actively working as a practitioner – a role that was never put on hold even in his academic appointments in Rome and Milan[12] or as president of the Venice Biennale during the 1980s – Portoghesi maintained a distinguished and international scholarly profile. In addition to a life-long focus on the architecture of Italian baroque, his studies ranged from the Renaissance, including an investigation of Leonardo's technical drawings[13] and the edition of Leon Battista Alberti's *De re aedificatoria*,[14] to the architecture of Michelangelo,[15] nineteenth-century Art Nouveau[16] and modern and contemporary architecture. At the same time, no other historian of Portoghesi's calibre could count on such pragmatic and technical insights gleaned from his years spent designing and building. His first built project was the Enpas building in Pistoia (1957–59). Shortly after its completion, in 1964, he established his practice with engineer Vittorio Gigliotti. Known as 'the office of via Pinciana',[17] Portoghesi and Gigliotti worked on a long list of residential and urban projects at different scales, culminating with the Mosque and Islamic Centre in Rome (1974–95) (discussed in Chapter 3). The office also carried out consultancy work for MEFIT Consulting Engineers, which maintained a presence in developing countries and which led to significant commissions abroad, including the International Airport of Khartoum (1973–82). Portoghesi considered these two vocational facets – historian and designer – as the two sides of his pendulum. Strategically balanced, they enabled him to carry out a specific experimental design method based on scientific historical premises that few other architects could boast. While dedicating considerable time to architectural projects and his declared vocation for design, interestingly, it was not until 1995 that Portoghesi was appointed Professor of Architectural Design at the Faculty of Architecture 'Valle Giulia' of La Sapienza in Rome.

It was in fact through practice that Portoghesi believed the history of architecture could be instrumentalized to free forms and expose design to new opportunities of spatial and linguistic expression. Unlike his colleagues Tafuri and Norberg-Schulz,[18] who deliberately chose to be historians, Portoghesi preferred to absorb and digest what was, only in appearance, a dichotomy of two subdisciplines which, for him, were indissolubly synergic.

Based on this constant oscillation between historical studies and design applications, Portoghesi would introduce himself as an architect, as he emphatically does in the foreword to his 1964 book *Borromini nella cultura europea* (Figure 2.3), which documents more than a decade of scholarly research into baroque architecture: 'This book, written by an architect, has been, in its time and in its chapters, a tool of methodological research, of clarifying issues, not only in respect

FIGURE 2.3 Cover of Paolo Portoghesi's foundational book *Borromini nella cultura europea*, 1964.

to critical and historical operations but also to the active intervention in the field of modern architectural culture.'[19]

Portoghesi would continue to deepen his interest in baroque architecture in the context of a broad disciplinary discussion devoted to the critical revision of seventeenth-century architectural heritage. He read authors and books that reassessed baroque culture and evaluated its relevance, such as Siegfried Giedion's *Space, Time and Architecture* (1941); Gillo Dorfles' *Barocco nell'architettura moderna* (1951) and *Borromini* (1952); Rudolf Wittkower's *Art and Architecture in Italy 1600 to 1750* (1958); as well as Giulio Carlo Argan's *L'architettura barocca in Italia* (1957) and *L'Europa delle capitali 1600–1700* (1964).[20] In electing the work of Francesco Borromini as his field of enquiry, Portoghesi found himself operating alongside other esteemed historians, such as Argan, James Ackerman, Hans Sedlmayr, Leo Steinberg and the then emerging American historian Joseph Connors.[21] But while the interpretations of these scholars – all art historians – operated on more stylistic foundations, Portoghesi as an architect offered a distinctive take on baroque architecture by leveraging Borromini's design strategies and use of geometry. At the same time, the analysis offered by Robert Venturi in *Complexity and Contradiction in Architecture* (1966) never stood on the same solid historical footing as that put forward by Portoghesi.[22]

Nearly a decade prior to publishing his volume on Borromini, Portoghesi turned his attention to the Piedmontese architect Guarino Guarini when embarking on his first trip to Piedmont as a university student, motivated, in part, by a desire to research his identity on his mother's side.[23] At the same time, he also intended to satisfy his intellectual eagerness to study Guarini as well as Bernardo Vittone, another baroque architect from the region.[24] What followed was Portoghesi's first published book, *Guarino Guarini 1624–1683* (1956),[25] which brought an analysis of its subject's buildings into conversation with those of Borromini, whose work Portoghesi claimed as a 'favourite issue'.[26] Modest in size, but comprising a richly articulated critical essay, the volume marked a transition away from more solitary research to a dynamic international exchange of ideas.[27] After its publication, the book was highly regarded by Argan and Wittkower, who both acknowledged the young Portoghesi as one of the leading experts on baroque architecture in the Italian postwar context – and a rising international star of architectural history.

Soon Portoghesi had positioned himself as one of the most enthusiastic and operative interpreters of baroque architecture in the twentieth century, turning its principles on contemporary architecture into a subject for debate. Portoghesi showed that the principles of baroque architecture, subject to a process of critical revision, had a surprising relevance for the present moment. His ambition was thus to establish a bridge between writing history 'indirectly' – that is, by design – and writing history 'directly', through a critical publishing activity. In *Le inibizioni dell'architettura moderna*, his first theoretical book, published in 1974, he elucidated his intentions:

In architecture you can build history, 'write it' in a metaphorical sense, by designing and building works of architecture: it is by designing, for example, that architects of the early Renaissance reorganised their knowledge of the classical heritage into a unified *corpus*; it is by designing that Borromini has brought to light such methods as Gothic diagonality, anticipating an analytical re-reading of medieval heritage. Each generation of architects, even without the direct and specific contribution of criticism, wrote history, interpreting it in a different way according to the problems of their time.[28]

In his endorsement for the book *Roma barocca*, Argan observed that 'Portoghesi, as an architect, puts in his critical vision an operative interest that gives to his prose a unique character in our criticism of architecture, unique because Portoghesi has the architect's sensibility for architectural form.'[29] This aptitude informed Portoghesi's reflections in his other book on the work of Victor Horta, where the arduous critical problem was to 'establish Horta's role in the line of development of the Modern Movement' and to clarify to what extent it could still contribute to the design method of architectural culture.[30]

Neoliberty polemic

When Portoghesi graduated, elsewhere in European and more so in American schools of architecture, history was still a marginalized subject. Yet, in Italy, the debate on the value of historical references in relation to design intensified as early as 1957 under the banner of the so-called Neoliberty polemic. An issue of *Casabella-continuità* published the same year ran the provocative editorial 'Continuità o Crisi?',[31] a text in which the Milan-based architect and director Ernesto Nathan Rogers invited the young generation of designers to reflect on a significant shift in their approach to the discipline of architecture:

> Considering history as a process, one could say that it is always continuity or always crisis depending on whether you want to accentuate permanence rather than emergencies ... the concept of continuity implies that of mutation in the scope of a tradition. Crisis is the rupture – revolution – that is, the moment of discontinuity.[32]

Rogers talked about the mistaken belief in the Modern Movement as a 'style' instead of a 'method' and the necessity to assess Liberty architecture in the context of its cultural reality.[33] In that very year, 1957, the BBPR office (Gianluigi Banfi, Ludovico Barbiano di Belgiojoso, Enrico Peressutti and Rogers) had completed the iconic Torre Velasca (1950–57) in Milan. With its explicit linguistic references to the surrounding medieval heritage, this controversial high-rise was a demonstration of Rogers' notion of 'continuity' – a word that he had emphatically added to the original name of the magazine *Casabella* during his editorship. This was also the year that Portoghesi began his career as a designer with his first built project, the Enpas Headquarters in Pistoia (1957–59). While other architects had informed the early years of Portoghesi's career – among them, the Roman architects Mario Ridolfi and Saverio Muratori, with their regional take on Italian rationalism, and Ludovico Quaroni with his research on the recovery of the vernacular language – Rogers constituted a vital point of reference when it came to integrating the memory of place within the design process to transcend modern architecture. Francesco Moschini observed that it was in Portoghesi's early commissions that 'the two different cultural matrices seem to merge: the Roman one in which particular attention is turned towards Ridolfi's lesson, and the Milanese one, always mindful of the profession as research, of the BBPR group'.[34] Rogers's method was based on the notion of the *preesistenze ambientali* (environmental pre-existences), according to which the design of a building establishes a tight formal relationship with its direct urban or natural surroundings. The aim was to achieve a 'synthetic' result, one that respected the memory of the past and allowed for the renewal of modern architecture as related to its direct surroundings – its language, typology, morphology and culture. According to Rogers, taking into account the environment in the design process means acknowledging its history. Conceptually oscillating between the past and the present, history was not considered as a passive copy, or dogma, but was incorporated with a dynamic approach to ensure both continuity and novelty.

In 1958, the year after Rogers's famous *continuità o crisi* dilemma, Portoghesi published a pivotal article in the magazine *Comunità*,[35] titled 'Dal neorealismo al neoliberty'.[36] After outlining a thorough historical analysis of the previous decades of Italian architecture, he attempted to critically name a new architectural experience – that of Neoliberty, which connected to Italy's neorealist cinema to provide a change of direction from the most established positions related to the Modern Movement. The notion of Neoliberty, of which the Torre Velasca, together with Roberto Gabetti and Aimaro Isola's Bottega d'Erasmo (1953–56) in Turin, are significant examples, was underpinned by the principles of continuity, renewed interest in the history of architecture, historical interpretation and a return to tradition – all ideas that were intrinsic to Rogers's theoretical line.

The definition of Neoliberty stirred up a tense debate, even beyond Italy.[37] 'Paolo Portoghesi seems to have been the first to call the style of the retreat by the apt term "Neoliberty" as late as the end of 1958,' boomed the eminent architectural critic and historian Reyner Banham from the pages of the authoritative *The Architectural Review*.[38] In that memorable article, Banham manifested all his disappointment with *Casabella-continuità* too, not only for its antimodern stance in publishing examples of Neoliberty architecture, but also for 'the whole body of Italian modernism [which] must share the blame'.[39] Nevertheless, the intention behind the neologism coined by Portoghesi was not to produce another stylistic label, 'so useful to the accusers',[40] but to acknowledge a moment of exploration in architectural design in postwar Italy. Portoghesi replied directly to the 'brilliant English critic' whose fierce attack, he said, had missed the opportunity to add to such a relevant debate.[41] Rogers also berated Banham, nicknaming him the 'custodian of refrigerators'.[42]

The altercation exposed the radical position of postwar Italian architecture towards the Modern Movement and framed it as a postulate for the postmodern turn to come. It also revealed young Portoghesi as an already significant critical voice within a broader conversation about architectural design that exceeded the confines of Rome and Italy. Years later, Portoghesi would write:

> The awareness that the continuity of historical development has not been definitively broken by the advent of the Modern Movement but – like a wound that continually heals – has, in the long run, substantially recomposed, makes it necessary once more to re-establish the building of architecture on new foundations.[43]

Despite the fresh inspiration brought about by the generation of Ridolfi, Gardella, Quaroni, Muratori and Rogers, over the years Portoghesi registered its limits – or, as Tafuri succinctly wrote, 'its lack of courage'.[44] There was an increasing exhaustion related to their questioning of modernity, which Portoghesi believed should be accessed with more irreverence, 'mixing the cards as long as it takes to find that right one to face the reality in continuous transformation'.[45] This feeling was shared by other representatives of Portoghesi's generation who were concerned that the innovations deployed in postwar architecture were increasingly caught up in nostalgia.[46] At this time of critical stagnation, Borromini's work burst onto the scene as a symbol of liberation for his freedom from conventions and his propensity for experimentation.

Instrumental value of the past

Portoghesi's turn to history was fortified by his intellectual encounters with the architectural historian Bruno Zevi and his line of 'operative criticism'.[47] In 1945, upon his return from the United States (where he graduated from Harvard and was introduced to the work of Frank Lloyd Wright), Zevi became a theoretician of organic architecture and one of the most intellectually inspiring and militant revisionists of the Modern Movement. He taught the history of architecture at the IUAV in Venice until 1963, and the following year moved his academic career to Rome.[48] In Venice, Zevi had worked to develop his students' critical capacities and had successfully experimented with a new didactic approach that consisted of understanding how, pedagogically, architectural history could serve as an 'intellectual and professional model for contemporary architects negotiating the post-war inheritance of functionalism'.[49] In other words, Zevi's approach to the teaching sought to bring a historical relevance to contemporary architectural culture.[50] Portoghesi had played a role in Zevi's new appointment with the Faculty of Architecture at La Sapienza in Rome,[51] and together they worked to disentangle the ossified academic system.[52]

Portoghesi and Zevi met as early as 1956, through the poet and art critic Leonardo Sinisgalli, founding editor of the magazine *Civiltà delle macchine*, to which Portoghesi was a regular contributor.[53] However, their real intellectual encounter occurred years later, in 1964, when Zevi was asked to organize an exhibition on Michelangelo celebrating the quadricentennial of the artist's birth. Held at the Palazzo delle Esposizioni in via Nazionale, in Rome, *Mostra critica delle opere Michelangiolesche* displayed the work of the artist in a strikingly innovative way, most notably by connecting his designs for fortifications with the more exuberant plastic forms of late-period Modernism.[54] Underpinned by an operative approach to read history in light of contemporary art and culture, the exhibition represented one of the most innovative reactions to the anti-historicist line put forward by the Modern Movement. If the show provided Portoghesi and Zevi with a platform to reconsider an important historical case – that of Michelangelo – it also allowed them to pursue a mutual desire to close the gap that separated history from the present moment[55] and shift the reading of buildings from a plastic analysis to a spatial one (Figure 2.4).[56]

The installation, designed by Portoghesi with Gigliotti, substantially reconfigured the interiors of the palazzo with alternating open spaces and compressed passages.[57] The traditional philological and chronological criteria for the sequencing of projects were discarded in favour of an interpretative selection based on the ideas of Michelangelo,[58] rather than his work, projecting the visitors into the artist's imaginative design process. Photographs of the buildings taken by Oscar Savio were enlarged, mounted on panels detached from the walls and tilted forward to spatially involve viewers – a technique that brings to mind Alvar Aalto's solution for the photos on the leaning and undulating wall of the Finnish Pavilion at the 1939 World's Fair in New York. Other photographs were hung by thematic associations. The exhibition aimed to establish a dialogue with the visitor,[59] a spatial immersion somewhat anticipating the degree of involvement and interaction of Portoghesi's memorable *Strada Novissima*.

Central to the exhibition were the so-called 'interpretative models' produced by Zevi's IUAV students under the guidance of Mario Deluigi, a Venetian painter who was part of the spatialist movement with Lucio Fontana. Composed of wire and set on metal stands to abstractly express the spatiality of Michelangelo's architecture,[60] the models exemplified Zevi's line of operative criticism, offering an original interpretation of the past.[61] Through the models, the exhibition revealed a

FIGURE 2.4 Paolo Portoghesi introducing the then president of the Italian Republic, Giovanni Gronchi, at the opening of the *Mostra critica delle opere michelangiolesche*, Palazzo delle Esposizioni, Rome, 1964. © Paolo Portoghesi Archive.

methodological affinity with Luigi Moretti's analysis of baroque architecture.[62] Neither the models nor the photographs were intended to be surrogates for Michelangelo's actual work but, rather, vehicles for implementing a critical historiography.[63] The overall interdisciplinary approach of the installation was enhanced by the decision to combine the visual experience with sound 'through the reading of contemporary chronicles and elaborations of electronic music, by the musician Vittorio Gelmetti, derived from the modular rhythms of the set-up to create an unsettling synthesis of acoustic and environmental geometries.'[64] Portoghesi and Zevi worked together on the layout of the drawings, reliefs and photographs and the drafting of captions while co-editing the hefty (nearly 1,000-page) catalogue: an imposing volume with contributions from historians Giulio Carlo Argan, Aldo Bertini, Sergio Bettini, Renato Bonelli, Decio Gioseffi and Roberto Pane. The collaboration with Zevi, which Portoghesi compared to the action of playing the piano with four hands, involved translating a specific critical interpretation of Michelangelo's work into the selection, sequence, hierarchy and the cutting of images.[65]

The exhibition and its catalogue represented the apex of the intellectual exchange and alignment between Portoghesi and Zevi.[66] As Portoghesi recalled:

Central to the exhibition were the projects for the fortification that Michelangelo had designed for the Florentine Republic as an artist politically engaged in a civil battle for freedom and justice. Perhaps out of opportunism, we preferred to ignore the fact that Michelangelo had abandoned his work halfway through.[67]

The exhibition proved that the two scholars could establish a strong alliance to rehabilitate architectural history within contemporary design: but whereas Zevi was more interested in the process of abstracting architectural elements, Portoghesi was committed to their formal and linguistic reinterpretation.

In 1967, during celebrations marking three hundred years since the death of Borromini, an international congress was organized at the Accademia Nazionale di San Luca in Rome. Portoghesi was invited to join two roundtables, 'Il rapporto fra Borromini e la Tradizione' and 'Il metodo di progettazione del Borromini', and he also edited the catalogue of Borromini's drawings.[68] His views were pulled sharply into focus during a debate with Zevi, a fellow attendee.[69] In contrast to the collaboration they had enjoyed working on for the Michelangelo exhibition, the conference revealed a growing discomfort as Portoghesi distanced himself from the assumptions of Zevi, 'who needed to hide some emergent aspects of Borromini's work in order to present him as a "subversive".[70] Portoghesi, instead, insisted on the recovery of Borromini's design process as a useful instrument for contemporary design. His aim was to formulate a historical interpretation of Borromini's architecture based on objective values, and he argued that philological analysis and critical observations were insufficient for the task at hand: it was necessary to enact what Portoghesi called the 'verification of the draughting table' in order to continue the interrupted research otherwise so full of promise.[71] In short, Portoghesi did not share Zevi's stretched view of Borromini as a subversive protagonist of the baroque. To support his thesis, Zevi had minimized dominant themes of Borromini's design research.[72] Portoghesi countered with a defence of a more contextual approach.[73] With the argument unresolved, Zevi continued to lambast Portoghesi in the pages of the architectural journal *L'architettura. Cronache e storia*, expanding the dispute to address matters of design for years to come.

While these disagreements on how to interpret Borromini's architectural design caused fissures in their relationship, it was Portoghesi's 1967 book on Borromini that precipitated his intellectual divorce from Zevi.[74] The pair had initially committed to co-authoring a book on the architect for Einaudi, but the volume was never realized.[75] Portoghesi's book *Borromini: Architettura come linguaggio*,[76] published by Electa, was the result of another exhibition, *Mostra critica delle opere Borrominiane*, curated at the Villa Ciani in Lugano, Switzerland, between September and October 1967.[77] Organized through photographs and drawings, the Lugano show took inspiration from the 1964 Michelangelo exhibition curated with Zevi. The emphasis on the use of photographic material was strong: mounted on a winding installation designed by Portoghesi and Gigliotti, the photo enlargements of Borromini's buildings in their contexts were absorbing, drawing the viewer into a vivid historical promenade. The exhibition concluded with a set of contemporary visual associations – from Antoni Gaudí and Frank Lloyd Wright to Alvar Aalto – to reiterate the topicality of Borromini's design method and language across different architectural epochs.

Despite their mutual interest in history, their embrace of the operative criticism and their innovative way of exhibiting architectural ideas, the partnership between Portoghesi and Zevi, so full of potential, came to a drastic and sudden end. 'You were for me the best, and I felt our collaboration would have been fecund, unbeatable. What happened afterwards, is almost worthless to dig up,'[78] admitted Zevi in a passionate three-page letter addressed to Portoghesi in 1978. Although their conversation continued sporadically until 2000, the year of Zevi's passing, what had been a productive intellectual exchange – and, even more, a coordinated plan to reinstate history at the centre of the architectural debate – ended up disintegrating into a set of mutual, sometimes groundless, attacks. After the fall-out with Zevi, Portoghesi remained fully attuned to history as his life's master – his *magistra vitae*[79] – and continued to develop his independent line of interpretation of baroque architecture to serve the language and methodology of contemporary design.

Technique of lap dissolves

At a time of intense debate concerning the role that the history of architecture should take in relation to design, of primary importance was the development of a valid method and approach to reference. Various Italian architects, including Portoghesi, took on this task. As discussed in Chapter 1, Aldo Rossi, who at the end of the 1970s was recognized as the theoretical linchpin of La Tendenza,[80] undertook a poetic recovery of historical forms that gained new meaning through a process of abstraction and juxtaposition. Similarly, Alessandro Mendini, a core member of Studio Alchimia, 'borrowed' popular forms from the history of architecture as if they were fragments which in turn were playfully and ironically reformulated. As for Portoghesi, he forged his own path based on blending historical sources from different periods, according to a non-hierarchical, eclectic approach.

Already tested in 1974 in *Le inibizioni dell'architettura moderna* (Figure 2.5), this approach is also clearly illustrated in the book *Paolo Portoghesi: Progetti e disegni 1949–1979*, edited by Francesco Moschini. As Portoghesi writes:

> The theory is that architecture, every architecture derives from other architectures, from a non-fortuitous convergence between series of precedents

FIGURE 2.5 Example of the lap dissolve technique applied to Sant'Ivo alla Sapienza and Casa Baldi, included in Paolo Portoghesi's book *Le inibizioni dell'architettura moderna*, 1974.

which combine by means of imagination in a process involving the solitude of thought and the nature of the collective memory.... Architecture was born of architecture *tout court*, the result of love stories woven among buildings far off in time and space, for which the architect is an indiscrete party, a best man, an indispensable catalyst, not a creator.[81]

In the attempt to clarify a seemingly ineffable process of historical associations, Portoghesi's projects are presented through analogical combinations across the book, with drawings and critical photographs of their respective precedents disclosing the sources that provided inspiration in the initial design phases. The technique for charting such source blending of the past was what Portoghesi referred to as the 'lap dissolve'. In cinematographic terms, a dissolve is an act of gradually moving from one picture to another – the fade-out of one scene that overlaps with the fade-in of a new scene, so that one appears to dissolve seamlessly into the other. For Portoghesi, who was profoundly influenced by films to the point of using a cinematic approach in the design of his architectural projects, this method meant bringing a dynamic and polyvalent dimension to the genesis of the building and its relationship with the history of architecture. The lap dissolves 'indicated possible, mysterious genetic connections to intentional repetitions ... One image penetrates the next and is, at the same time, crossed, in a movement from within evoking the invisible mechanisms of visual thought'.[82] Some of the photographs used for the lap dissolves, fragmentary, distorted, washed out, sentimental fog, poetic, casual, spectacular,[83] were taken by Portoghesi himself. Despite their technical imperfections, these critical pictures revealed the way the historian was looking analytically at buildings, extrapolating their essence. The values intrinsic to this technique were the right to explore and progress the design process where others had stopped, granting the architect the freedom and the agency to evolve the architectural discourse, as indicated in the cover of the book dedicated to Vittone.[84]

For instance, the project for the Mosque of the Royal Palace of Amman, designed by Portoghesi between 1973 and 1975, sits next to photos of the dome of the Chapel of the Sacred Shroud by Guarini, and Borromini's Sant'Ivo alla Sapienza. The visual juxtaposition on the printed page, with all its limitations of analytical reduction if compared with the cinematic effect of an actual lap dissolve, nonetheless communicates the process of source blending, as it occurred at the very inception of the project's design stage.[85] Page after page, case after case, one realizes the depth of knowledge and uniqueness of these combinatory experiments. If, at first glance, Portoghesi's associative process seems informal, on a closer analysis one is impressed by the rich historical repertoire from which Portoghesi drew – an extremely informed mental collection of precedents that ranged from the ancient to contemporary architecture across different geographical and cultural regions. The visual reading deployed by Portoghesi through his juxtapositions of images is reminiscent of Aby Warburg's *Mnemosyne Atlas* but also of Sigfried Giedion's *Space Time and Architecture* and informed by Norberg-Schulz's 'polemical idea that architectural history was grasped more truthfully in images than in words'.[86] It entailed decades of rigorous and continuous scholarship, to the point that 'the game has turned into a ritual'.[87] And yet despite the intellectual dedication to the project, this photographic approach – shared also with Zevi and Leonardo Benevolo – was condemned by Tafuri for the risk of 'becoming an end in itself'.[88]

Through the blending of precedents and geometric formulas from the past, Portoghesi attempted to generate opportunities to free the architectural language from what he saw as a series of inhibitions: 'We do not intend an organised tendency endowed with an orthodoxy of its own, but rather a grasped phenomenon coming into being,' he wrote in 'The End of Prohibitionism', the introduction to the catalogue for the 1980 Venice Architecture Biennale.[89] Baroque culture in particular had introduced a design method that had broadened the formal historical repertoire.

Geometria borrominiana

Despite Portoghesi's eclectic approach to history and blend of sources, permeated by a sense of inclusion and curiosity, his preferred field of investigation was the baroque. This choice was certainly not the result of any aesthetic assumption but was rather based on the importance that geometry gained in the development of his personal design poetic, as well as on the courage to advance new design solutions.[90] At the time Portoghesi was reasoning on the instrumental value of geometry in baroque architecture, the Roman group GRAU (Gruppo romano architetti e urbanisti) was concurrently referring to geometry as the means to re-use forms from the past.

For Portoghesi, the figure of Borromini stood out as an 'ideal master', particularly for his original take on the Renaissance tradition. 'While claiming responsibility for the right to invent new things,'[91] Portoghesi observed, Borromini sought always for a dialectic between the new and the ancient – a method that Portoghesi was determined to absorb in his design poetic. This was a goal pursued with the same determination by Borromini's follower, Guarini, in whom Portoghesi recognized the merit of the study of geometry and statics with a spirit of universality which was one of the most fruitful conquests of the baroque period.[92] In the wake of the example of these authoritative masters, and with the support of the technique of the lap dissolves, Portoghesi was attempting to find the logic in which the architecture of the past could be revealed to the modern consciousness as a problem of contemporary culture.

> Before being an occasion of historical and philological analysis, the knowledge of the work of Borromini is a tool for the self-criticism of modern culture. Against its own intentions for the expansion of classical orthodoxy, Borromini's controversy ultimately undermines the very foundations of the linguistic conventions restored by the Renaissance, overcoming, in its most intense moments, hesitations and inhibitions that still weigh, like mortgages, on modern architecture itself.[93]

The shared interest of Borromini and Guarini in the dialogue between 'revolution and tradition, rule and freedom'[94] indicated a way to avoid a contemplative or revival-like approach to history. Borromini, in Portoghesi's eyes being a defender of free will in the interpretation of the classical code, would appear as an ideal companion.[95] He was captivated by the critical attitude that his maestro Borromini deployed when using the classical tradition on new premises. Reflecting on his own epoch, Portoghesi observed:

> For Borromini it is no longer only to rebuild and restore a legacy, but to widen it from the inside and to deny the dogmatic and authoritarian character

claimed for it by its contemporary interpreters.... [He] bravely faces, without compromise, the problem of redeeming the culture of his time from dogmatism, shallowness, and the passive celebration of the present.[96]

The art historian Giulio Carlo Argan has suggested that Portoghesi's architecture is dedicated to the investigation of form 'and' its meanings.[97] History of architecture was perceived as a 'repertoire' of forms and design solutions using neither direct 'quotations' nor formal 'mechanical transpositions'.[98] Hence, Portoghesi's buildings do not suffer from *borrominismo* – a stylistic approach to Borromini's oeuvre – but comprise the considered return to those matters in the baroque that proved useful for the renewal of the modern language of architecture. The control of space and light, the use and definition of the curve and the re-instatement of the corner (questions often disregarded by the modernist orthodoxy) were re-appropriated by Portoghesi and liberated as design tools of direct pertinence to his own architectural production.[99] In particular, the curve – an element that Borromini interpreted in experimental ways – is what then motivated Portoghesi to devote parts of his studies to Art Nouveau, as his book on Victor Horta demonstrates.

Where the technique of the lap dissolves constituted a visual process of blending different sources, Portoghesi has suggested another step, crucial to equip the historian's tool kit: that of the 'documentary analysis'.

> The moment of documentary analysis has as its purpose, after the collection of sources, their verification based on every possible testimony. The documents ... allow the reconstruction, albeit incomplete, of the self-critical path that led the author to the design result. This of the self-critical path is probably ... the most important of the historical-critical operations because it tends to trace the architectural thought that guided the author within the work.[100]

Key to the documentary analysis is the 'critical drawing', a graphic tool that allows one to clarify the design construction and composition of the actual project under scrutiny.[101] This modus operandi informed the exhibition *Disegni di Francesco Borromini*, which Portoghesi curated at the Accademia di San Luca in the *anno borrominiano*.[102] In the preface to its catalogue, Portoghesi acknowledged his fascination with the analytical technique of representation that unified Borromini's drawings on display, as well as the systematic geometrical construction of forms. Borromini's drawings not only revealed an exceptional 'drawing ability' but also 'a rigorous design logic'.[103] The analytical tables included in the catalogue help to clarify what Portoghesi meant by 'drawing ability'. For instance, he regarded the drawing of table number 50, representing the section and the front of the lantern of Sant'Ivo alla Sapienza,[104] 'as one of the most fascinating accounts to date of the art of construction'.[105] In this drawing,

Borromini's skill lies in the simultaneous representation of structural and formal development of the architectural element. For Portoghesi, this elegant and complex drawing, with its transparencies and veiling, serves as an X-ray that shows 'the internal structure, qualifying itself as a section or describing the surfaces as an elevation, or both together'.[106]

Beyond Borromini's exceptional ability to capture the spatial, structural and formal dimension of a building in a single architectural drawing, was his rigorous design logic that was regarded by Portoghesi as the ultimate instrument for dealing with the problems posed by history. With Borromini's method, the design phase occurred at two different points: first, the design genesis (or ideational phase), based on an approach of typological and linguistic synthesis; second, the geometric verification (or control phase), implemented through the scientific geometrical formulation of the construction of plans and facades.[107] In other words, Portoghesi was thrilled to discover the way in which architects of Michelangelo's and Borromini's calibre arrived at defining their projects – that is, the steps involved and how they related to each other.[108]

Portoghesi admired how Borromini's projects were both *verified*, through the geometrical construction deployed by the maestro, and *verifiable* by others, through that very geometrical construction, since architecture embraces geometry as 'a means of extending to wider and wider fields the process of rationalising visual knowledge'.[109] As Portoghesi more recently observed, 'Geometry gains in Borromini profoundly innovative aspects ... [as] it helps to analyse and separate the parts, for then combining them harmoniously'.[110] In other words, through geometry, each of Borromini's drawings was decipherable and therefore accessible to his and future generations. The practice of the geometrical construction – or the rational sequence to construct a drawing – did not leave room for approximation of the form or whim of invention, but instead traced each drawing back to a universally legible formula.

As both a historian and an architect, Portoghesi believed that he should operate a historical analysis of Borromini's drawings through interpretative graphics as well as analytical essays to reveal the artistic process going on in the architect's mind.[111] By redrawing the geometrical steps of San Carlo alle Quattro Fontane church (also known as San Carlino), for example, Portoghesi could retrace Borromini's 'problem of defining the scheme through a rigorous method capable of minimising empirical choices'.[112]

Portoghesi clearly verified the geometrical principles of Borromini's work in his book *Borromini nella cultura europea*, whose first section, 'La geometria borrominiana. Saggio di analisi sintattica',[113] uses a series of analytical panels to point to the origins of the architectural ideas underpinning San Carlino, Sant'Ivo alla Sapienza, Sant'Andrea delle Fratte and the Collegio di Propaganda Fide. Portoghesi patiently redrew plans and details of these four buildings, following their geometrical traces step by step. His interpretative diagrams reveal

Borromini's design principles, which, in turn, rely upon the combination of regular forms, dominated by curved lines generated by choices that are far from arbitrary. In their own research, Wittkower and Argan were likewise engaged in the discovery of the genesis of Borromini's work. Portoghesi's studies, however, retracing the original drawings, reveal an originality of method – one whose scholarly significance is distinct from the approaches of the earlier generation.[114]

Portoghesi, who could also rely on his professional skills and sensibility, started from the original San Carlino drawing kept at the Albertina Museum in Vienna and published in the very first pages of *Borromini nella cultura europea*. Unlike Wittkower and Argan, who suggested the hall of the Piazza d'Oro in Villa di Adriano at Tivoli as the main reference for this project,[115] Portoghesi argued that the origin of the church's design lay in Michelangelo's scheme for St Peter. Although he concurred with Wittkower's assessment that the geometrical foundation of the plan was a pair of equilateral triangles with a common base,[116] Portoghesi took his explanation further:

> Plate B – San Carlino 2.... The first phase of the layout concerns the design of the oval of the dome, constructed with the rule of equilateral triangles; the vertices of two raised triangles determine the centres of the four segments of the circle that form the oval, while their bisectors mark the horizontal axis and the intersection of curves of different radii. Thus, the equilateral triangle, a symbol of the Trinity, occurs as a latent form, at the origin of the compositional process.[117]

The same analytical fervour informs the verification of the design process underpinning the project of Sant'Ivo alla Sapienza. Portoghesi read the geometric scheme of the church, wherein an equilateral triangle contains a hexagon. Wittkower provided an overall picture of the religious complex and a plan of the church showing the rhythmic construction of the alternating convex and concave niches, yet Portoghesi focused on redrawing the layout of the church, starting from the equilateral triangle and the inscribed hexagon to generate its overall shape (Figures 2.6 and 2.7). To this extent, Portoghesi agreed with both Wittkower and Argan. While a comparative reading of the three respective interpretations could well result in a sharp exchange between peers, Portoghesi's analysis added to the discussion through the development of his analytical drawings.

> Panel G – S. Ivo 1. The geometric matrix of the interiors of S. Ivo is the equilateral triangle. The illustrations in this panel show the different steps of its geometric genesis. (1) The triangle is divided into sub-triangles. (2) On the intermediate triangles of each of the sides is set a semicircle of corresponding diameter.[118]

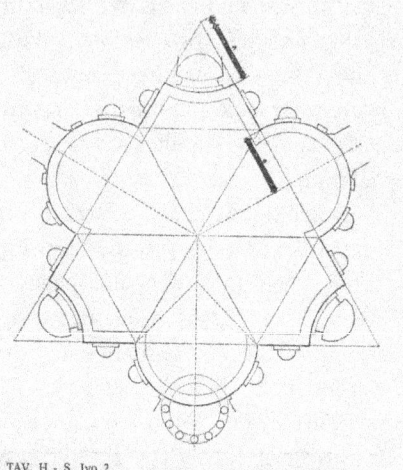

TAV. G - S. Ivo 1.

La matrice geometrica dell'interno di S. Ivo è il triangolo equilatero. Le illustrazioni di questa tavola illustrano i vari tempi della genesi geometrica: 1) Il triangolo è scomposto in triangoli sottomultipli. 2) Sui triangoli intermedi di ciascuno dei lati viene impostato un semicerchio di diametro corrispondente.

TAV. H - S. Ivo 2.

Tracciate le tre absidi semicircolari, sugli altri lati dell'esagono, inscritto nel triangolo generatore, si appoggiano altri nuclei spaziali dal contorno mistilineo; in parte essi si avvalgono dei lati del triangolo che in tal modo determina direttamente parte del perimetro fondamentale. Le terminazioni convesse sono realizzate con archi di cerchio che hanno il loro centro sui vertici dello stesso triangolo. Il raggio di questi archi è però diverso da quello delle absidi semicircolari. L'abside colonnata presente nel primo progetto fu soppressa nella realizzazione.

FIGURE 2.6 Panel G – S. Ivo 1, from the section 'La geometria borrominiana', in *Borromini nella cultura europea*, 1964. Diagrams by Paolo Portoghesi.

FIGURE 2.7 Panel H – S. Ivo 1, from the section 'La geometria borrominiana', in *Borromini nella cultura europea*, 1964. Diagram by Paolo Portoghesi.

In drawing up these schemes, Portoghesi sets himself in the role of the humble scholar executing a task of self-discipline through which he aimed to absorb a logical and rational method of design to secure the 'freedom' to transgress he was after.

Zevi recognized in Portoghesi's totalizing research on and devotion to Borromini a 'relationship of affinity and almost of identification' with his subject.[119] This proximity was sublimated in an 'impossible interview' between Portoghesi and Borromini 'recorded' in 1975.[120] The imaginary dialogue was part of the radio show *Le interviste impossibili*, a subgenre of posthumous colloquia broadcast between 1974 and 1975 on Radiotelevisione Italiana (RAI).[121] In each twenty-minute episode a living expert communed with the ghost of a well-known historical figure (played by an actor) in an effort to clarify certain mysteries and interpretations from the past. Most of the guest hosts came from literary backgrounds: Italo Calvino interviewed Neanderthal man and Montezuma, while Umberto Eco had conversations with more than half a dozen subjects, including Diderot and Pythagoras. One of the reasons for Portoghesi's involvement in the programme (he was the only architect to appear), besides his reputation as an esteemed scholar of the baroque, was his connection to the interdisciplinary avant-garde literary movement Gruppo 63, which counted many of its members, including Eco and Edoardo Sanguineti as hosts of *Le interviste impossibili*. For his first interview, broadcast on 8 April 1975, Portoghesi's subject, a reluctant Gian Lorenzo Bernini, articulated a partisan description of Borromini and his relation to contemporaneity: 'I recognise his ability, and imagination,' said the ghost of Bernini, 'but the proportions he uses seem drawn from the body of a chimera rather than from a beautiful human body, in some cases even reminiscent of gothic architecture.'[122]

One week later, on 17 April 1975, Portoghesi met with an earnest Francesco Borromini, impersonated by the theatre and film actor Roberto Herlitzka. The riveting interview, directed by writer Andrea Camilleri, was a repartee fully constructed around Portoghesi's design agenda.[123] One of the first topics discussed was the attempt to adopt an inclusive attitude towards history and the right for freedom in architecture, a theme very dear to Portoghesi. Here the Roman architect, as the interviewer, longs for his master and invokes his authoritative support while experiencing a moment of difficulty in his own work and career:[124]

Portoghesi 'So, between Classicism on the one hand and Gothicism on the other you have sought a compromise that maintains a kind of ambiguity?'

Borromini Even though so much time has passed, why do you persist in thinking in such a foolish way that tends to divide things, to classify, to separate and is never able to grasp the unity of what is only apparently contrary? When I fought to defend my architecture from these accusations of contamination, I believed that the future would prove me right, that man would give up on imposing artificial rules that humiliate freedom and transform men of genius into miserable copyists.

Portoghesi It is not that the future has not proved you right, Maestro, but that yours is a battle that continues to be fought today, and the enemies are as numerous as they were then.

Borromini It should be clear that time is like a great circle where everything has already been and can return: truth is curvilinear.

Portoghesi It is clear only to some, Maestro; and whoever has a different opinion is always, as in your day, intolerant.

Borromini Oh, intolerance, I have been a victim of it!

Before entering an enquiry on his relationship with Bernini, the discussion lingers on the notion of geometry.

Portoghesi   And the heptagon is the seven-sided polygon. Is it possible that you have also used this polygon always rejected by architects?

Borromini   Precisely for this reason, history is full of waste, of experiences that have been abandoned or interrupted.

The impossible interview was the perfect formula for the moment – a time when history was commonly accepted as a resource for the present. The past was a place of multiple narratives and creative attitudes, and the present had the tools and the intellectual freedom to instrumentalize the past. History was appreciated as a 'friend', a repository for inspiration and a playground for architects, writers, artists and intellectuals. Portoghesi embraced this format to divulgate the history of baroque architecture and talk in a simplified way of processes he had long studied as historian and designer.

Casa Baldi, or the rehabilitation of the curve

With work on *Borromini nella cultura europea* spanning a period of more than twelve years, some of the design themes the book explores were on Portoghesi's desk when he was starting his very first projects as a practitioner. Among these early works sits Casa Baldi (1959–61), his first built residential project which offers an eloquent example of the instrumentalization of Borrominian methods and forms for contemporary design (Figure 2.8).

Located in Labaro, a small municipality on the outskirts of Rome, Casa Baldi is nestled in a plot adjacent to via Flaminia, the ancient Roman road that leads over the Apennine mountains all the way down to the Adriatic coast. Before the rampant urbanization of the 1960s overtook the neighbourhood, the house overlooked a bight of the River Tiber from above a tuff stone hill. The small residential building was commissioned by the Italian producer, director and screen writer Gian Vittorio Baldi,[125] whom Portoghesi met in 1957 when the pair worked on *Automi e macchine*, a short film dedicated to the relationship between automata and machines.[126] Both client and architect were young and ambitious and, while the budget was limited, Portoghesi was granted freedom in the design. The house was built by the construction company of Portoghesi's father, allowing the architect to keep a daily track of progress.[127] Appropriating Rogers's notion of *preesistenze ambientali* and Norberg-Schulz's *genius loci*, Portoghesi reacted to the natural environment of the site for Casa Baldi of tuff and pozzolana rocks and historical artefacts, such as the ruins of a nearby Roman theatre.

Casa Baldi was developed as a manifesto of rebellion against the modern orthodoxy. Sketches of the house and image juxtapositions show how the

FIGURE 2.8 Casa Baldi during construction works, Rome, 1960. Photograph by Paolo Portoghesi. © Paolo Portoghesi Archive.

principles of modern architecture were mediated through the use of baroque design and, vice versa, where the forms of baroque architecture were absorbed through the modern language. As Portoghesi has explained:

> The attempt in my building is that of using the forms not in their autonomy but the interpretation of those forms through a critical approach that belongs to the period I have lived in.... When I use a theme from Bramante or Borromini, I do so by looking at those models through the experiences of Gaudí, Le Corbusier, Terragni, Ridolfi, Kahn, Pietilä and Gehry. Without the lesson of the zeitgeist offered by these protagonists, those very forms would not yield the same meaning.[128]

Casa Baldi's overall project intentionally referred to the syntactic process of De Stijl and, more specifically, to the Schröder House (1924), designed by Gerrit Rietveld and Truus Schröder-Schräder. Nevertheless, the rigidity of Rietveld's orthogonal scheme was overtaken by way of Borromini – his boldness in breaking the rules and his awareness of the limits of action. While Rietveld's space, with the orthogonal juxtaposition of its walls, resulted in a rigorous layout, Casa Baldi's curved walls allowed Portoghesi to achieve the effect of a pulsating space[129] that could accommodate and emphasize the movements of its residents. The space of Casa Baldi was in fact defined by the combination of undulating walls that led to moments of 'expansion' and 'contraction'.[130] Through this curvature the walls absorb and retain the natural light; at the same time, the dialectic relationship of their concave-convex forms renders the space as 'fluid but articulated'[131] with cinematic attributes. Windows result from the encounter of the walls – the so-called dialectic-windows – establishing a swift flow of continuity between the interior of the building and its landscape.[132] The juxtaposition of curved elements is conceptualized in a desk designed especially for Casa Baldi, a sort of didactic miniature that concentrates the project's main design ideas. In the 'Lap dissolves' section of Moschini's book, the neoplastic model serving as the main precedent for Casa Baldi is matched to Le Corbusier's Ronchamp Chapel (1950) and Ludwig Mies van der Rohe's house for the Berlin exhibition (1930) – two strong examples of the juxtaposition of surfaces.

In his most recent book *Poesia della curva*, Portoghesi has observed that 'the straight line and the right angle are unique, they do not admit variations, the curves are infinite, as many as the imagination can identify, they represent the multiplicity, the variability, the difference' (Figure 2.9).[133] Through his use of the curve, Portoghesi not only challenged the lessons of De Stijl but also broadened its thematic horizons. The comparison between the lantern of Sant'Ivo alla Sapienza and the soffit edge of the Casa Baldi[134] suggests that the cornice obtained by the alternation of concave and convex lines in Sant'Ivo was elaborated by Portoghesi as an element to join the scalloped walls and to amplify their expressive power.[135] The

FIGURE 2.9 Casa Baldi, detail of the corner. Photograph by Paolo Portoghesi. © Paolo Portoghesi Archive.

final spatial effect of the house was dynamic, with its walls embodying the flow of the wind.

When completed in 1961, the residence was one of the few buildings in the international context to emphasize the use of the curve, rehabilitating it as a design element. Beyond the curved line, Casa Baldi expressed many other aspects of postmodern architecture including the recovery of traditional materials, such as tuff and brick; and the formal and linguistic references to baroque architecture such as, for example, the use of pronounced cornices and the manipulation of space and natural light.

Despite Portoghesi's relative inexperience and the house's somewhat hidden location on the edge of Rome, Casa Baldi drew international attention. Both *Architectural Forum* and a 1964 article by Thomas W. Ennis in the *New York Times* argued whether the house marked the beginning of 'a new wave',[136] anticipating the condition that almost fifteen years later Charles Jencks would identify in his seminal book *The Language of Post-Modern Architecture* (1977). In fact, Jencks locates the beginning of Postmodernism in late 1950s Italy, in what Banham had qualified as the Italian retreat from Modern Architecture. Casa Baldi features as a persuasive example of this turning point:

> One of the most convincing historicist buildings of the Fifties was Paolo Portoghesi's Casa Baldi, 1959–61, an essay in free-form curves definitely reminiscent of the Borromini he was studying, yet also unmistakably influenced by Le Corbusier. Here is the schizophrenic cross between two codes that is characteristic of Post-Modernism: the enveloping, sweeping curves of the Baroque, the overlap of space, the various focii of space interfering with each other and the Brutalist treatment, the expression of concrete block, rugged joinery and the guitar-shapes of modernism.[137]

For Portoghesi, the ambiguity of the project – the 'schizophrenic cross' as per Jencks – was programmatic. Through Casa Baldi he claimed the right to incorporate complexity in architecture. Incidentally, Casa Baldi was completed the same year as the Vanna Venturi house built by Robert Venturi for his mother in Chestnut Hill, near Philadelphia. Like his American counterpart, Portoghesi used the site of a small residential project to erect a manifesto that undermined the canonization of modern architecture. Standing as two ideal entrance columns, these houses heralded the beginning of the postmodern turn through their two different approaches: in the first instance, through the interpretation of baroque architecture; in the other, through a more American tendency towards historical and primitive forms, emphasizing the use of complexity and ambiguity, colour and irony.

While international critics welcomed Casa Baldi as an early example of postmodern architecture, in Italy the small house turned out to be 'one of the most problematic events of the whole architectural debate',[138] considered with perplexity and resistance, even judged by some as reactionary. In 1962, Zevi published an article on Casa Baldi in his magazine *L'architettura: Cronache e storia*. Despite the ten richly illustrated pages that were dedicated to the project, the piece, 'Un edificio problematico: Polemica con l'autore',[139] was critical in its analysis of 'a highly controversial piece of work' whose 'design shows some late-antique, Baroque, Art Nouveau as well as Wright's and Le Corbusier's influences'. It argued that 'it is questionable whether the path it proposes is a fruitful one or remains a "unique" and ambiguous case', somehow anticipating the divergence that would soon occur between the agendas of Zevi and Portoghesi.

Despite its critics, Casa Baldi led to a series of other design opportunities for Portoghesi, '[following] one upon the other at regular intervals, to the point of marking a change of course every time in his designing trajectory'.[140] These included the unbuilt Casa Baldi II (1966), the completed Casa Andreis (1964–69) in Scandriglia, Rieti, the project for Cagliari Theatre (1965–66) and the completed Casa Bevilacqua (1966–67) in Gaeta. Each one constituted a step forward in Portoghesi's definition of his design method.

One of the common traits of the above-mentioned projects was their use of geometric construction, characteristic of the baroque tradition, illustrated in the catalogue of the exhibition *Paola Levi Montalcini, Paolo Portoghesi and Vittorio Gigliotti*, held at Palazzo Farnese in 1969. Early sketches for Casa Baldi II reveal its geometric construction through the placement of generative dots of curve segments – 'force fields', as Christian Norberg-Schulz defined them. They are fixed within the perimeter of a hexagon (the hypothesis of the pentagon was soon abandoned).[141] The 'force fields' generate 'grammatical chords' obtained by the juxtaposition of inflected walls that determine the various openings in the plan.[142] The use of generative dots appeared in Casa Baldi but became more structured in Casa Baldi II and even more so in Casa Andreis, one of Portoghesi's clearest attempts to mediate between language and geometry, setting the theoretical basis for the definition of a 'system of places' (Figures 2.10, 2.11, 2.12).[143]

The drawings of Casa Andreis are exemplary for their articulation of a geometrically constructed 'regulating layout' and its volumetric development. It has been observed that baroque architecture represents a sophisticated example of proto-parametric architecture.[144] In line with this approach, Portoghesi developed a *teoria dei campi*, or fields theory: 'From the observations of the ornaments of the altars in baroque churches, [he] reflected on architectural elements that can "emanate" waves, as if they were magnetic fields, which affect the surrounding spaces of the church.'[145] This produced a series of diagrams in which rippling waves propagated in concentric circles. Following a strictly algorithmic logic, these spatial diagrams produced fields of lines that then became 'the model in which walls, structure and dividing elements can be arranged'.[146] An initial sketch shows Portoghesi working on a grid of modular squares, the vertices of which generate concentric circles. That drawing evolved into a second layout wherein three adjacent scalene triangles lead

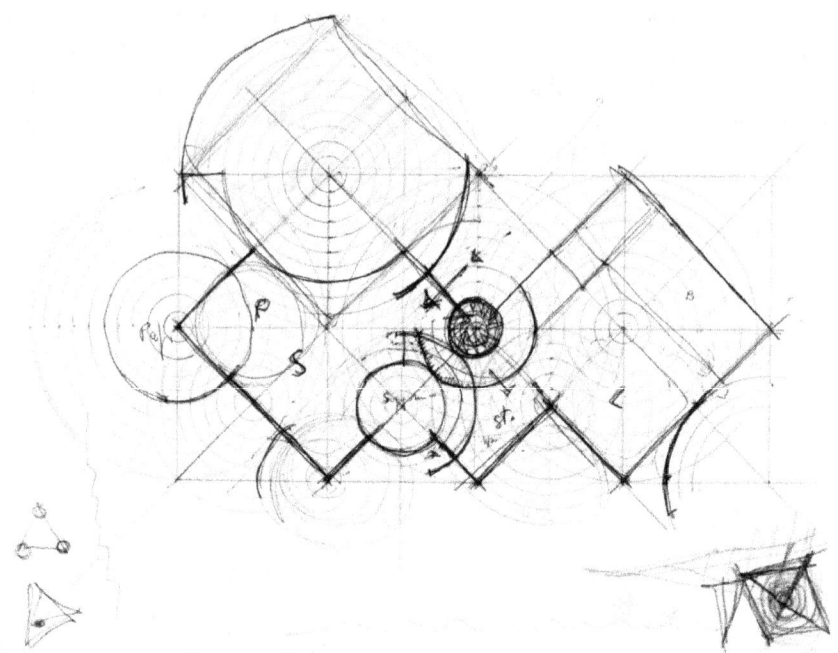

FIGURE 2.10 Geometrical construction of the plan for Casa Andreis in Scandriglia, sketch by studio Portoghesi-Gigliotti, c. mid-1960s. © Centre George Pompidou.

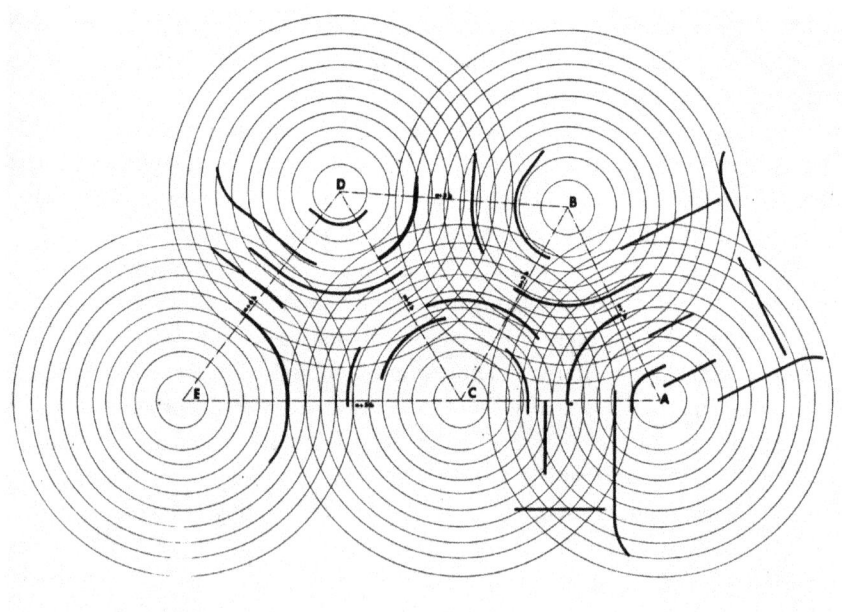

Tracciato regolatore

FIGURE 2.11 Geometrical drawing of the plan for Casa Andreis in Scandriglia, by studio Portoghesi-Gigliotti, c. mid-1960s. © Paolo Portoghesi Archive.

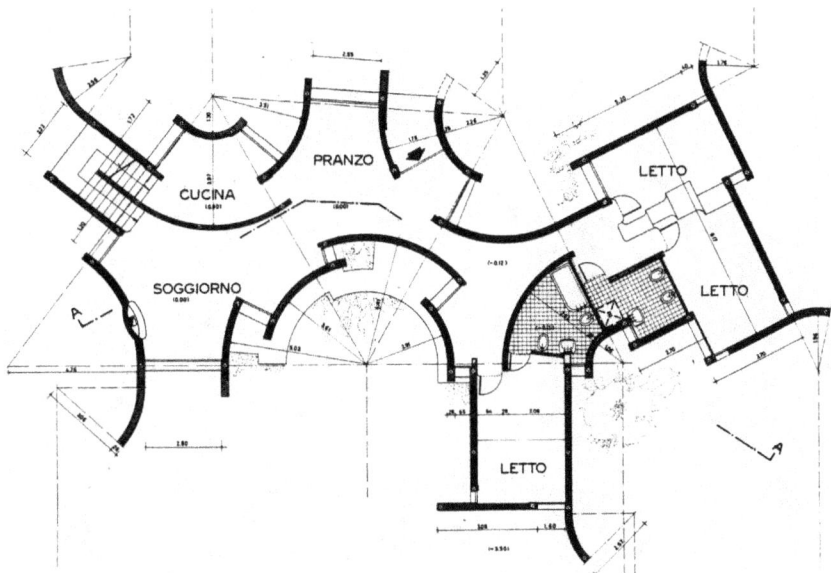

FIGURE 2.12 Plan of Casa Andreis in Scandriglia, by studio Portoghesi-Gigliotti, c. mid-1960s. © Paolo Portoghesi Archive.

him to fix the 'centres of curvature'.[147] Only the geometric organization of the plan can bring a rhythm to the surface and to the overall volume, the disposition of which is ruled by a principle of 'order in movement'.

In Casa Bevilacqua, the use of a geometrical scheme in plan gains volumetric emphasis. Conceived as a Michelangeloesque fortress set on the Mediterranean coast, the inflection of the walls forcefully connects the building to the dramatic landscape with great assertiveness but lacking the elegance and dynamism of Casa Baldi. Not only does the building look as if it is stacked into the sloping ground, but the tension emerging from the walls shapes the roof with its white, open-air steps. The order of the curvilinear system is here called up by the pinnacle: at once linchpin of the house and marker of the maritime landscape (Figure 2.13).

This series of projects culminated in Casa Papanice (1966–70) and, even more convincingly, the Chiesa della Sacra Famiglia (1969–74) in Salerno[148] – arguably the most mature of this series of works based on geometric diagrams. In the former (discussed in depth in Chapter 4), the geometrical choices transcend into a highly cinematic sequence based on the forms of the circle and cylinder, leading to an unprecedented spatial dynamism and fluidity. Here the spatial rhythm becomes almost hypnotic, and the overall volume of the building, generated through the fast repetition of variations on the theme of the cylinder, assumes a deliberately exuberant character (Figures 2.14, 2.15 and 2.16).[149]

FIGURE 2.13 View of Casa Bevilacqua, looking onto the maritime landscape. © Paolo Portoghesi Archive.

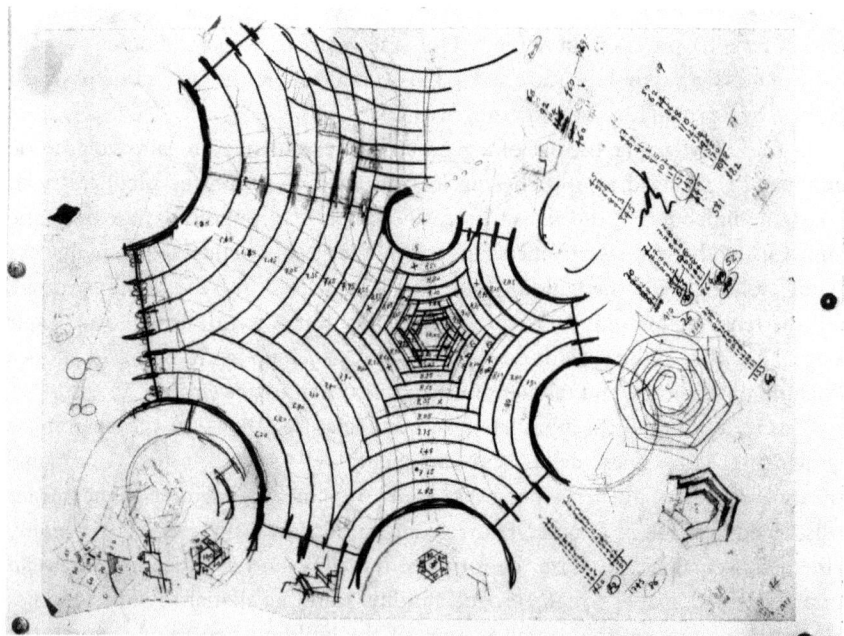

FIGURE 2.14 Study plan for the Sacra Familia Church, Fratte, Salerno, c. mid-1970s, by studio Portoghesi-Gigliotti. © Paolo Portoghesi Archive.

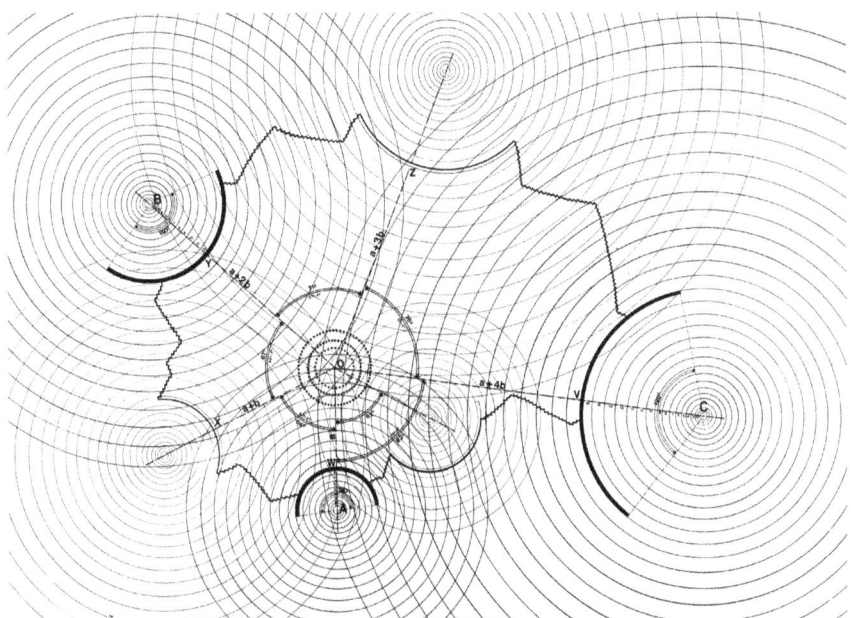

FIGURE 2.15 Geometrical drawing of the plan for the Sacra Familia Church, Fratte, Salerno, c. mid-1970s, by studio Portoghesi-Gigliotti. © Paolo Portoghesi Archive.

FIGURE 2.16 Interiors of the Sacra Familia Church, Fratte, Salerno, c. mid-1970s. Photograph by Paolo Portoghesi. © Paolo Portoghesi Archive.

In the Chiesa della Sacra Famiglia (1969–74), the geometric scheme of the plan that in Casa Andreis had dictated the inflection of the walls becomes the formal matrix for the ceiling and the piers of the domed room, which establish an 'absolute continuity'.[150] Externally, the same elements are adapted to the structure to connect to the morphology of the surrounding landscape.[151] And differently from Casa Baldi and Casa Andreis, the disposition of the centre of magnetic fields is in this project verified against the plan of Sant'Ivo, as Portoghesi's hand-drawn, colour diagram demonstrates through the overlapping of the ground plans of the two buildings.[152]

These experiments are confirmed in other urban projects, which present real tests for Portoghesi and Gigliotti's approach in the city: the competition for the Opera House in Cagliari (1965) and the extension of the Chamber of Deputies in Rome (1967). In Rome, to control the process of rooting the building in its context and to obtain a dialogue with its surroundings, the designers proposed a plan system generated by a central core that coincides with the axis of vertical paths and around which an aggregation of triangular modules grows into a broken spiral. On this project, Manfredo Tafuri wrote that Portoghesi:

> has been for a long time theorising the need for a rigorous, programmed structure of geometric types, in which it is possible to recover the irrational and a sensitivity to the morphology of the place. In his competition project, the modular grid and the spiral that generates the contraction of the vitreous volume sloping upwards serves to confirm and criticise one another, as if to prove that unique and true freedom lies in the rigor with which the limits are set.[153]

* * *

As soon as Portoghesi became president of the Venice Biennale in 1983, the idea of history as *magistra vitae* permeated the other sectors of the institution too. The appointment of Maurizio Calvesi[154] (like Portoghesi a historian and academic) as the director of the visual arts sector was a sign of how he intended to extend his postmodern project and turn to history across the Biennale, cutting through the different disciplines. The name of the 41st International Art Exhibition of the Venice Biennale in 1984 was *Arte e arti: Attualità e storia* and the Central Pavilion at the Giardini di Castello contained a show titled *Arte alto specchio*. International in scope and curated by Calvesi,

> 'Art in the Mirror' was a self-reflecting exercise about art that looks at the history of art, with contemporary artists referring to their *maestri* and relying on the notion of memory.... The historical part of the exhibition included 'De

Chirico who copies Watteau, Picasso who refers to Velazquez, Duchamp who draws moustaches on the Gioconda, De Pisis who remembers Goya'.[155]

With this exhibition on display, other sectors of the Venice Biennale became venues for Portoghesi to pursue once more the centrality of history for contemporary cultural practices, unwavering as it was seamless.

3 SOCIALISM FOR FREEDOM

FIGURE 3.1 Bettino Craxi, Mario Rigo, Giovanna Massobrio, Pietro Longo and Paolo Portoghesi at the Marco Polo airport of Venice for the opening of the 37th International Art and Architecture Exhibition, Venice Biennale, 1976. © Lorenzo Cappellini.

A photo from 1976 encapsulates some of the dynamics and alliances that would influence Italian architectural culture of the late 1970s and 1980s (Figure 3.1). Pictured are Benedetto 'Bettino' Craxi, national secretary of the Partito Socialista Italiano (PSI), Mario Rigo, mayor of Venice, Giovanna Massobrio, Pietro Longo, national secretary of the Partito Socialdemocratico Italiano (PSDI), and Paolo Portoghesi. The group is shown arriving at Marco Polo airport in Venice for the opening of the 37th International Art and Architecture Exhibition of the Venice Biennale. Their pace is confident, their attire sophisticated and their mood jolly.

The image adds another dimension to Portoghesi's role as impresario of Italian postmodern architecture: not only was he deftly navigating the cultural politics of his discipline; he was playing a part in the actual politics of Italy – and in doing so he influenced the making of the country's postmodern architecture and its public reach.

In order to interpret the intricacies of the Italian postmodern architectural scene, of which Portoghesi was one of the main figures of power,[1] it is necessary to delve into the complex intersection of Italian architecture, politics and ideology – a relationship that makes the country a distinctive 'case' in the international context of the second half of the twentieth century. While Portoghesi's alliance with the PSI is recognized, less well known are the ways in which he operated within the party, and how politics in general were useful to the formulation and spread of his design ideas and theories. There were multiple mechanisms by which postmodern architecture in Italy related to the new socio-political agenda and the neoliberal economic context promoted by the PSI between 1976 and 1993. During this period, Italian socialists orchestrated a novel marriage of politics and architecture, allowing for a renewed image of their party while popularizing new forms of aesthetics and design ideas.

Rise and leadership of the PSI

If modern architecture in most European countries and the United States has been predominantly associated with a social agenda and the implementation of the welfare state, then postmodern architecture is often seen as a direct consequence of the rise of free market economies and the liberal right, making architecture and urbanism an integral part of the neoliberal turn. In the United States, for example, 'postmodernism became the new corporate style',[2] while collectively postmodern architects have generally exhibited a marked indifference to social policies. Yet, some contexts, such as Italy, France and Belgium, have offered alternative scenarios.[3] At the end of the Second World War, the Italian PSI, a minor left-wing party with a long history going back to 1892, found itself operating in the shadow of the Partito Comunista Italiano (PCI), the largest communist party outside the Soviet Union. At the time, the Italian cultural debate revolved around the ideology promoted by the PCI. Recognized as the only possible interlocutor for renewing the discussion of social issues affecting the nation,[4] the PCI counted members of the Italian intelligentsia among its ranks – such as artists and filmmakers as well as architects. A young generation of architects, urbanists, historians and critics, including Aldo Rossi, Guido Canella, Vittorio Gregotti and Gae Aulenti[5] (all active in the Milanese editorial board of Ernesto Nathan Rogers's *Casabella-continuità*), as well as Giuseppina Marcialis, Manfredo Tafuri and Carlo Aymonino, joined the PCI and actively engaged in its cultural initiatives and administrative roles. In 1951, Rossi travelled to Russia on a trip organized by the party – 'a modern grand tour for the communist intellectuals of the time'.[6] He also wrote for the communist magazines *La voce comunista* and *Società*. Aulenti and Canella, too, visited Moscow in 1961.[7] These trips led to issue 262 of *Casabella-continuità* dedicated to the architecture in the USSR, which familiarized Italian architects with the relationship between Soviet ideology and the built environment. In 1963, Marcialis travelled to Havana to attend the International Congress of Architects (UIA), broadening the Italian architectural communist network abroad. Underpinned by a participatory spirit promoted by Marxist philosopher Antonio Gramsci,[8] this group of dedicated, intellectual and engaged architects, through their personal trajectories and individual projects, buildings, publications and conferences, bridged the communist ideology to architecture and, at the same time, facilitated the strategic role of architecture in the making of the city and its urban scenarios.

The practice of becoming a member of the PCI and assisting with administrative and cultural roles outside the profession and academia eventuated in strategic political appointments, pushing the commitment of architects, critics and historians to the next level. The most illustrious cases included the art and architectural historian Giulio Carlo Argan, who was elected the first communist mayor of Rome (1976–79). Argan, in turn, appointed the communist architect Renato Nicolini as the city's culture councillor (1976–85),[9] while Aymonino served as councillor of Rome's historic centre (1980–84). The architects who 'served the party' aspired towards a culture based on communist ideology. The role of the architect as 'intellectual', with its strong political connotation, was thus recognized also outside the discipline of architecture.[10] But with the USSR's invasion of Hungary in 1956, the Italian Left began to crumble. At that time, the PSI started to gradually withdraw from its alliance with the PCI and intensify its relationship with the Democrazia Cristiana (DC). This alteration in the political spectrum created new possibilities for Italy's political development.[11] As observed by Pier Vittorio Aureli:

> What was taking place in Italy and throughout Europe in the 1960s was what had occurred in the United States in the 1930s: the system of production was becoming more efficiently organised. This meant a more generalised and extensive dissemination of industrial production beyond the factory to the whole of society.... Neocapitalism became the organic link between the capitalist system of the accumulation and the programs of the welfare state.[12]

Portoghesi belonged to this generation of politically engaged intellectuals. But while others were joining the PCI, as early as 1961 he enrolled in PSI (Figure 3.2).

Within the PCI, architecture had aroused little interest from the party establishment,[13] which failed to recognise the link between architectural discourse and the party's cultural programme. In 1964 the journalist Alberto Cavallari,

FIGURE 3.2 Paolo Portoghesi's enrolment card in the PSI party, issued in Rome, 1961. © Paolo Portoghesi Archive.

lamenting the lack of cultural spaces in Milan, observed how those managing the city's cultural organizations 'were all social democrats or socialists'. The suggestion of a lack of communist control over the cultural system of one of Italy's main cities made it clear that the cultural system of Milan was already a political matter.[14] The PSI, instead, offered more dynamic cultural possibilities, and other architects began to turn their attention to the party. For instance, Milanese architect and urbanist Michele Achilli, who had taught at the Politecnico di Milano as an assistant of Piero Bottoni in 1965, was an active representative of the PSI at a national level in the 1960s and a decisive operator in the reform process of urban legislation. His partnership with Canella, a member of the PCI, eventuated in the office of Achilli Canella Brigidini, which used architectural projects to pursue a set of social ideals and political ambitions.[15] As a result, the Segrate Townhall (1963–66), the IACP Housing in Bollate (1974–81) and the Townhall in Pieve Emanuele (1979) were all seen as occasions to design places of social and political aggregation in the Milanese hinterland and to create socialist-inspired communities. As Achilli later observed, it was the PSI's practice to involve committed young people with specific expertise to join the boards of the municipalities of Milan in order to directly handle the contradictions between the existing legislation and the needs of the local bodies.[16] Despite its long subordination to the PCI, by the mid-1970s the PSI had taken on a new identity, establishing itself as an alternative voice in the national political debate. Its leadership initiated a radical ideological shift within the Italian Left by fostering a progressive socio-political programme that shared some characteristics with right-wing values, including a greater liberal stance and a call for individual freedom.

Years of the protests

Portoghesi's involvement in the political scene intensified in 1967, when he moved north to take on a position as Professor of History of Architecture at the Politecnico di Milano (from now on Politecnico).[17] In 1968, the year of the infamous student protests, he was elected dean of the Faculty of Architecture and became fully immersed in the political arena. At the time, Milan was the national epicentre of extra-parliamentary groups[18] and the Faculty of Architecture their strategic fortress – an example of how deep infiltration of politics in Italian universities was during the 1960s and 1970s.[19] While the student riots in Milan were becoming more intense and inflammatory, Giacomo Mancini, then the PSI's secretary, invited Portoghesi to join the party's Central Committee, which Portoghesi regularly attended from 1969, positioning himself in the decision-making frontline.[20]

At the time of Portoghesi's arrival at the Politecnico, there were two major groups that enlivened the cultural scene of the Faculty of Architecture: the heirs of the Modern Movement, situated on the left of the political spectrum, and the lecturers of scientific subjects, situated on the centre-right. In August 1968 the Milanese architect and academic Carlo De Carli, then dean of the Faculty, was removed from his role by the Ministry of Education. His dismissal was caused by his close collaboration with the student assembly in relation to the controversial *Sperimentazione* – a courageous attempt to reform the Faculty's teaching system in order to produce a different model of teaching and learning and, within this, different approaches to the discipline.[21] This collective programme of students and lecturers, in the first instance authorized by the Ministry of Education in 1967, was calling for the reorganization of the Faculty of Architecture's curriculum, which led to a form of self-governance encouraged by some of the extreme fringes of the students groups.[22] In 1968, the Faculty board asked for the officialization of the *Sperimentazione*.

When the board convened to elect the new dean to replace De Carli, the Faculty was dominated by leading figures such as Franco Albini, Piero Bottoni and Ludovico Barbiano di Belgiojoso, all well-established members of Milan's architectural circles and ideal candidates – with the exception of Ernesto Nathan Rogers, who was absent due to health issues. The election of a new dean after the revocation of De Carli's position and the interim position (held, as per law, by the eldest professor of the Faculty, Arnaldo Masotti) was seen as an action of primary importance by the Faculty in retrieving control from the Ministry of Education and those aligned with it, including the Chancellor of the Politecnico, Bruno Finzi.[23]

To everyone's surprise, on 20 October 1968, Paolo Portoghesi – the youngest candidate – was appointed dean. In his words it was 'an unusual, extreme practice, that of electing the youngest candidate, which is adopted only when one feels under siege'.[24] At just thirty-six years old, Portoghesi's initial task was to quell the hostility between the conservative part of the teaching body, the more progressive staff members, the different groups of students and the administration – different groups that were also pursuing distinct agendas. The job was made particularly arduous by the fact that the boundaries between the political and ideological orientations of the different factions were not always clear-cut (Figure 3.3). Coming from Rome, Portoghesi could offer a fresh perspective on the troubled and chaotic academic dynamics of the Politecnico. More importantly, he operated within the PSI, which meant that, despite his alignment with left-wing political parties, the authorities of the Politecnico and the Ministry of Education did perceive

FIGURE 3.3 The executive board of the Faculty of Architecture of the Politecnico di Milano, sitting at the table for a meeting, 1971. At the head of the table, the dean, Paolo Portoghesi, reading a document. Anticlockwise, Lodovico Barbiano di Belgiojoso, Carlo De Carli, Franco Albini, Guido Canella, Vittoriano Viganó and Piero Bottoni. The meeting was attended by the students. © Paolo Portoghesi Archive.

him as more balanced than some of his colleagues who were members of the Communist Party or gravitating towards the extra-parliamentary groups. Rather, this 'outsider' – equipped with exceptional skills as a mediator, associations with the Roman political salons and an international reputation as a historian of architecture – was viewed as the person who could effectively negotiate with the authorities on behalf of the Politecnico community during the time of the student occupation.

Reflecting on the period immediately following his arrival at the Politecnico, Portoghesi described the Faculty of architecture as:

> The most disastrous and anachronistic Faculty, managed by the 'fascist architects' who had invented it. It was a kind of limbo – of Parnassian jealously – guarded until almost the '60s, in the midst of a dramatic social and economic reality in evolution. You cannot study architecture without doing politics.[25]

These obstacles did not stop Portoghesi from joining the Milanese community of architects and establishing long-lasting professional and personal relationships. Portoghesi taught history of architecture with Virgilio Vercelloni who, like him, worked across history and design. The two shared the same interest in the use of history to critically understand the present moment and in their joint course offered intellectual tools from a cultural perspective (Figure 3.4), according to a Marxist political definition of architecture and urban planning.[26] Vercelloni and the most progressive lecturers of the Faculty of Architecture including Luciano Patetta, Massimo Scolari and Ezio Bonfanti became also part of the Milanese editorial board of *Controspazio*, the architectural magazine that Portoghesi founded in 1969 as one of the tools to interpret contemporary architecture for the students (see Chapter 4).

In 1970, the Faculty of Architecture started testing new methods of teaching, including group work, which coincided with a spike in enrolment numbers (from 632 to 1,307 students).[27] However, this increase should be contextualized in the broader national phenomenon of the so-called 'mass university' initiative, which counted 500,000 students all over the country in 1967–68, compared with the 268,000 of 1960–61.[28] Thanks to Portoghesi's vision, between 1969 and 1971, the process of pedagogical modernization was carried out on relatively productive terms, helped by the Codignola National Law (11 December 1969) – the institutional attempt to respond to and regulate students' demands for didactic renewal and liberalize the access of students to the university system. The student–staff conflict was performed as a sort of a weekly liturgy – twice per week over three years. Assemblies gathered up to 1,200 very agitated and vocal students, organized as the Movimento studentesco and the Autonomi, two groups characterized by an irreverent anti-authoritarianism (the Movimento was also anticapitalistic and strongly critical towards the PCI).[29] It fell to Portoghesi, as dean, to manage the tense discussions of strongly opposed views between the student body and part of the staff (Figure 3.5).

FIGURE 3.4 *La rivoluzione culturale*, booklet produced by the research group led by Paolo Portoghesi at the Politecnico di Milano, academic year 1970–71. © Archivio Storico Politecnico di Milano. Servizi Bibliotecari e Archivi, Politecnico di Milano, ACL.

FIGURE 3.5 Dean Paolo Portoghesi surrounded by the students of the Politecnico di Milano, during a moment of tense discussion, 1971. © Paolo Portoghesi Archive.

On more than one occasion, Portoghesi stood up for the students, criticizing the top-down, hierarchical style of the university in its management of the turmoil that could sometimes involve the police to suppress the students' voices.[30] He operated in continuity with the *Sperimentazione* launched by De Carli and yet was able to work on different terms, bringing together the institutional legal structure and the experimental approach of the university with the support of many of the Faculty's lecturers.[31] Nevertheless, the atmosphere in the Faculty was restless, and the students had set their sights on a cultural revolution.

On 21 April 1971, the new chancellor of the Politecnico, Francesco Carassa, prepared a report on the Faculty of Architecture's current turmoil. This 'false portrait',[32] as Portoghesi described it, resulted in a ministerial inspection. Not long after the report was issued, in June 1971, Portoghesi found himself taking part in the occupation of the Faculty of Architecture, standing shoulder-to-shoulder with his colleagues Canella and Fredi Drugman and a mass of students as they faced off against a squad of police in full riot gear. A photograph of the moment shows Portoghesi wearing his signature checked jacket while holding a megaphone, once more a sign of his role as a mediator (Figure 3.6).

At the time, the Politecnico had just one computer, with its own dedicated space in the engineering department. 'It was massive – recalled Portoghesi – it took up a whole

FIGURE 3.6 Dean Paolo Portoghesi facing the authorities during a protest at the Politecnico di Milano with, from left to right, Fredi Drugman, Guido Canella, Federico Oliva and Pierluigi Nicolin, 1971. © Paolo Portoghesi Archive.

room and needed Niagara Falls to cool it down!'[33] The computer was prized by the university, and the engineers considered themselves the custodians of this technological treasure. The architects understood that the computer symbolized both their education and their struggle – Portoghesi even gave a lecture on the importance of the computer and its relevance to the socialist world.[34] And so when the police threatened to enter, they were warned of the dire consequences of upsetting the computer's delicate environment. When this tactic failed, Portoghesi resorted to other – architectural – means; at one point insisting that the mass of police and students congregating on a concrete ramp far exceeded the ramp's structural capabilities and would surely result in its imminent collapse. The police dutifully retreated.

The stressed relationships within the Faculty of Architecture and between the Faculty and the authorities descended further on the night of 6 June 1971. In Milan, between 1968 and 1970, approximately 40 per cent of the 100,000 families living in social housing refused to pay their rent, or self-reduced it, in protest of the prohibitive fees and lack of services.[35] As a result, police evicted eighty families from a block of flats located in via Tibaldi, and a child tragically lost his life. On the night of the 1971 eviction, students who supported the far-left extra-parliamentary organizations Lotta Continua and Il Manifesto, as well as dean Portoghesi and members of the Faculty, collectively decided to house within the Faculty of

Architecture the newly homeless families – approximately 200 people.[36] At that time, 'attention was directed, much more than in the past, to the necessity for greater social justice and to the formation of communities with a strong sense of the collective and solidarity'.[37] Consequently, the homeless, the students and teachers spent the night together in the Faculty. To prevent the police from bursting in, professors lectured continuously on the topic of housing problems – the only legal way of keeping the Faculty open and the police out: 'There was the delusion that the police would not enter because there were on-going activities. If they did, one could have said that the police were preventing public officials from performing their role,' recalled Portoghesi.[38] Umberto Eco, who joined for solidarity, remembered that:

> At four in the morning, Paolo Portoghesi was able to raise the general spirit by holding a two-hour lesson with the projection of colour slides on popular construction in its correlation with elite construction and on the relationship between architecture and the lower classes. It was a learned lesson, at times precious, that was needed to restore everyone's attitude.[39]

Portoghesi was giving a lecture on neorealist architecture when the police broke in and expelled everyone.[40] Molotov cocktails and rocks were thrown from the roof of the Faculty of Architecture, injuring forty-one policemen.[41] The police responded with tear gas, and the ensuing battle turned into urban warfare that extended to the area surrounding the Politecnico. The scene was tense, violent and bloody, constituting one of the most dramatic points of conflict between governmental and academic power. Portoghesi became a national symbol of political resistance to social injustice.[42] He appreciated how both professors and students had defended 'the democratic freedom established by the Constitution and the University's autonomy from the political power, which is the opposite of autonomy understood as neutral detachment from reality'.[43] The historical 1971 event resonated across the nation and was captured in Anton Virgilio Savona's 1973 song 'La Ballata di via Tibaldi', which conveyed the sense of social injustice experienced that night.[44]

The attempt by the Faculty to collectively redefine the role of the architect in light of the real needs of society, against speculation and the capitalist use of the territory, was finally judged as subversive by the government, and inspectors were sent to the Politecnico. On 23 November 1971, in the 'manner of the Spanish Inquisition',[45] Minister of Public Education Riccardo Misasi, a Christian Democrat, suspended eight professors including dean Portoghesi from their academic activities for two and a half years and even reported them to the authorities.[46] In the wake of the government's 'coup' against the Faculty, an engineering professor, the Christian Democrat Corrado Beguinot, was chosen to bring the Faculty of Architecture back to a 'state of order'.[47] This top-down action to normalize the

Faculty substantially neutralized the attempts – facilitated by Portoghesi – for renewal from within the teaching and student bodies.

It was in these very years that discussions shifted from ideological to political terms, with the newspaper *Corriere della Sera* observing that politics played a role in teaching suspensions.[48] Although Portoghesi was readmitted as dean in 1974, he would resign two years later, citing radical changes to the Politecnico and the disappearance of the student movement.[49] At the end of such a heroic academic and political journey at the Politecnico di Milano, Portoghesi was described as:

> Professor of Baroque who chose the protest … clinging to the gates of via Bonardi, the megaphone in his hand and a hat on his head from which fell very black hair. The Faculty was teeming with innovative ferments and protests, the student movement proposed debates and meetings, organised parades along the streets of Milan and he – the dean who had opposed the police evictions – showed up next to Mario Capanna, signed dazibaos and manifests and was the most convinced animator of the cultural debate.[50]

According to Portoghesi, the events related to May '68 marked 'one of the last phenomena of vitality displayed by the middle class'.[51] The moment was now over, and he recognized that the collective impetus of the 1960s was taking the form of 'isolated revolts'.[52] In the mid-1970s, Italian universities underwent a systematic process of depoliticization, and Portoghesi no longer found it inspiring to administer the complex machine of the Faculty of Architecture. Freed from the commitment that had kept him occupied for a decade, he now possessed the credentials of a cultural and political operator of national stature. By the time he resigned from the Faculty, he was on the list of the PSI in the 1976 elections, thus confirming his involvement in the party well beyond its connections in the academic world.[53] He was also listed among the new 'Milanese who count in the PSI'[54] and started preparing the next chapter of his political and institutional career: the directorship of the Venice Architecture Biennale.

Craxismo and the end of prohibitionism

On 16 July 1976, at the Midas Hotel in Rome, Bettino Craxi was elected leader of the PSI. This election, in which Portoghesi had taken part,[55] represented a watershed moment in the history of Italian socialism and the Left in general. Craxi's role as the secretary broke with the socialist establishment, and for the first time in the history of the party, he managed to transition the PSI out of the PCI's dominance, bringing it to the forefront of the Italian political scene. During the second half of the 1970s, the Socialist Party was redefined to become autonomous from the dogmas of the

Marxist-Leninist ideology. The PSI distanced itself from most economic theories of communism and focused instead on its own liberal reform – a reorientation dedicated to the middle classes and trading the need for social justice for a new desire for individuality. What Craxi and the 'new PSI' were first to recognize was the changing status of Italian society. Following the postwar economic boom – the so-called *miracolo economico* –[56] a de-proletarianization and expansion of the tertiary sector fuelled the rise of secular, liberal and modernist forces, as well as a general consumerism and a strong sense of individualism. This swerve in Italy's political trajectory coincided with a shift from years of deep political and social crises, terrorism and financial difficulty (including the first and second international oil crises) to a new phase of economic revival and social progress.

In June 1983, after seven years of internal transformations, the PSI won the national election. Craxi was appointed Prime Minister of Italy by the then President Sandro Pertini – the first socialist to become president of Italy (1978–85). From a subaltern and marginal party, the PSI became the force governing the country, offering a convincing alternative to the exhausted political agendas of the once-dominant parties, the Christian Democrats and the PCI. By the end of the 1980s, Italy's economy had outdone that of Great Britain, making the country the fifth industrial world power after the United States, Japan, West Germany and France. However, Italian public debt soon outgrew gross domestic product (GDP), with the country living beyond its financial means. Craxi's political changes also had consequences for the building industry. Extensive construction activity had overturned the landscape of substantial Italian rural and coastal areas, and the country was marred by recurrent cases of speculation, deregulation and inflated prices. As a result, by 1989 the economic bubble had burst as the national debt climbed.

But in the years prior to his appointment as prime minister, Craxi, in his role as PSI secretary, undertook a full reform of the party, ushering in a new attitude or *Craxismo*, as journalists called it.[57] When he was elected in 1976, Craxi set out to revise the communist ideology in order to put forward a socialism that was neither of 'misery' nor of 'bureaucracy' but that would promote social justice, political freedom and productive efficiency.[58] What Craxi defended was liberal socialism – a far cry from almost all of Italy's leftist parties. If originally the socialists and communists had shared a disdain for consumerism and commercial entertainment, Craxi captured and exploited the widespread desire for change. As observed by historian Paul Ginsborg: 'More than any other Italian politician of that decade, Craxi possessed an innate skill of comprehending the ongoing mutations of Italian society, to which he offered a spectacular response […].'[59]

In 1978, Craxi published his revolutionary text 'Il Vangelo Socialista' (remembered as the 'Essay on Proudhon'). The article placed the French socialist Pierre-Joseph Proudhon in opposition to Lenin, thus distinguishing the socialists from the communists in order to trigger an ideological battle that could finally free the PSI from its subordination to the PCI.[60]

The contrast between socialism and communism is very profound. Leninist communism has palingenetic aims: it is a religion disguised as science that claims to have found an answer to human life. Therefore, it does not want to tolerate rivals and is in a word 'totalitarian'. For this reason, communism cannot come to terms with the critical spirit, the methodical doubt, the plurality of philosophies, with all that represents the cultural heritage of the secular and liberal Western civilisation. Compared to the communist orthodoxy, socialism is democratic, secular, pluralist. It does not intend to raise any doctrine to the rank of orthodoxy, it does not intend to place limits on scientific research and intellectual debate.[61]

This ideological provocation – a 'cannon ball' as it was defined at the time – likely represented a moment of inspiration for Portoghesi, who described Craxi as having a great 'sense of the State, fighting to free Italians from the inertia of jammed institutions'.[62] That sensibility towards freedom was not dissimilar to Portoghesi's own; he had written *Le inibizioni dell'architettura moderna* in 1974 pursuing a line of disciplinary liberation from the orthodoxy imposed by the Modern Movement. Thus, with his slogan 'the end of prohibitionism',[63] Portoghesi aimed to use this political stance to free the discipline of architecture (Figure 3.7).

The PSI's political values soon became the operative ground for many Italian architects, and the instrumentalization of architecture and politics therefore went in both directions. As observed by Franco Purini, politics for Portoghesi was necessary to turn change into reality and to avoid making merely abstract hypotheses.[64] In Craxi's politics Portoghesi saw the possibility of support and the legitimization of the radical disciplinary reorientation he was putting forward. Portoghesi consistently defended the cause of postmodern culture for its capacity to reflect the heterogeneous qualities of the city at large, where the triple forces of politics, ideology and architecture converged.

'Questione di feeling', a popular Italian song by Mina and Riccardo Cocciante released in 1985,[65] describes the mutual understanding and affinity between two friends. Likewise, over the years, a *questione di feeling* emerged between Craxi and Portoghesi, based on their political comradeship, professional collaboration and personal friendship (Figure 3.8). Although the two met in Milan, they became closer when Craxi, the Milanese, started spending long periods in Rome as leader of the PSI and prime minister of Italy.[66] Paolo and Giovanna Portoghesi, who had a deep knowledge and understanding of Milanese culture from their years at the Politecnico, introduced Craxi to the eternal city. While Paolo Portoghesi and Craxi had their own distinct personalities and came from different backgrounds, they shared certain traits that can partly explain their ideological affinities. For example, Craxi wanted to open Italian politics, economics and culture to a broader international horizon – a desire that Portoghesi shared when it came to Italian architectural culture, especially through his cultural programme deployed at the Venice Biennale during the 1980s.

FIGURE 3.7 Paolo Portoghesi at his desk at the Politecnico di Milano in front of the book *Dieci Posters Del Partito Socialista Italiano 1905–1925*, 1971. © Adriano Alecchi, Mondadori Portfolio/Getty Images.

FIGURE 3.8 From left, Giovanna Massobrio, Anna Maria Moncini, Paolo Portoghesi and Bettino Craxi, Como, 1984. © Paolo Portoghesi Archive.

Far from conservative, the two men had a similar passion and insatiable curiosity for the ideal of 'difference' and 'the other'. As mass media took hold in the late 1970s and 1980s Craxi and Portoghesi made a constant effort to cultivate their public personas. Both were gifted speakers who were profoundly keen on communication strategies and the art of persuasion, and their natural charm, whether on TV shows, radio programmes or in the press, made their ideas and interventions accessible to a broad audience. Craxi communicated using a simplified, unsophisticated language that shirked traditional political jargon. Equally, Portoghesi's language was more accessible than the impenetrable *architettese* spoken by his colleagues. This architectural jargon, developed in Italian faculties of architecture, was a mix of the disciplinary, political and artistic languages, and reflected the demiurgic attitudes of intellectual architects. While the art of rhetoric displayed by Portoghesi took its major inspiration from Bruno Zevi (see Chapter 4), it also drew upon the argumentative strength typical of Craxi's style.[67]

Staging the PSI

Craxi was the very first Italian politician to genuinely understand the power of television as a tool to promote a form of soft propaganda. A showman, he loved appearing on screen or attending interviews, often in informal attire, and used his charisma to exert influence over the party membership. His public image created a new perception of the politician for the Italian electorate. As the journalist Philip Willan has recalled, 'Craxi's spectacular style of politics was costly. Party conferences were not gatherings of earnest socialist working men, but theatrical productions frequented by a social elite of fashion designers, architects, financiers and intellectuals.'[68] Far from communist sobriety, Craxi gave licence to Italians to experience a period of financial buoyancy. Hedonism, excess, abundance and accumulation became common features of 1980s Italian culture, which had a direct impact on the arts, design and fashion.

The PSI's ideological shift coincided with an unprecedented displacement of the political power from Italy's capital, Rome, to Milan, the financial centre of the country. With its international connections, efficient public transport, busy stock exchange and experimental showrooms, Milan was a privileged social observatory and perfect urban stage to deploy Craxi's liberal programme. During the early 1970s, design production of Milanese companies and designers became internationally renowned as industrial manufacturers exported products all over the world. The Milan Furniture Fair, first opened in 1961, was recognized as the official stage of international design and as a great showcase for the 'Made-in-Italy' campaign, emblematic of 1980s Italy. During Milan Design Week, national and international furniture companies and designers converged on the city, setting up independent events outside the official venue of the fair – in their showrooms or in unusual locations. Ephemeral installations and spectacular parties generated luxurious and dream-like atmospheres, turning Milan into one of the most creative cities in Europe.

It was during this period that architectural discourse became increasingly intertwined with popular culture – fashion, food, scenography, photography, music and art – and generated new and transgressive scenes.[69] With their inclusive attitude, enthusiasm for heterogeneous materials and curiosity for experimentation, two Milanese postmodern design collectives, Studio Alchimia and Memphis, were at the forefront. Their products, characterized by an ironic approach to design and a fascination for surface decoration, introduced a high degree of freedom, a liberation from the constrictions of the Modern Movement, which Portoghesi certainly appreciated. This general excitement was encapsulated in an advertisement for the Ramazzotti liquor, released in 1985 and titled 'Una Milano da Bere' (Milan to drink). In the short promotional video, smiling people rush through the city as the day starts. Milan is described as everyday, different, pulsating, positive, optimistic and efficient. Milan was a city to experience, dream about, enjoy – 'Una Milano da bere'.[70]

Craxi understood that the kind of ideology his party was attempting to instill in the Italian population – an ideology that marked a clear distance from previous political eras – required a new aesthetic sensibility to match the progress that Italy was undertaking. As Mary Macleod has observed, 'just as architecture is intrinsically joined to political and economic structures by virtue of its production, so, too, its form – its meaning as a cultural object – carries political resonances'.[71] From the

1970s, Craxi and his socialist comrades embraced the ephemeral as a formal strategy for connecting with the electorate. In this context, ephemeral architecture gained a new cultural significance for its 'lightness', 'rapidity', 'exactness', 'visibility' and 'multiplicity' identified by Italo Calvino amongst those values guiding the course of Italian postmodern society.[72] Where, in the first part of the twentieth century, architecture had been used to communicate the idea of power and leadership predominantly through the erection of monumental buildings meant to impress a political message over time,[73] it was now scenography – as sensational as temporary – with exuberant postmodern aesthetics and forms shaping the expression of the new liberal ideology. The successful urban festival *Estate Romana* (1977–85) by Renato Nicolini had already shown the potential for cultural transformation through the use of temporary structures for urban events in the city of Rome.[74] The use of the ephemeral was nothing new: from antiquity to revolutionary France, for example, ephemeral architecture was used for urban rituals, including celebrations, funerals and victories – all functions that appropriated the public space and spectacularized reality. Significantly, in 1979, Italian designer Gianni Pettena published the book *Effimero Urbano e Città*, an historical study on the relationship between ephemeral architecture, urban environment and political events.

The deployment of ephemeral design for political celebrations was certainly not limited to postmodern Italy, but was widespread towards the end of the twentieth century. In 1989 Paris, for example, to mark the bicentenary of the French Revolution, socialist President François Mitterrand staged a three-hour commemorative parade – an effort to democratize culture and instrumentalize public space – choreographed and supervised by the prolific designer and advertiser Jean-Paul Goude. The event went down as one of the most spectacular happenings of the late twentieth century.[75] However, if the embrace of ephemeral structures was common in the postmodern work of European and American architects in the late 1970s and early 1980s, the bond between this type of aesthetic strategy and political imperatives has played a particular role in Italy due to Craxi's work with architects, artists and graphic designers to forge a new image of the PSI and its ideology during the 'time of the ephemeral'.[76]

Besides Portoghesi, these collaborators included the Sicilian artist Filippo Panseca, whose participation proved especially fruitful for the PSI. Not only did he redesign the party's logo in 1978,[77] he also produced scenography for the party's annual events. For example, Panseca transformed the hall of the 1984 Congress in Verona into a rocking discothèque, with mirrors and neon lights. Three years later, in 1987, for the 44th party congress arranged in the warehouse of the trade fair in Rimini, he designed a stage shaped like a Greek temple with a frieze that turned into an LED screen projecting a flow of messages. If they initially seemed unconventional, venues like warehouses were ideal settings for gathering large masses of comrades and communicating, through TV, the success of the PSI conventions.

The 1984 'disco-themed' congress also marked another significant shift in the history of the party.[78] The old Central Committee that had long provided a forum for discussion and political decisions taken by party officials was no longer front-and-centre. Instead, a new National Assembly, comprising a range of personalities including intellectuals, entrepreneurs and TV celebrities, assumed more of a profile, and despite its lack of decisional power, it advocated for Craxi's new programme of reformism.[79] Portoghesi, active in the Central Committee for years, was now part of the Assembly, which included art critic Achille Bonito Oliva, theatre director Giorgio Strehler, fashion designer Nicola Trussardi, actor Vittorio Gassman and pop singer Ornella Vanoni, for example. These personalities were called upon to bring new perspectives to the party and were seemingly allowed to retain a high degree of intellectual freedom. In exchange, the PSI intended to extend its reach to the centres of cultural production and into various sectors of society and the economy – a new mechanism perceived as unconventional by the Italian political establishment. It was the first time since the postwar years that a political party had shown such dynamism in promoting its messages so directly to different audiences. That energy reached new heights at the 45th PSI congress, held in the former Ansaldo factory in Milan in 1989. The event would become a sort of emblem of the successes – and excesses – of Italian postmodern politics. This time Panseca produced a spectacular stage dominated by an LED pyramid (Figure 3.9). Its form and colossal dimensions – it was eight metres in height – conveyed the idea of a stronger hierarchical party structure and, at the same time, a change of strategy in terms of political communication, with images of Craxi and other speakers, including Paolo Portoghesi, presented as if they were popstars (Figure 3.10).

FIGURE 3.9 45th congress of the PSI, LED pyramid designed by Filippo Panseca displaying the logo of the PSI, Ansaldo, Milan, 1989. © Lorenzo Capellini.

FIGURE 3.10 Paolo Portoghesi talking at the 45th congress of the PSI. LED pyramid designed by Filippo Panseca displaying the face of Paolo Portoghesi giving a talk, 1989. © Filippo Panseca Archive.

With Panseca's designs, the PSI officially adopted a new popular language, which in turn spoke of the specific aesthetics of the 1980s, both within and beyond the party. Although Portoghesi's collaboration with Craxi and the PSI was carried out on a more institutional level, one can appreciate the close affinity between the provisional character of Panseca's evanescent stages and Portoghesi's twenty facades of the *Strada Novissima* at the First International Architecture Exhibition at the Venice Biennale. The *Strada*, curated with the assistance of Francesco Cellini and Cladio D'Amato, Portoghesi's young collaborators, was a highly innovative form of exhibition that combined the political and social space of the street with the idea of individual facades, or spaces for self-representation. It was, as Portoghesi recalled, 'an exhibition of real architecture in three dimensions: showing the houses of the architects invited to compete with each other exposed to the judgment of all the inhabitants.'[80] Using the power of the ephemeral architecture, typical of Venice's history and dear to the ideology of the PSI, the *Strada* was built in papier mâché by cinema set designers from the Roman studios of Cinecittà,[81] conveying the sense of individualism and the socialist value of freedom together in a new aesthetic (Figure 3.11).

And yet, the *Strada Novissima* was only one of the ephemeral projects – albeit by far the most impactful – on which Portoghesi was working in those years, showing once more how the relationship of architecture and politics travelled in

FIGURE 3.11 In the foreground, the crowning element of Paolo Portoghesi's facade for the *Strada Novissima*, revealing the temporary constructive technology, Venice Biennale, 1980. © Paolo Portoghesi Archive.

FIGURE 3.12 Paolo Portoghesi's frontal photograph of the gate he designed for the pavilion at the festival of antique in Todi, 1982. © Paolo Portoghesi Archive.

both directions. For example, the *Pallone* was a temporary pavilion for the 1982 Todi Antiques Festival, enriched by two small timber gates at either end – one designed by Portoghesi and the other by Aymonino – and respectively referencing the Renaissance and medieval language (Figure 3.12).[82] Similarly, Giancarlo Priori, one of Portoghesi's pupils, designed the *Porta della Pace*, a temporary gate with classic motifs, for the 1984 national festival of the communist newspaper *L'Unità* in Rome.[83] Moreover, during the 1980s, Portoghesi initiated a solid collaboration with RAI to produce scenography for urban shows in different Italian cities, confirming the consolidated public use of ephemeral architecture in Italian postmodern culture.

Control over the lagoon

In 1976, Craxi kicked off his mandate with a controversial decision. He came out in support of his party comrade Carlo Ripa di Meana, president of the Venice Biennale since 1974, to go ahead with the organization of the provocative *Biennale del Dissenso nei Paesi dell'Est*.[84] This unconventional Biennale,[85] announced in the middle of the Cold War era, was touted as 'a brave Biennale that anticipated the fall of the Berlin wall'.[86] On the one hand, it represented the culmination of a cycle of initiatives held to implement the institution's new democratic statute (adopted in

1973), developed to replace the previous and obsolete statement.[87] On the other hand, it was meant to be the largest and most comprehensive documentation of alternative cultures in the USSR and in Eastern bloc countries to date – recovering the interest of the United States for the institution of the Biennale.[88] By exhibiting artists who were considered dissidents in their native lands, the exhibition turned into an explicit *j'accuse* of the absence of intellectual freedom in the USSR and in other Eastern countries. Moscow, directly and through the PCI, accused the exhibition of hindering collaboration between Eastern and Western countries and pressured the Italian government to cancel the event. Despite the opposition – not least the resignations of Vittorio Gregotti, Giacomo Gambetti and Luca Ronconi from their respective posts as directors of this controversial 'anti-communist Biennale' –[89] the exhibition opened in November 1977 at Museo Correr in Piazza San Marco.[90] The initiative not only marked a step forward in the PSI's programmatic distancing from the PCI's line but also revealed the importance of the Biennale as a cultural venue for the promotion of ideological and political messages and values. At the 1977 Biennale, key concepts dear to the PSI, such as those of autonomy of thought and individual freedom, were represented in their fullness.

During these years, Portoghesi operated as one of the most active 'front men' of the PSI on the national cultural scene. His disciplinary status, alongside his flair for communication, made him an ideal fit for cultural roles on behalf of the party, and despite his Roman roots, he was seamlessly enmeshed in the Milanese scene. By the mid-1970s, his standing as an architectural historian, critic and designer was acknowledged at national and international levels. He had just won the competition for the Mosque of Rome (1974–95), an intricate project to be carried out as an entreaty to diplomatic discussion between Italy and the Middle East, but even more importantly, his skills as a mediator between different political and cultural parties, as demonstrated during the difficult years at the Politecnico, had granted him the reputation of a successful 'institutional man'.

In 1978, Portoghesi started to take part in events dedicated to the cultural role of the Venice Biennale. He gave a speech at a convention dedicated to future directions of the institution,[91] such as the one organized at the Rotonda della Besana in Milan, an event promoted by the Club Turati, the Milanese meeting place of the anti-communist Left, of which Ripa di Meana had been secretary.[92] At this venue, Portoghesi spoke of the need for the institution to broaden its cultural horizons and reclaim its international reputation – an attitude that was perfectly aligned with Craxi's foreign policies, which aimed to globally expand Italy's political and economic relationships. Portoghesi also took part in a public discussion about the Biennale at Palazzo Taverna in Rome organized by the IN/ARCH, alongside the then director of the Art and Architecture sector Vittorio Gregotti (Figure 3.13). These two events marked the lead up to Portoghesi's institutional involvement in the Venice Biennale.

FIGURE 3.13 Biennale – Architettura_INVITO_(recto-verso). INARCH Istituto Nazionale di Architettura, 23 October 1978. Palazzo Taverna, Via Monte Giordano, 36 – Rome. I lunedì dell'architettura: Biennale – Architettura. Tavola rotonda, con la partecipazione di: Enrico Crispolti, Vittorio Gregotti, Francesco Moschini, Paolo Portoghesi e Lara Vinca Masini. © FFMAAM | Fondo Francesco Moschini A.A.M. Architettura Arte Moderna.

In 1979, historian Giuseppe Galasso succeeded Ripa di Meana as president of the Biennale. The Argentinian Tomás Maldonado was the strongest candidate to replace the previous director of the Visual Art and Architecture sector, the communist Gregotti, whose programme was perceived as too elitist, but it was Ripa di Meana who added Portoghesi's name to the list of possibilities.[93] Then, in February of that year, Portoghesi was nominated to direct the architecture sector – newly split from the discipline of art. If, on the one hand, this was a great step up in Portoghesi's disciplinary leadership at a national level, on the other, his role as the director of the Architecture Biennale ensured the PSI's agency in the forging of Italian postmodern design culture – in that the Venice Biennale, together with RAI, were amongst the most influential venues of national cultural production.

Like Craxi, Ripa di Meana saw in Portoghesi a reliable socialist capable of setting up progressive initiatives.[94] The three men had made one another's acquaintance in Milan. Both Portoghesi and Ripa di Meana experienced their Milanese phase in the 1960s and early 1970s, during Craxi's escalation to the party's secretariat. Often taking part in the same cultural initiatives, Portoghesi was operating at the Politecnico while Ripa di Meana was part of the administrative board of La Scala Theatre. As Gregotti observed:

> Craxi was a really good friend of Portoghesi, who was also a friend of Ripa di Meana. So, the cycle was really simple, it was political. But this does not diminish the quality of Ripa di Meana's and Portoghesi's work: Ripa Di Meana was a really good president and Portoghesi is a brilliant critic.[95]

Portoghesi acted as the director of the architecture sector until 1983 when he was elected as president of the Biennale. A factor for his appointment was his enrolment in the party. By the 1980s, enrolment in a political party was practically mandatory for anyone to pursue a public career in Italy. Nominations were endorsed directly by the parties. In an article for *La Repubblica*, journalist Natalia Aspesi, who was covering the opening of the 42nd Venice Cinema Festival, described the tightly intertwined relationship of culture and politics in (postmodern) Italy: 'Critics and people of the cinema, bizarrely still without the party badge, know that by now the games are done and that every institutional career, even if cultural, will be to them always precluded.'[96]

In his 1978 song 'Ambarabaciccicoccò', the pop singer Vasco Rossi highlighted the centrality of the party in Italian postmodern culture, as it could support people, since the party was considered a social achievement and an institution – no small feat considering the profound social trust in political parties in Italy at the time.[97] As the critic Ricky Burdett has observed of the Biennale's election system:

> The appointment of the directors for the different sectors – art, architecture, theatre and film – reflects the entire breath of the Italian political spectrum. . . . Such explicit political involvement would be frowned upon in more Calvinist northern climates, but in Italy the political importance of cultural and artistic activities has a long and well-established history.[98]

Portoghesi joined the incumbent Giuseppe Galasso (supported by DC and PRI), as well as Cesare De Michelis (supported by the PSI) on the ballot.[99] Despite the fact that De Michelis already represented the PSI, the party's cultural leaders (specifically Claudio Martelli, then deputy secretary of the PSI[100]) backed Portoghesi.[101] On 11 March 1983, at Cà Giustiniani, the Venice Biennale's headquarters, Portoghesi became president with the support of all the parties involved – the PCI included.

Alongside the task of reconciling different political forces within and around a central cultural institution, Portoghesi played a key role in fostering a cultural programme of international relevance. This included the retrospective exhibition on the Viennese Secession as well as reinstating the cinema festival following its closure in 1968. He also presented Luigi Nono's *Prometheus*, conducted by Claudio Abbado with lyrics written by Massimo Cacciari and scenography by Renzo Piano. With these interventions, Portoghesi endeavoured to promote a cooperation among the different sectors of the Biennale (architecture, theatre, cinema, music, art, dance). And yet, looking back on this period, he bitterly commented that his main ambition to establish an interdisciplinary dialogue on the themes of modernity within the institution did not achieve the desired result.[102]

The Venice Biennale was heavily attended by politicians from Rome. Invitations were sent from Portoghesi's office to officials for the various events.[103] The Italian president opened and closed proceedings, and the first few rows of seats at the cinema festival were always occupied by politicians. Their physical presence stressed the Biennale's role in relation to the centralized political power of the capital city. It was also customary for political parties to publicly express their disapproval of the selection of some artworks or films – an attitude that had manifested with particular intensity around the Biennale del Dissenso.[104]

The fact that the Venice Biennale was seen as a kind of protectorate of Rome was reflected in the tense relationship between the institution and its host city – a dynamic with a long history.[105] Venice and the Biennale accused each other of not engaging in an open and trustworthy discussion – even though the deputy president of the Biennale was, by statute, the mayor of Venice. If Venice reproached the Biennale for not paying attention to the real problems of the city, the Biennale blamed the city for looking with suspicion at the cultural initiatives organized by the institution.[106] All of this was fuelled by political interests. Even on bipartisan issues such as the restoration of buildings, including the Biennale headquarters and the Cinema Palace at Lido – interventions that were urgently needed – the Venetian authorities were slow with their replies, which often took the form of polite refusals.[107] Despite the 1985 Architecture Biennale's focus on Venice and the surrounding region, as set out by the director Aldo Rossi, the project was never regarded by the city as an olive branch but was instead the subject of a bitter review by the architectural historian Cesare de Seta.[108]

The Istituto Universitario di Architettura di Venezia (IUAV) added another level of complexity to the discussion on the Biennale. According to Portoghesi, the presence of professors such as Tafuri, Aymonino and Gregotti – all members of the PCI – seemed to produce a 'hypnotic atmosphere' and a 'stagnant balance'[109] that he believed should be challenged. Whether or not those at the IAUV recognized it, Portoghesi immediately understood the huge potential of the Biennale as an international architectural showcase, and he quickly oriented it around a message advertising the end of modernist prohibition and celebrating architecture's plurality. Central to this, of course, was his 1980 *Strada Novissima*, the idea for which originally came from a visit to a street market in Berlin's Alexanderplatz with fellow architects Rossi and Aymonino. To confront the architectural fortress of IUAV, Portoghesi thought of exhibiting 'architecture' as opposed to its representations – photos, drawings or models. As Portoghesi recalls, it was first necessary to undermine the *status quo*: 'Throwing a stone into the pond has always been a familiar and liberating gesture for me.... The first stone thrown into the Bacino di San Marco was the Teatro del Mondo.'[110]

Although the Teatro-shaped stone was positively received by the establishment of the IUAV, with an article by Tafuri elaborating on the floating pavilion as a poetic appearance,[111] taken as a whole, the First International Architecture Exhibition of the Venice Biennale was condemned by the professors of the IUAV for not establishing a solid dialogue with the city.[112] Nevertheless, despite the polemics, the exhibits were as popular as they were spectacular. In 1987, with unanimous consensus, Portoghesi was confirmed to carry out a second mandate as president of the Biennale which would end in 1992, coinciding with the beginning of the PSI's fall.[113]

The Mosque of Rome, between religion and oil

Among Portoghesi's first ambitions as director of the architecture sector of the Venice Biennale was the idea to broaden the coverage of the architectural thematic beyond the Westernized world, including the Middle East.[114] Venice has always been seen as the hinge between Eastern and Western culture and the common ground for revising their historical encounters. The 1982–83 exhibition *Architecture of the Islamic Countries*, curated by Portoghesi with the assistance of Francesco Cellini and Attilio Petruccioli among others, explored contemporary architectural production while retaining a historical perspective (Figure 3.14).[115]

Writing in the catalogue, Portoghesi explained how Islamic culture had served as a precedent for architects such as Antoni Gaudí, Joseph Olbrich and Raimondo D'Arondco.[116] Special sections in the forms of homages – borrowing a formula already tested in *The Presence of the Past* (and discussed in Chapter 2) – were dedicated to the work of Mimar Sinan, Le Corbusier, Louis Kahn and Fernand Pouillon in relation to Islamic culture, with a special section looking at the Islamic architecture of Sicily. The context, the spiritual component and the social purpose of Islamic architecture were characteristics instrumentalized by Portoghesi to argue against the coldness, repetitiveness and self-referentiality of modern architecture, fostering once more his agenda of opening up the discipline to new possibilities. In so doing, Portoghesi presented some of the cross-cultural influences that made up his architectural poetic. Space was therefore given to the Egyptian

FIGURE 3.14 Paolo Portoghesi's photograph of the installation of the second International Architecture Exhibition of the Venice Biennale dedicated to the Islamic culture, 1982. Photograph by Paolo Portoghesi. © Paolo Portoghesi Archive.

architect Hassan Fathy, whose work pursued a different idea of modernity based on the research of the vernacular and an attempt to express the quintessential idea of *arabité*.[117] The exhibition also presented a series of built and unbuilt projects by Islamic architects, as well as Western architects invited to build in Arab countries. From Reima and Raili Pietilä's extension of the Ministry of Foreign Affairs (1969–70) in Kuwait, to the Bab-Al-Sheikh development (1982) in Baghdad by Ricardo Bofill, and Hans Hollein's Museum of Glass and Ceramics (1977–78) in Tehran, local constructive traditions were blended with innovative technologies and contemporary languages. With the support of the Aga Khan Foundation, the University of Geneva, Harvard and MIT, the overall exhibition engaged in a broad conversation with international interlocutors.[118]

At the same time, the Biennale brought to the Venetian lagoon a core topic dear to Rome's political authorities: that of the negotiation with the Middle East following the period of the oil crises of 1973 and 1979. Some condemned this choice: Bruno Zevi described it as the 'exhibition of the petrodollars of the construction industry',[119] while Gregotti downplayed the existence of an identity of modern Islamic architecture and criticized the validity of the work designed by Western architects in Arabic countries.[120]

However, Portoghesi's long-lasting interest in Islamic culture, reflected in the second edition of the Venice Architecture Biennale, shall be intersected with a strategic project that shows the profound political implications of architecture in 1970s and 1980s Italy. While working on the 1982–83 exhibition he was in fact developing the project for the Mosque of Rome. Spanning two decades, from 1975 (the year of the competition) to its official opening in 1995, the Mosque, alongside its Islamic Cultural Centre, remains Portoghesi's most acclaimed work – and more than any other, it epitomizes his cultural relationship with politics. Beyond its symbolic value, the mosque is the result of a complex and delicate 'political project', one that deliberately contributed to strengthening Italy's pro-Arab politics.[121] Indeed, the story of the Mosque unfolded over the 1973 oil crisis and the embargo imposed by the Organization of Arab Petroleum Exporting Countries (OAPEC), and the 1979–82 dispute between the Italian multinational oil and gas company Ente Nazionale Idrocarburi (ENI) and the Saudi Arabian Petromin.[122]

In the 1970s, Saudi Arabia was a strategic partner for Italy – the nation supplied one-third of Italy's oil, and Italy was its fourth-largest commercial partner. The bilateral agreements on oil between Italy and the Middle East were at the centre of Italian foreign policy during that decade and the following, coinciding with the rise of the PSI. Requested and funded by Arab countries, the mosque (along with the Islamic Cultural Centre) was the first to be built in the pulsating heart of Catholicism[123] and marked an epochal turning point in the history of the eternal city. In the 1970s, Rome was still one of the few European cities without an Islamic centre – an issue that had been debated since the days of fascism.[124] Therefore the project held political and social implications.[125] As Portoghesi observed, 'the creation of such a structure is more than justified, not only for the significant presence of Muslims in the capital, but also with respect to circumstances no longer of contrast, existing between the Christian and Islamic world'.[126]

In 1973, King Faysal of Saudi Arabia visited Rome to negotiate the construction of a mosque for a community of nearly 40,000 Arab Muslims. Following his visit, an international design competition was organized to build on a 30,000-square-metre site in the northern area of Monte Antenne, donated by the city council to the Italian Muslim community. In 1974, the ambassador of Saudi Arabia announced that the country was prepared to cover the seven-million-dollar construction budget, in the instance that the funding already offered by other Arab countries did not suffice.[127] In 1975 the international competition for a mosque and Islamic centre opened with a jury comprising authorities from Rome and the ambassadors of Saudi Arabia, Kuwait, Egypt and Indonesia,[128] showing the substantial political extent of this initiative. Of the forty-six submissions received from all around the world, four projects were selected ex-equo.[129] Out of these four, two groups, Paolo

Portoghesi-Vittorio Gigliotti and Sami Mousawi, an Iraqi architect practising in the UK, eventually jointly collaborated on the general design scheme between 1976 and 1977, as official authors of the project.[130] The two project teams represented the double-soul of this ecumenic enterprise: on the one hand, Portoghesi-Gigliotti had to guarantee harmony with the Western architectural world and the city of Rome; on the other hand, Mousawi acted as a cultural guardian of the Muslim tradition. Portoghesi and Gigliotti took the role of project directors during the construction works until the completion of the building. Portoghesi, who had already been involved in two other projects for a mosque,[131] took on the task of managing the crucial, and at times arduous, dialogue with the press (Figure 3.15).

The project for the Mosque of Rome received the approval of the Italian government as well as the placet of the Vatican, which had a significant voice in the process of negotiation.[132] However, the project came with two conditions: there would be no speakers for the call to prayer and the dome had to be lower than that of San Pietro. The mayor of Rome, Portoghesi's close friend Giulio Carlo Argan, was decisive to the success of the entire enterprise; he associated the building process to a 'battle' with many elements and made a point of advocating that such

FIGURE 3.15 Paolo Portoghesi next to the model of the Mosque of Rome. © Paolo Portoghesi Archive.

an international city as Rome, traditionally open to all religions, should have a mosque.[133] As for Portoghesi, Rome's future was based on the mediation between the Mediterranean Basin and European civilization.[134]

Portoghesi's design proposal for the Mosche of Rome was guided by a search for 'encounters': between Italy and the Middle East, and between Christian and Muslim traditions. This last encounter was embodied by two forms at the heart of the project: the square, symbolizing the earth, and the circle, referring to the sky and divine perfection.[135] Portoghesi also looked to traditional Muslim forms in Roman architecture,[136] locating points of contact across different building cultures and establishing dialogues that blended materials, stylistic motives and compositional solutions[137] with typologies dating back to the classical period.[138] He called this process the 'architecture of listening' – even more profound given the political need to bring two global financial systems closer through cultural action (Figure 3.16).

For Portoghesi a difference between church and mosque lies in the interpretation of the structure and the focus of gravitational phenomena, from the relationship between what carries and what is carried:[139] 'By re-proposing the woven ribs in the Mosque of Rome, I wanted to offer to the mind of the observers a back-and-forth itinerary from East to West, to evoke encounters that have already taken place between Islamic culture and Italian culture, and to resume a dialogue that has been

FIGURE 3.16 Paolo Portoghesi's sketch for the Mosque of Rome. © Paolo Portoghesi Archive.

interrupted many times.'[140] Portoghesi drew inspiration from Borromini's use of woven arches, which characterize the vault of the Cappella dei Re Magi in the Collegio di Propaganda Fide (a similar system was used by Guarino in San Lorenzo; by Vittone in the sanctuary of Vallinotto; and more recently by Pier Luigi Nervi in his sport palace in Rome). He used the stepped dome for the mosque – a system that he and Gigliotti had tested in the church of the Sacra Famiglia in Salerno (1969–74)[141] and which referenced the Pantheon, Sant'Ivo alla Sapienza and Vittone's project for the regional church of Chierici in Turin. Guarini also inspired the lighting of the domes via multiple sources, pursuing an anti-gravitational effect. At the same time, Portoghesi embraced a rich repertoire of precedents from the Middle East, such as the model of the Ottoman mosque interpreted by Mimar Sinan, and the ancient mosques of The Maghreb and South Spain. The mosques of Kairouan and Córdoba in particular inspired the use of pillars for the prayer room[142] – thirty-two in total for the Mosque of Rome, each formed by the juxtaposition of four prefabricated elements (Figures 3.17 and 3.18).

The project, officially signed by Portoghesi and Gigliotti in collaboration with Mousawi, was approved in early 1979 by the Rome city council. That same year construction was blocked by a decision from the Tribunale Amministrativo Regionale (TAR),[143] and work restarted only in 1984.[144] The groundbreaking ceremony in December 1984 was attended by the Italian authorities, including President of the Italian Republic Sandro Pertini and Minister of Foreign Affairs Giulio Andreotti, as well as Secretary of the League of the Islamic World (RABITA) Abdallah Omar Nasseef and other representatives of Islamic countries.[145]

When the building works began, journalists reiterated the highly political and diplomatic role of the project that could 'give a push to the dialogue between Muslims and Christians that still experience considerable difficulties'.[146] In his speech at the groundbreaking ceremony, Portoghesi emphasized that the project 'was the concrete expression of the "culture of peace"; of that culture based on tolerance, reciprocal understanding, recognition of the differences and the identities of peoples'.[147] Indeed, the project was another manifestation of the idea of cultural freedom, so relevant in Craxi's socialist programme, which liberated the city from its monoreligious principles.[148] 'It is the work in which the "poetics of listening" is best expressed,' wrote Portoghesi: 'the building must speak an accessible language and therefore, in this case, speak to the citizens of the Islamic religion recalling their great tradition, and to the Romans showing openness to a culture with which there has already been a dialogue rich in reciprocal exchanges in the past'.[149]

The Mosque has been recognized as a success in political terms, confirming Portoghesi as a dextrous negotiator of cultures and parties, as well as an effective diplomat between far away regions of the world. When the construction of the mosque was finally completed, Argan wrote to Portoghesi:

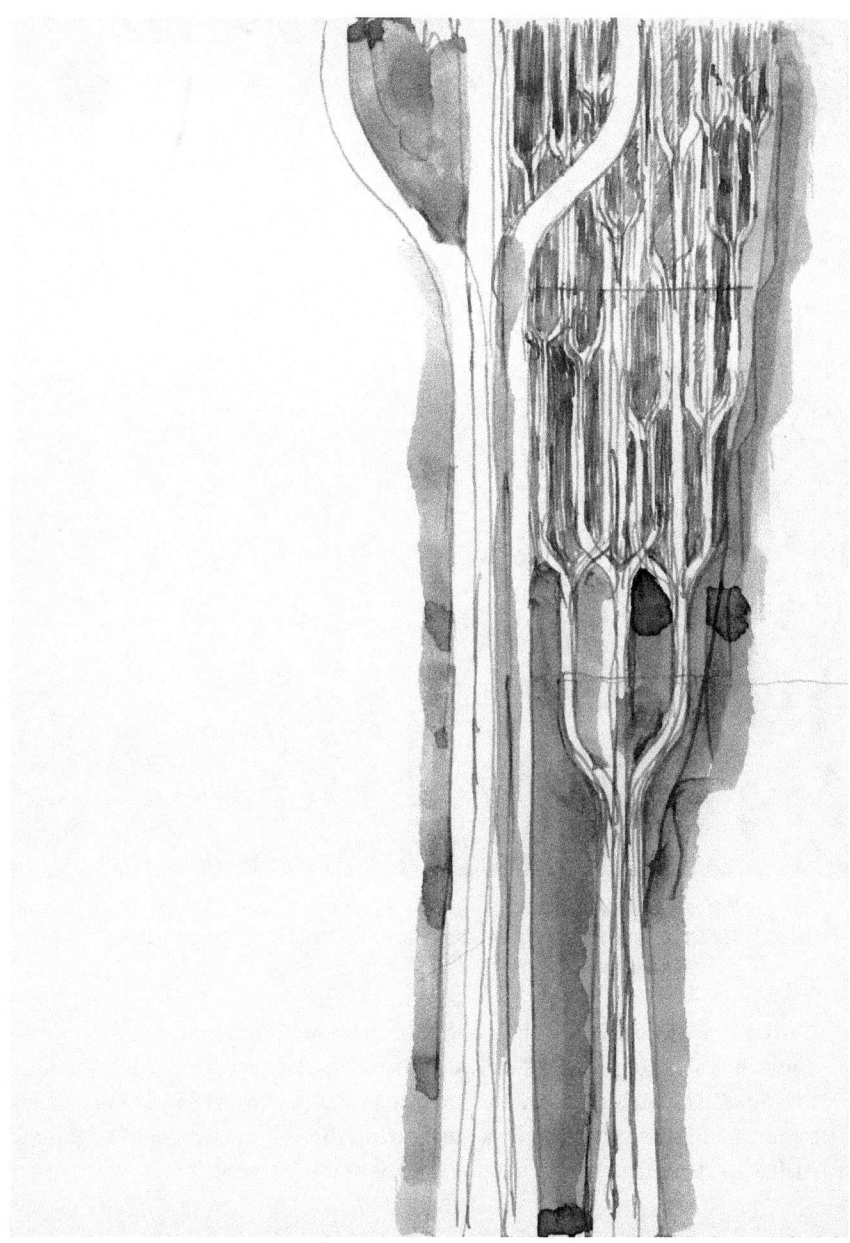

FIGURE 3.17 Paolo Portoghesi's study for the pillars of the Mosque of Rome, sketch, 1979. © Paolo Portoghesi Archive.

FIGURE 3.18 Paolo Portoghesi's low-angled shot photograph of the Mosque of Rome, showing the effect of the natural light in the space. © Paolo Portoghesi Archive.

> *Carissimo* ... I wanted to tell you that the Mosque impressed me. There is no doubt: it is a masterpiece. ... I tell you: until a few days ago, I admired you more as an architectural historiographer than as an architect. Maybe I was not entirely wrong, then: now yes. But only a great architectural historian could have done such a great architectural oeuvre, as the one you have done.[150]

While these personal lines from the former Mayor of Rome add to the many confirmations of the appreciation of Portoghesi as an architectural historian and designer, they also attest to the synergy that politics and history played in Portoghesi's overall postmodern project.

4 EMBRACING MASS MEDIA

FIGURE 4.1 Still from the movie *Pizza Triangle*, showing Monica Vitti looking down from the balcony of Casa Papanice, 1970. © Fondazione Papanice.

A scene from the 1970 comedy *Dramma della gelosia* (The Pizza Triangle), directed by Ettore Scola, shows the actress Monica Vitti leaning on the balustrade of a balcony made of slender white tubular elements of different heights (Figure 4.1). Shot from below, the view accentuates her character's despair while giving particular prominence to the architecture that frames the scene. In the film, partially set in an eccentric house in Rome, Vitti plays Adelaide Ciafrocchi, a florist stuck in a love triangle. The house belongs to Adelaide's rich fiancé, the butcher Ambleto Di Meo (Hércules Cortéz), but she is in love with two other men: construction worker Oreste Nardi (acting Marcello Mastroianni) and pizza maker Nello Serafini (played by Giancarlo Giannini). Scola's legendary images depict not only one of the most famous stars of Italian cinema but also the features of an entirely unconventional Roman house, one of the most celebrated dwellings of its time: Casa Papanice, designed in the late 1960s by Paolo Portoghesi with Vittorio Gigliotti.

Vitti's balcony scene at Casa Papanice speaks, albeit indirectly, to Portoghesi's flair for using media to take architecture beyond its disciplinary boundaries.[1] Portoghesi was fascinated by mass media throughout his career. His penchant for popular culture as well as radio and television, alongside more traditional disciplines such as architecture, cinema and poetry, fuelled his desire to use new communication modes and channels to inform his design. Moreover, because Portoghesi very clearly understood the importance of 'staging' architecture, he was fully attuned to the growing importance that images, whether static or cinematic, would play in postmodern culture.

Mediatization of the building

The Teatro del Mondo, exhibited at the first International Architecture Exhibition of the Venice Biennale in 1980, is perhaps Portoghesi's most famous – and literal – staging of architecture. In 1971 Portoghesi had commissioned Aldo Rossi to design a small floating theatre meant to implement an agenda based on the synergy of history and design (see Chapter 1). However, beyond the relatively well-known narrative of the pavilion's design and construction, its staging was informed by the postmodern tendency to turn art – and, consequently, architecture – into events. In the case of the Teatro, Portoghesi's plan to transform an ephemeral building into the protagonist of a rich artistic season went far beyond all expectations. What is less known of the Teatro is the long journey that it eventually made to Dubrovnik, in former Yugoslavia, to take part in the city's theatre festival.[2] From a floating theatre docked in the Venetian lagoon (Figure 4.2), the Teatro became a travelling chamber orchestra hall, navigating the waters of the Adriatic Sea for almost two weeks in August 1980.[3]

Berthing all along the Croatian coastline and touring like a celebrity, the Teatro was one of the few buildings in the history of architecture to leave its original site, only to then become ubiquitous, in a sort of illusional ever-present state. Enjoying a privilege normally reserved for photographs, models, texts, drawings and design objects, the Teatro was a direct and literal embodiment of the idea of architecture as media. Its formal simplicity and temporary nature, combined with its singular floating condition, generated the production of photographs that circulated around the world – it even surfaced on the covers of popular magazines such as *Casa Vogue*.[4] Maurizio Scaparro, director of the Biennale's theatre sector, praised the Teatro's mobility for:

> discovering new, 'non-Venetian' territories, contrasting other 'external' monuments, meeting new people and traditions, introducing oneself, becoming a different theatre in diverse places.... And it is with this spirit that the Teatro del Mondo begins its voyage, both real and fantastic, towards [former] Yugoslavia.[5]

FIGURE 4.2 Aldo Rossi's Teatro del Mondo floating in the lagoon of Venice, Photograph by Paolo Portoghesi. © Paolo Portoghesi Archive.

More recently, another postmodern building has offered a similar live spectacle. Originally designed by Robert Venturi in 1967, the Lieb House cruised up the East River towards Long Island in 2009, in a two-day interstate journey recorded by the cameras in the presence of its designer.[6] However, if the Lieb House had been relocated as a result of a threatened demolition and its heroic rescue by a new buyer, the show performed by the Teatro was of a pure mediatic nature. In this respect, the Teatro spoke – and still speaks today through its legendary reputation – of Portoghesi's acute understanding of mass media's ability to disseminate the latest postmodern news: the end of the modernist prohibition and the celebration of architecture's plurality.

In her seminal book *Privacy and Publicity: Modern Architecture as Mass Media* (1996), Beatriz Colomina argued that modern architecture became truly modern only through its engagement with media.[7]

To think about modern architecture must be to pass back and forth between the question of space and the question of representation. Indeed, it will be necessary to think of architecture as a system of representation, or, rather, a series of overlapping systems of representation. This does not mean abandoning the traditional architectural object, the building. In the end, it means looking at it much more closely than before, but also in a different way. The building should be understood in the same terms as drawings, photographs, writing, films and advertisements; not only because these are the media in which more often we encounter it, but because the building is a mechanism of representation in its own right.[8]

Yet, by the 1960s, media had become ubiquitous in people's lives and representation often became more important than any spatial consideration.

Portoghesi's academic career started only four years prior to the publication of Marshall McLuhan's ground-breaking writings on media. *Understanding Media: The Extension of Man*, first published in 1964 and translated into Italian in 1967 under the misleading title of *Gli strumenti del comunicare*, focused on the media effects that permeated society and culture. Its main thesis – that the media, rather than the message it carries, is what affects society – quickly circulated and had a profound impact on intellectuals worldwide. There is little doubt that Portoghesi was embedded in this critical discourse. Through Gruppo 63, which gathered the new literary vanguard, he encountered Umberto Eco, a thinker who 'produced, both as a journalist and at a more specialist level, a constant flow of acute, forceful and entertaining articles and essays on specific topics in broadcasting, publishing, advertising and related aspects of modern mass culture'.[9]

From his base in Rome (the home of RAI/TV and Radio and Cinecittà), Portoghesi became an active participant in these new modes of communication – as illustrated by his radiophonic 'impossible interviews' recorded for RAI (see Chapter 2). The physical proximity to these new centres of media production as well as his intellectual immediacy with emerging discourses on communication enabled Portoghesi to eschew otherwise conventional and rigid disciplinary boundaries to instead boost his postmodern project, giving his architectural message substantial scope while overlapping different languages for new audiences.

As Andreas Huyssen has explained, with postmodernism 'emerged a vigorous, though again largely uncritical attempt to validate popular culture as a challenge to the canon of high art, modernist or traditional'.[10] Portoghesi built his body of work as much through disciplinary channels as through those dedicated to the general audience. Looking beyond conventional exhibition spaces, he unreservedly operated between television and radio studios, discothèques, cinemas, theatres and magazine editorial boards, as well as cultural happenings and glitzy society parties that gained exposure in newspapers – one media foregrounding the other. These were the type of popular venues that flourished during the 1970s and 1980s. All welcomed artistic performances as part of their programmes, and while this 'new creative relationship between high art and certain forms of mass culture' still involved the use of photography and film, it increasingly embraced screen-based, video and computer elements.[11]

Portoghesi's affiliation with the Venice Biennale, first as director of the Architecture sector and then as president, made him a figure of significant media exposure. From the 1980s to the early 1990s he leapt from the national domain into an international orbit. No other Italian architect before him had had the opportunity – or the audacity – to access such positions at the top of one of the world's most prestigious cultural organizations. Portoghesi frequently appeared on television, and his projects, as well as his private life, were recorded in detail by newspapers and magazines. *Corriere della Sera* and *La Repubblica* reported on the suits and ties Portoghesi wore at the openings of the Biennale festivals; his weekly trips to local markets to buy second-hand Liberty furniture and his jet-set friendships across the socialist networks of Rome and Milan. He was the subject of international magazine articles, television reports and documentaries, and he even played the protagonist in an architectural docu-fiction, *Utopia, Utopia* (1969), with Renato Nicolini.[12] Beyond Portoghesi himself, four buildings – three houses, Casa Baldi, Casa Andreis, Casa Papanice, and the Mosque of Rome[13] – became the stages for feature-length Italian films.

The cinematographic 'roles' played by both Portoghesi and his architecture show his natural affinity with the seventh art. This extended beyond pure cinema to mass media in general, and he used this dimension to inform the overall strategy for his postmodern project. In so doing, Portoghesi was one of the first architects in Italy to make intentional use of mass media, embracing its forms, languages and mechanisms to disseminate his architectural message, stage his own projects and cultivate his public profile.

Ars oratoria

The figure of the architect as a communicator – the *architectus verborum*, according to John Evelyn – is as old as the profession.[14] But in the postwar period, with the advent of mass media facilitating different forms of expression, architects such as Philip Johnson based their reputations not just on how well they built but on how well they spoke. In turn they achieved architectural stardom thanks mainly to their abilities as verbal communicators.[15]

The power of verbal communication has always informed Portoghesi's modus operandi. The famous photograph taken at the Politecnico di Milano immortalized him as a national hero, speaking through a megaphone to mobs of angry students while facing the police. Portoghesi would carry a proverbial megaphone with him to promote his postmodern project, although in contrast to the university turmoil, this time his methods as a communicator were more sophisticated. On the one hand, his social and cultural life in Roman society, with its links to the city's political circles and its jet set,[16] provided the ideal environment for promoting architecture beyond professional and academic circles – an environment that found its natural stage at the Galleria Apollodoro (see Chapter 1). On the other, his understanding of the mechanism by which mass media could convey a message and explain architecture to the public was an aspect he had absorbed from his master and mentor, Bruno Zevi.[17]

In the postwar period, Zevi emerged as the European interpreter and advocate of American architecture and was among the most persuasive critics of modern design in Italy.[18] From 1955 until his death in 2000, he held great influence over public opinion thanks to his regular weekly column in the left-wing magazine *L'Espresso*.[19] Following his years in the United States (having escaped the racial laws in 1940s Italy), Zevi was convinced that architecture should be presented to the broadest possible audience using every means necessary, from newspapers and glossy magazines to radio and television.[20] He took a didactic approach – distinctive of the postwar Italian TV agenda – to 'explain' architecture to the masses. As author of a popular 1948 book, *Saper vedere l'architettura* (Architecture as Space: How to Look at Architecture),[21] Zevi had provided the general audience with some understanding of the environments in which they spent their lives. In Rome, he was a regular at the debates 'I Lunedì dell'Architettura', which were convened every Monday at Palazzo Taverna, the headquarters of the National Institute of Architecture (In/Arch).[22] The platform was successful in critically opening the disciplinary debate to the arts, urbanism and politics, and Portoghesi was often in attendance.[23]

Zevi was also a habitual speaker on television programmes, such as the *Maurizio Costanzo Show*, the longest running and most popular talk show on Italian television, broadcast on Silvio Berlusconi's Canale 5.[24] Wearing his distinctive bow tie, Zevi would stand on stage among showmen and opinionators, proselytizing the architectural message in one of Italy's most popular televised parlours. On the 9 June 1994 episode, Portoghesi appeared as a discussant proffering a comment about the responsibility of the supposed failures of Italian architecture that triggered a furious reaction from Zevi.[25] By comparison, Portoghesi came across as a more diplomatic yet provocative orator, with a calmer tone than Zevi's militant speeches, so proving himself a good fit for the camera. Thirteen years younger than his master, Portoghesi was attuned to an audience that was less concerned with grasping absolute truths and more interested in open dialogues through entertainment.

Television was a comfortable medium for Portoghesi to spread his knowledge of architecture. He initiated his TV career as early as 1967, collaborating with director Stefano Roncoroni on a documentary film marking the third centenary of Borromini's death. In the hour-long black-and-white film, Portoghesi appears as 'one of the most qualified experts' on the architect.[26] Conceptualizing architecture using lay terminology, he put forward his core argument: that it is the similarities between Borromini's work and modern architecture that have contributed to contemporary interest in the baroque architect. Portoghesi also appeared in a series of television reports with Folco Quilici, such as, for example, *Festa barocca* (1980-82) and two short films: one dedicated to music and architecture, the other to genius loci.[27] In 1987 he consulted on the documentary *Roma imago urbis – le mura*, directed by Luigi Bazzoni.

In 1980 Portoghesi took to the TV screen to promote the events of the Venice Biennale. The architecture exhibition was the subject of two documentary films: *La presenza del passato*, directed by Azio (Maurizio) Cascavilla,[28] and Marcello Ugolini's *Viaggio nella Biennale: Architettura*.[29] Broadcast across Italy, the documentaries promoted the exhibition while explaining the 'new' postmodern architecture to a wider public. While *La presenza del passato* shows Portoghesi in the middle of a Roman street, advocating for the return of public space, *Viaggio nella Biennale: Architettura* features an antagonistic debate between Zevi and Portoghesi, the protagonists belligerently responding to each other (although they were filmed separately) while walking along the *Strada Novissima*. As much promotional tools as invaluable archival documents, both films comprised part of a complex media strategy based on the innovative blending of two video-based genres: the documentary and the advertisement.

Through the pages of the magazines

In a 1983 article published in *Domus*, Portoghesi poetically described architectural magazines as 'the most vain and inconvenient inhabitants of those small cities of words and images that are our libraries'.[30] For a scholar who had built his admirable expertise and inviable scholarly reputation on the publication of rigorous studies based on the analysis of archival sources (see 1964 *Borromini nella cultura europea* or his 1966 *Roma barocca*, for example), magazines may have not necessarily been the prime place for historical disputes or assessments. Yet Portoghesi valued the intrinsic potential of this medium to develop specific lines of thought about design and gather architects, historians, critics and cultural operators to generate a collective debate. Cleverly instrumentalizing the accessible nature of magazines at the highest points of his leadership, Portoghesi generated his own channels rather than taking part in the already established editorial ventures that, at the time, dominated the Italian landscape of architecture and design with their specific agendas.[31] His main contribution to this cultural landscape was the founding of two magazines: first *Controspazio* (1969-81), launched during his heroic period at the Politecnico, and then *Eupalino* (1983-90), coinciding with his political escalation in the PSI and institutional roles at the Biennale.

Decades earlier, Portoghesi had made his own debut on the Italian magazine publishing scene in the pages of *Civiltà delle macchine*,[32] founded in 1953 by Leonardo Sinisgalli – an engineer by education, writer by vocation.[33] Portoghesi admired Sinisgalli, not only for his brilliant intellectual and poetic attributes, but also for his inspiring interdisciplinary approach and understanding of media.[34] Sinisgalli, like Portoghesi, had a protean nature, being an author and, at the same time, a poet, art critic, translator, art director, radio broadcaster and documentary filmmaker.[35] In *Civiltà delle macchine*, Portoghesi wrote on topics as varied as locks, standardization, Vitruvius and optical illusions. Despite the small quantity of articles he published – including his first piece, 'Borromini in ferro'[36] – this early experience remained foundational for the breath of approaches and topics.

It was, however, a position on the executive board as chair for the Architecture section of a different magazine, *Il Marcatrè. Rivista di cultura contemporanea* (from now on *Marcatrè*),[37] that put Portoghesi into contact with a wider network of intellectuals. Active between 1963 and 1972, *Marcatrè* was an interdisciplinary journal founded in Genoa by the art and architectural historian Eugenio Battisti and closely linked to the neo-vanguard Gruppo 63. Contributors included semiologists Gillo Dorfles and Umberto Eco as well as the poet and writer Edoardo Sanguineti. What united the authors of *Marcatrè* was their predilection for philological and historical research. All held specialized knowledge of a great historical 'moment' and recognized that by acting on the historiographical interpretation of the past one could incisively operate in the present.[38] Portoghesi's expertise on baroque culture and architecture fully aligned with the ethos of the journal, which, in turn, reinforced the intentions underpinning his postmodern project, at the time in its early phase. From 1965 onwards, Vittorio Gregotti also contributed to the magazine's Architecture section, representing one of the first encounters between the two architects.

When *Marcatrè* was launched, the popularity of *Casabella-continuità*, whose reverberations had been felt across Italy's schools of architecture, was dwindling.[39] Under the directorship of Antonio Bernasconi, the legendary magazine went through a quiet phase. Meanwhile, Gio Ponti's *Domus* – essentially ecumenical in character in its value system and in its singular faith in architecture – was sticking to its traditional line of reporting on the achievements of Italian and international design. But by the end of the 1960s, with the protests at their height, the lack of leadership in architectural design was palpable, and a new architectural journal was needed. In the same years, while dean of the Faculty of Architecture at the Politecnico di Milano, Portoghesi was ready to establish a journal of his own – one that would push the disciplinary debate within the country. A number of design journals were already coming out of Milan, prompting Portoghesi to look elsewhere not only for a publisher but also for a model from which to draw. The editorial project of *Casabella-continuità*, which had successfully established a cohesive design theory while attracting the best young intellectual minds, still seemed relevant. Following its example, in February 1969, Portoghesi signed an agreement with Bari-based publisher Dedalo for the publication of a new architectural magazine that he named *Controspazio. Rivista di architettura e urbanistica*.[40] Translated as 'Counter-space' or 'Anti-space', the name itself was pure invention, combining *spazio* from the cult magazine *Spazio* (edited by Luigi Moretti 1950–68) with *contro* (counter), which tapped into the counter-cultural sentiment of youth culture of the time. *Controspazio* was also a political and ideological reference – or reaction – to the short-lived *Contropiano. Materiali marxisti*, edited by Alberto Asor Rosa, Massimo Cacciari and Antonio Negri, printed in Florence from 1968 to 1971. As Portoghesi explained in his editorial for the very first issue:

> Choosing *Controspazio* as the title of a magazine – a word that does not appear in vocabularies – means placing as an object of analysis and information that in architecture is not space but its objective and historical place in reality; it means proposing as an objective the hypothesis of other spaces, alternative to the present city, subversive of its absurd balance.[41]

A canny response to the market of glossy magazines, *Controspazio* adopted a tabloid format, a bold, narrow sans serif font on the cover, and cheap paper (Figure 4.3). It was sold for just a few Italian liras, guaranteeing its immediate success among architecture students. Though scheduled to launch in April 1969, the first issue of *Controspazio* appeared in June, but it immediately provided 'a space for articles in which design, history and theory frequently gave rise to passionately ideological criticism'.[42] The magazine was co-edited by Massimo Scolari with Ezio Bonfanti, who worked on it until his death in 1973. The editorial board was based in Milan, where Portoghesi could count on the assistance of young graduates from the Politecnico, 'many of whom were former students of Rogers'.[43] Over the years, the editorial board changed, but it was always composed of a series of young architect-researchers pursuing both writing and design activities and who saw the knowledge of the history of architecture as an indispensable foundation of design.[44] Like Rogers, Portoghesi used his platform to gather brilliant young collaborators, such as Scolari and Bonfanti, as well as Virgilio Vercelloni and Luciano Patetta, all of whom were connected to the Faculty of Architecture at the Politecnico di Milano.[45] Together, they published 'a good mix of projects, theoretical ideas, essays of architecture history, establishing a real continuity with the magazines that had come out in Europe between the two wars'.[46]

Controspazio was influential from the start, and in the aftermath of the political movement of 1968 it became the centre of disciplinary debate in Italy.[47] The content was based on a pluralistic approach to design, as well as a dialectic historical-critical discourse concerning the dogma of the Modern Movement – an issue dear to Portoghesi.[48] Articles addressed the work of Italian and international figures including Louis Kahn and Mario Ridolfi, as well as emerging architects such as Aldo Rossi, Antonio Monestiroli and Gianugo Polesello. The magazine also presented historical research on central episodes of modernity such as Futurism and the Bauhaus, writings by figures such as Jeremy Bentham and unpublished works by Sebastiano Serlio and Giovanni Battista Piranesi. During these first three years, and over twenty-six issues, Bonfanti and Scolari mainly focused on Italian

FIGURE 4.3 Cover of the first issue of the architectural magazine *Controspazio*, June 1969.

schools of architecture and the phenomenon of urban studies that had their stronghold in Venice. Importantly, *Controspazio* was also soon identified as the journal of La Tendenza, a position that, according to Scolari:

> Does not discover new truths, but aims at the elimination of errors in a process of knowledge centred on historical and formal analysis, on the study of the city

as a product, and on the characteristics that lead a certain kind of architecture to be projected onto a certain part of society.... From Aldo Rossi's book to the contributions of Giorgio Grassi and Carlo Aymonino, to the work of diffusion conducted after 1969 by a few editors of *Controspazio* (up to the dissolution of the Milanese editorial staff in 1973), the Tendenza succeeded in providing a real alternative to the facile utopias, to the abstraction of 'revolutionary' discourse, and to geometrical research as an end in itself, and in finally confronting the sovereignty of the most accredited Italian professionalism in the field (Gio Ponti, P. L. Nervi).[49]

Controspazio was meant to challenge the modernist view of architecture as a tool for social reform. In fact, Portoghesi 'refused to consider any deterministic relationship between architecture and society, challenging what he called the "moralist" and "dogmatic" attitude of the modern movement'.[50] Ultimately, he 'wanted to give voice to the many objections born within modernity, to deepen to its self-criticism'.[51] Portoghesi also insisted on his intention to reach 'another' audience located outside the circle of initiates in order to explore the ways in which architectural thought collided with social reality – in other words, to look at architecture from the point of view of those who use it.

The work of La Tendenza was presented in 1973 at the 15th Milan Triennale – an exhibition developed around the pioneering thinking of Aldo Rossi and recorded in its catalogue *L'architettura razionale*. Similarly, in the pages of *Controspazio*, Rossi immediately became the architect through whom Portoghesi and his acolytes intended to disseminate a new line of design, as a real alternative architecture.[52] *Controspazio* was moved to Rome after the turmoil of the early 1970s, when Portoghesi was temporarily suspended from his academic activity at the Politecnico. This period is remembered as the 'Roman phase'. During this time, with the assistance of Renato Nicolini, the editorial board attracted the most talented young architects – amongst them Maurizio Ascani, Alessandro Anselmi, Claudio D'Amato Guerrieri, Daniela Fonti and Laura Thermes, to mention just a few – of the school of Rome, who gave voice to the deep transformations of 1970s Italy.[53]

In the 1980s' context of accumulation and acceleration, architectural magazines proved to be the perfect vehicles for enhancing the circulation of ideas and images while framing a nation-wide discourse. Less intellectually demanding than books and more aesthetically appealing with their numerous images, big titles and increasingly large formats, these publications better suited the new, dynamic postmodern lifestyle. But by around 1980, *Controspazio*'s mission to catalyse the Italian disciplinary discussion was coming to an end. Once the rebellious dean of the Faculty of Architecture in Milan, Portoghesi had advanced to the prestigious institutional position at the Venice Biennale; he needed a different tool to foster his postmodern project at a time when the centrality of architectural language was gaining momentum. This tool took the form of a second architectural magazine,

FIGURE 4.4 Launch of the architectural journal *Eupalino. Cultura della città e della casa*, at the Italian cultural institute in New York, 1985. Paolo Portoghesi with the then Italian Minister of Foreign Affairs, Giulio Andreotti (first from the left). © Paolo Portoghesi Archive.

Eupalino. Cultura della città e della casa. Unlike the tabloid style of *Controspazio*, the bilingual *Eupalino* was issued quarterly between 1983 and 1990, and distributed internationally from New York to Hong Kong, Rotterdam to Buenos Aires, testifying to Portoghesi's determination to go international. The editorial board, which included a pool of Rome-based architects and intellectuals, such as Giancarlo Priori, Guglielmo Bilancioni, Stefania Tuzi, Antonio De Bonis and filmmaker Egidio Eronico (also Alessandra Latour as a correspondent from New York), gathered in via Gregoriana 25, Portoghesi's residence and office in Rome. Promoting itself as 'a magazine that will record and promote the great change that has contributed to link architecture to history and that will start a dialogue between architecture and other fields of culture and communication',[54] *Eupalino* marked a more affirmative phase for postmodern architectural culture, when, after the launch of the architecture sector at the Biennale, it benefited from a wider international scope.

Paying homage to Paul Valéry's *Eupalinos ou l'architecte* and drawing on the elegance of *fin de siècle* magazines *Pan* and *Ver Sacrum*,[55] Portoghesi's latest editorial project was a lavish publication that fully reflected its exuberant cultural context. It presented architecture – alongside other disciplines such as industrial and interior design, cinema, music, art and poetry – through long articles and lush images, including large colour photos and fold-out drawings. Far from the sparse look of *Controspazio*, whose form and content reflected the period of intense ideological and political transformation of 1970s Italy, *Eupalino*'s generous format offered a rich interdisciplinary journey across the most sophisticated examples of Italian and international postmodern culture, all based on Portoghesi's network. These physical qualities and intellectual ambitions contributed to the magazine's elitist reputation – a status that was further confirmed by a photograph of Italian Prime Minister Bettino Craxi holding the first issue of *Eupalino* at the magazine's official launch in New York, also attended by Italian Minister of Foreign Affairs, Giulio Andreotti (Figure 4.4).

Architecture on the dance floor

Despite *Eupalino*'s highbrow tendencies, Portoghesi believed in a greater democratization of architecture and design through the utilization of public spaces as media platforms – particularly spaces dedicated to popular culture. If architecture was going to appeal to the masses, it had to conquer spaces like discothèques – places for entertainment as well as cultural and social venues of the city.[56]

It was the release of the song 'Stayin' Alive', written and performed in 1977 by the Bee Gees for the *Saturday Night Fever* motion picture soundtrack, that had a tremendous effect on popular culture, while discothèques became hotbeds of contemporary urban life.[57] As a sign of this new cultural phenomenon, internationally renowned architectural and design magazines – such as *Domus* and *Modo*, directed by Alessandro Mendini – started to pay attention to discothèques from a typological and aesthetic point of view. For example, in 1978, the photographer Gabriele Basilico was commissioned by *Modo* to explore the phenomenon of dancing in central Italy – from Piacenza to Rimini. According to Basilico, discos were 'a real revolution in the mass entertainment system', inspired by the architecture and clichés of Las Vegas and kitsch to build a world articulated in events and attitudes.[58] In 1981, *Modo* published photos of the inauguration of Filippo Panseca's project for the club Studio 54 in Milan.

Panseca's aesthetic interest in the disco space was part of the *zeitgeist* and would be exploited by the PSI in 1984, when Craxi held the 43rd PSI party congress in Verona. Designed to match the aesthetic of a nightclub, Panseca's stage was composed of steps covered in mirrors that formed the speaker's podium. From this gleaming pulpit, Craxi was visible to and consumed by his mass audience. In the background, a neon light in the form of a carnation was presented with the slogan 'A right society'. The party's 'disco' was also reminiscent of a television studio, and the overall spatial setting suggested an atmosphere closer to that of an American political convention than a traditional Italian political assembly. For the first time since the end of the Second World War, the Italian political spectacle was taking shape with triumphant tones, all while referencing nightclubs.

If politics appropriated the aesthetic of the discotèques, conversely, discos themselves became spaces for cultural explorations. Opened in 1965 in via Tagliamento 9 in a chic neighbourhood of Rome, the legendary Piper club gained a reputation as the most experimental and transgressive night venue in the country, staging foreign groups, including early performances by Pink Floyd and Genesis, and displaying work by Italian and international contemporary artists such as Mario Schifano, Piero Manzoni, Andy Warhol and Robert Rauschenberg. In 1979, the club's founder Giancarlo Bornigia commissioned Roman architect Giovanni Rebecchini to carry out a major refurbishment of the Piper. Rebecchini not only designed a brand new polyvalent and multimedia venue, but also organized a set of events to bring culture and dancing together. Architecture and urbanism, painting and sculpture, photography, cosmology and cinema were presented through initiatives such as nightly shows and interior design lessons, run by Rebecchini himself.[59] The idea was to exploit the space and equipment of the Piper – loudspeakers, maxi screens and the stage of the room – to present talks and debates of a high intellectual standard. In the early 1980s, the Piper thus became the theatre of a series of playful and cultural experimentations known as 'Frivolo e Sublime'. These 'incursions' in the cultural and entertainment scene adopted a dynamic and ironic mode to provide insights into the fields of art, architecture, fashion, photography, cinema and design.[60] After the talks, people were invited to dance to loud music, an initiative that triggered a dramatic increase in female attendance at architectural events, contributing to a reduction in the gender imbalance that characterized the discipline at the time.[61]

Portoghesi was regularly involved in these events – a testament to his appreciation for popular culture and its ease in engaging with different groups of audiences. Rebecchini, who met Portoghesi for the first time at the Piper, admired his experimental attitude and recognized a rare openness to new situations.[62] Portoghesi himself was the protagonist of some of the nightclub's cultural shows, including a series of inventive 'architectural trials'. For a 1981 edition of the series 'Processo al Postmodern', he stood as the main 'accused', appearing on stage while being scrutinized by five authoritative 'judges' including the art critic Achille Bonito Oliva, as well as architects Costantino Dardi and Franco Purini. On that occasion, 1,800 people took part in the two-hour event (1,300 inside the venue and 500 outside)[63] – confirmation of Portoghesi's popular appeal. Another memorable trial was organized in 1983 'against' the Catalan architect Ricardo Bofill, who was judged by Rebecchini and the actress Sandra Milo (Portoghesi played Bofill's defence attorney; Figures 4.5, 4.6, 4.7).

The idea of organizing trials of architects and buildings was so successful that the format was borrowed in other venues across Rome. The trial of the, allegedly, ugliest monument in Italy, the Altare della Patria (formerly the monument to King

Vittorio Emanuele II), received sponsorship from Mediocredito Lazio bank at Palazzo Venezia in 1986. With Portoghesi, alongside Claudia Conforti and Gugliemo Bilancioni, defending the monument, and Bruno Zevi and Klaus Koening prosecuting, the verdict came in for the monument to be saved but with a change of function.[64] Intriguingly, among those who testified sat Christian Democrat Giulio Andreotti, then Italian Minister of Foreign Affairs, and Republican Giovanni Spadolini, then Italian Minister of Defence,[65] a striking example of the intertwining of history, politics and media in postmodern Italy.

The magazine and the nightclub were even showcased together in 1984, when the Piper hosted a presentation of *Domus* (Figure 4.8).[66] Rebecchini's idea was to turn the publication's cover and articles into a live show with animated discussions between Alessandro Mendini and Bruno Zevi, Pierre Restany and Achille Bonito Oliva, among others. Artist Luigi Ontani and the pop group Matia Bazar both participated.[67] As a consequence, an issue of *Eupalino* was launched at the Piper that same year.[68] Taken together, the confluence between the highly public yet subversive design of the discothèques, the ephemeral space of the dance floor, and the pages of the magazine created a wholly new postmodern media apparatus on which architecture could capitalize.

FIGURE 4.5 Paolo Portoghesi, in his white suit at the centre, at the Piper, during the trial with Ricardo Bofill, Rome, 1983. © Paolo Portoghesi Archive.

FIGURE 4.6 Flyer for the invitation to the trial with Ricardo Bofill at the Piper, 1983. © Paolo Portoghesi Archive.

FIGURE 4.7 Trial with Ricardo Bofill at the Piper, 1983. Paolo Portoghesi, speaking on the microphone, and Bofill sitting on the chair of the accused. © Paolo Portoghesi Archive.

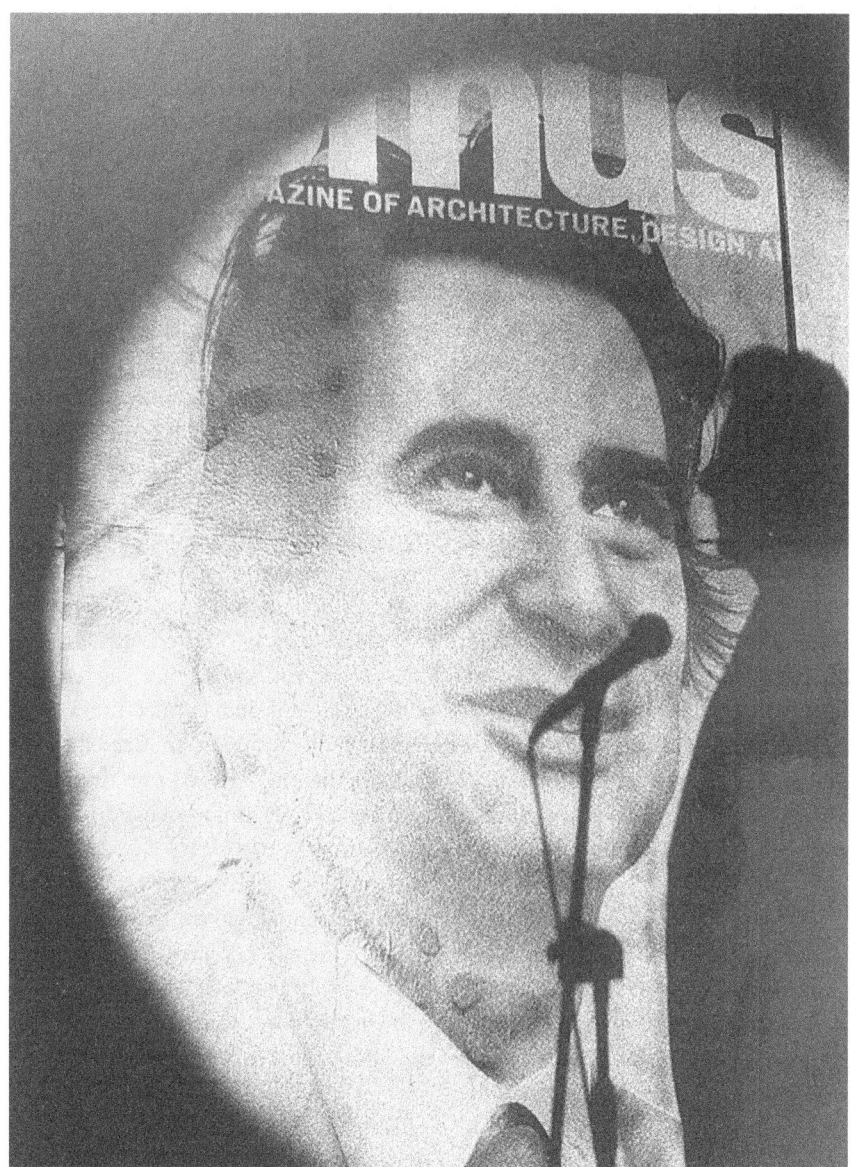

FIGURE 4.8 Paolo Portoghesi speaking at the *Domus* party at the Piper, Rome, 1980. © Paolo Portoghesi Archive.

From movie protagonist to stage set

In postwar Italy, cinema and more particularly the tradition of neorealist films provided a rich source of inspiration for intellectuals, artists and architects.[69] Revealing the difficult economic and moral conditions of society during the years of the reconstruction, neorealist cinema was characterized by stories set among the working class. They were shot on location, frequently featured non-professional actors and often explicitly included architecture.[70] This combination of 'real' life on the film screen was straightforward and unsparing compared with prewar Italian cinema, portraying changes in the material conditions and psychological environments of working-class Italians – from poverty to oppression, injustice to depression. A famous example, and one of Portoghesi's first cinematic influences, is the 1948 film *Ladri di Biciclette* (Bicycle Thieves), directed by Vittorio De Sica, of whom the young architecture student appreciated the intellectual capability of combining historical value with lightness. In its images, architects found an accurate visual description of Italian urban peripheries, which would become the natural field of action for their early projects.[71] For Portoghesi, neorealist films were fundamental; they represented the first documented instances of the city and the interactions of people in the street. Some, however, viewed the films as mannerist retreats into formalist involution – an accusation that suggests an interesting parallelism between the disciplines of cinema and architecture.

'Like every one of my generation, I have been a movie fanatic, motivated by the desire of getting hold of what we considered the language of our time,' said Portoghesi.[72] Over the years, cinema's media specificity influenced Portoghesi's way of thinking, designing, and even seeing the world:

> I am passionate about movement; for me it is essential that things move, either directly or virtually. This is the strength of cinema: to represent movement. Painting, however dynamic it may be, is fixed, immobile. While the image flows, this ability to use this feature of the eye to see the succession as a continuity is a miraculous thing. Indeed, for my generation, the birth of cinema was still considered a new dimension of life.[73]

Portoghesi's interaction with the world of cinema took multiple forms: he directed documentaries, acted in films, and a few of his major buildings served as backdrops or sets. Moreover, through the institutional context of the Venice Biennale, he cleverly made use of the language of cinema to display architecture effectively, before becoming a leading figure of cinema culture through his organization of the prestigious Mostra del Cinema, Venice's annual international film festival.

But what really captivated Portoghesi was how cinema could move between the real and the virtual:

The virtual has always interested me: it's a terrific tool for conveying ideas. Obviously with the real you can convey ideas, but it is much more difficult. Instead, the virtual is programmatic in itself. There is this alternation; a virtual project like that of (X) is absolutely separate from reality and from the possible, but it would like to affect reality and make us reflect on the world in which we live. With the virtual you can stimulate reflection, with the real you work on Earth, you try to do something that remains and you put yourself into a relationship with life.[74]

Making another important use of the format and language of cinema at the service of architecture, Portoghesi blended the two disciplines by conceiving the *Strada Novissima*, the seventy-metre-long artificial street built inside the Venice Arsenale for the First International Architecture Exhibition of the Biennale in 1980. The ephemeral facades that formed the *Strada Novissima* were neither stand-ins for real buildings nor were they projections of a potential future. They were both tangible yet virtual, stimulating a reflection on the actual streets around and leading to the Arsenale.

At the same time, Portoghesi's buildings became literal film sets. In 1962 Casa Baldi was the first to appear on-screen. Its owner, the film director Gian Vittorio Baldi, used the residence in *Luciano. Una Vita Bruciata*, a black-and-white drama featuring the interior of the Roman house.[75] Five years later, in 1967, Casa Andreis in Scandriglia, became the stage for Marco Ferreri's movie *L'harem*, a comedy-drama in which a seductive architect invites several of her male lovers to holiday with her in her elegant villa. With its labyrinthine and curved forms, Casa Andreis embodied the spirit and fantasy of the film's heroine who lived her life in a decidedly original way. Casa Papanice became not only a stage but also a protagonist of several movies, as analysed further in this chapter, while in 1990, the Mosque of Rome made an appearance in Giuseppe Tornatore's movie *Stanno tutti bene*.

While at the Politecnico, Portoghesi himself featured in *Utopia, Utopia* (1969), directed by his long-time friend Maurizio (Azio) Cascavilla. The film tells the story of Renato (played by architect Renato Nicolini), a twenty-eight-year-old Roman architect obsessed with geometry and urban questions. Renato visits 'an important professor' – Portoghesi indeed – with whom he engages in a serious conversation about the difference between geometry and architecture. As Portoghesi's character explains: 'The city is made of fragments of elementary geometrical forms, which combined together create complexity.'[76]

During his nine-year tenure as president of the Venice Biennale (1983–92), Portoghesi became the representative of perhaps its most important festival, the Venice Film Festival, still today one of the most prestigious festivals of Europe, with global standing and participation from all over the world. Actors from Hollywood would land at the Lido, turning the lagoon into an international stage. Portoghesi would attend with Massobrio who described the experience as 'a wonderful opportunity to meet actors, directors, in a unique Venetian atmosphere, between the Excelsior and the Lido Hotel that recalls the Belle Époque'.[77]

Given the popularity of the Venice Film Festival, the cinema sector of the Biennale received the most press and exposure, and Portoghesi needed a strong agenda for it to compete internationally. His primary intention was to better integrate the genre with other sectors of the Biennale: 'The logic ... was that of multidisciplinary or interdisciplinarity – as they say today: that is, to establish a relationship between sectors that historically ignored each other.'[78] In the wake of the success of the 1979 exhibition *Venezia e lo Spazio Scenico*, based on the collaboration between the architectural and theatre sectors, Portoghesi aimed to bring together different disciplines, while generating new cultural opportunities. One significant occasion was the international competition Portoghesi launched for the new Palazzo del Cinema in Lido (1990), seen as another opportunity for collaboration between the cinema and architecture sectors. The project would give more prestige and visibility to the Venice Film Festival and at the same time provide the lagoon with a new building – a rare chance for Venice. The competition was won by the Spanish architect Rafael Moneo, and the proposals of the ten finalists were exhibited at the fifth International Architecture Exhibition of the Venice Biennale in 1991.[79] Although the winning scheme was never built, with this initiative Portoghesi instrumentalized his institutional role at the Biennale in the attempt to provide both Venice and Italy with a significant postmodern building. In the same year, a similar strategy was adopted to establish a connection between the art and architecture Biennale with the competition for the reconstruction of the Central Pavilion in the Giardini di Castello and the Ali installation at the Arsenale by Massimo Scolari.[80] Again in 1991, the Biennale bookshop in the Giardini was built according to the design of English architect James Stirling. Like Moneo, Stirling was complex figure deeply immersed in the postmodern discussion of the use of history in contemporary design. Both Portoghesi and the then Director of the Architecture sector Francesco Dal Co were perfectly aligned in their efforts and ambitions to de-provincialize the Italian architectural scene by fostering the construction of buildings designed by representatives of international postmodern architecture. They shared the same conviction that, beyond essays, books and talks, it was by means of iconic buildings in strategic venues that Italian postmodern culture could be pushed to an international level.

Casa Papanice framed by the camera

In the opening of his book on Victor Horta, Portoghesi spends a few lines reflecting on the nature of one of Horta's most important clients, the Belgian engineer Emile Tassel:

Bachelor, passionate of projections with a magic lantern, Tassel accepted, and maybe wanted a house-spectacle, a house as a manifesto to gradually discover as a plot of a romance. But to what extent did he understand the intentions of his architect, and in which way did he [Tassel] decodify the signs chosen with such coherence and with such love?[81]

Writing these lines, Portoghesi, who was completing the construction of his eccentric residential project for Casa Papanice, was most probably identifying with the subject of Horta. The iconic house – commissioned by Pasquale Papanice, an entrepreneur from Taranto who had made his fortune in construction – was built with Vittorio Gigliotti between 1966 and 1970 in via Giuseppe Marchi on the Gianicolo hill in Rome. Similarly to Casa Baldi, translating the lessons of 1920s neoplasticism into a contemporary language, Portoghesi proposed a house that simultaneously returned to the origins of the Modern Movement while becoming radically novel; a house characterized by the use of the curve and designed with the principle of flexibility. As Portoghesi described it:

The greatest element of inspiration for this house was thinking about the kids who passed by on the street. There was no school nearby, but I have always thought with interest about a man's training. Childhood and adolescence are often considered unimportant periods in life. I turned to these young passers-by and thought 'What can a house say to these people?' First of all, it can mean the dream of a different city. In this sense, the house has succeeded in its intent: it does not combine with anything, it is an object with no relationship with the surrounding area, indeed, it represents the rejection of what is around it.[82]

Like Tassel, Pasquale Papanice had asked for his own house-spectacle, one that could even become a film set;[83] a building both cinematic and photogenic and whose conception would be dictated by the idea of movement. Unlike Baldi, however, Papanice offered a better budget for the house – but he did not give Portoghesi and Gigliotti full freedom with its design. 'I dreamed of a house like the Schröder house, absolutely flexible, in which almost all the walls were movable.... Then [the client] later asked for caesurae: bedrooms, and I had to redesign the entire house.'[84]

Spanning three levels, Casa Papanice included one apartment on each floor and a small attic (Figure 4.9). Unlike Portoghesi's previous residential buildings, the whole house was characterized by its use of vivid colours. Part of the exterior walls was covered with vertical majolica bands – in a palette that went from white to blue, green, brown and golden – to soar the urban profile of the building. In contrast, the internal walls were painted with horizontal-coloured bands to visually dilate the space. The generous rooms were dominated by the geometrical theme of the cylinder, producing inventive patterns on the ceilings as well as increasing the sense of tension and dynamism of the lateral walls. The balconies also reflected this matrix, both in

FIGURE 4.9 Exterior view of Casa Papanice, Rome. Photograph by Paolo Portoghesi. © Paolo Portoghesi Archive.

their shape and in the use of thin tubular elements for the balustrade. By curving the walls, Portoghesi and Gigliotti obtained a forceful dimension of the space that welcomed human movement. Like prior buildings, Casa Papanice was designed following the principle of fields theory (see Chapter 2). The direct relationship with nature was another component in the design process of the house. As Portoghesi explains, the work was done with respect for the natural surroundings:

> There was a beautiful tree, an old cedar, which was almost completely cut down. I decided to leave it and make it a direct interlocutor of the house. Indoors, coloured stripes represent the relationship with the sky (with the blue stripes that descend from above) and the earth (with the green stripes that rise from below and stop at a certain point). The brown stripes are dedicated to the trunk of this tree which was still part of the image of the house.[85]

For an architect-designed building to feature in movies is certainly not unusual in the history of the twentieth century. Frank Lloyd Wright's houses in Los Angeles, for example, have appeared in a range of famous Hollywood films, such as the Ennis House starring in the now classic movie *Blade Runner*, released in 1982. However, what stands out as a singular aspect of Casa Papanice is that this truly cinematic house was intentionally built to also be used as a film set. Its completion in 1970 was soon followed by the staging of three movies: a comedy, *Dramma della gelosia* (1970), and two thrillers, namely *Lo strano vizio della signora Wardh* by Sergio Martino (1971) and *La dama rossa uccide sette volte* by Emilio Miraglia (1972). This temporal proximity between the end of its construction and the use of the house as a set shows a perfect alignment of the design of the building with its time and culture.

In *Dramma della gelosia (tutti i particolari in cronaca)* (*The Pizza Triangle*), Casa Papanice, beyond its cinematic appeal, represents the social ambitions of the main character Adelaide (Monica Vitti), who, in order escape a love triangle, runs off with a third man. This new lover, Ambleto, is a butcher who, on making his fortune, bought Casa Papanice to give himself an air of sophistication and cachet. The film's director, Ettore Scola, was an excellent observer of cities and their architecture. Unlike Federico Fellini, who invented his own Rome, Scola preferred using real sets for his films, giving architecture a precise historical and social connotation (Figure 4.10). The shots taken in the house show Adelaide in her new life, elevated to a higher social status (*The Marriage of Figaro* plays in the background). Ambleto's well-rehearsed seduction of Adelaide involves a detailed explanation of the importance of geometry in the design of his house. While Adelaide looks out onto the terrace she asks about the unique architecture of his villa: 'What are all these reeds?' she asks of the white tubes that form the facade. 'It is a precise geometric qualification,' Ambleto replies. 'Or so it was written in the description of the project.'

In 1971, just one year after its completion, Casa Papanice became part of another set, this time for the mystery movie *Lo strano vizio della signora Wardh*

FIGURE 4.10 Interior of Casa Papanice, the lounge, 1970s. Photograph by Paolo Portoghesi. © Paolo Portoghesi Archive.

(The Strange Vice of Mrs Wardh; originally released as *Blade of the Ripper* in the United States). In this thriller the titular heroine (Edwige Fenech), wife of the diplomat Neil Wardh (Alberto De Mendoza), is stalked by her abusive former lover. Although the film is not set in Rome, some scenes were shot there, and Portoghesi's colourful house was used as the set of the diplomatic residence (Figure 4.12). Once again, the house symbolizes the status of its owner, in this case a diplomat who, at least initially, seems more respectable than Signora Wardh's ex-lover. The tension cutting through the thriller is emphasized by the spatial compression generated by filming the curves of Casa Papanice in rapid succession.

Then, in 1972, Emilio Miraglia released *La dama rossa uccide sette volte* (The Red Queen Kills Seven Times), another thriller in which two sisters, Kitty (Barbara Bouchet) and Evelyn Wildenbrück (Pia Giancaro), are cursed by a family painting

FIGURE 4.11 Still from the movie *The Pizza Triangle*, 1970, showing Ambleto Di Meo (Hércules Cortéz) and Adelaide Ciafrocchi (Monica Vitti) inside Casa Papanice.

FIGURE 4.12 Still from the movie *The Strange Vice of Mrs. Wardh*, 1971, showing heroine (Edwige Fenech), wife of the diplomat Neil Wardh (Alberto De Mendoza), inside Casa Papanice.

FIGURE 4.13 Still from the movie *The Red Lady Kills Seven Times*, 1972, showing Martin Hoffmann (Ugo Pagliai) and one of his employees in Casa Papanice.

that depicts a hundred-year cycle in which a red queen is raised from the dead to go on a killing spree. The film was predominantly shot in Würzburg and Weikersheim in Germany, but one of the main characters, Martin Hoffmann (Ugo Pagliai), lives in Casa Papanice. In this film, as well as *Lo strano vizio della signora Wardh*, Casa Papanice's suggestive coloured bands of the walls amplify the sense of suspense and tension within the house (Figure 4.13). The main character, Martin, is the director of a fashion business. Like in the two other movies filmed in Casa Papanice, in *Lo strano vizio della signora Wardh*, he embodies the postmodern middle-class individual displaying social status through the house he inhabits, and in doing so effectively conveys the ethos of his time.

Interestingly, the house itself was moveable, in a sense. In *Dramma della gelosia*, the house is ostensibly shown in its real urban context and connected to its surroundings. In the two thrillers that followed, Casa Papanice was used as a classic studio set instead, representing a domestic space located elsewhere. Similar to the case of Rossi's Teatro, the displacement of Casa Papanice freed the building from its environment, allowing it to gather an autonomous life through images in the history of cinema.[86] The house, like some of the characters who resided in it, suggests a form of libertarian attitude. It fully represents the postmodern emancipation from purely functionalist dictates, to stand up to a more sophisticated aesthetic plan and complex spatial dimension.

In 1972, after the death of its owner, Casa Papanice was sold to the publishing house Giunti. Just a few years later, it was acquired by the Jordanian government to host the country's embassy. Since then, the house, which has made history in postmodern architecture as well as in Italian cinema, has been considerably altered and is now in need of repair and protection. Through the current polemic on its preservation – with combative articles published in national newspapers, Portoghesi's public disappointment and *j'accuse*, and the current travelling exhibition organized by Papanice's nephew, Edmondo Papanice – Casa Papanice has triumphally entered the twenty-first century. Like Rossi's Teatro del Mondo, the Roman house continues to have a presence through both static and moving images. Yet, for the heirs of Papanice, who launched a media campaign to preserve and heritage list the house, the visibility of the building should be reinforced through a proper restoration of its original postmodern language. Through the controversy – in which even Her Majesty the Queen of Jordan, Rania Al Abdullah, and the Italian Minister of Culture, Dario Franceschini, took part[87] – Casa Papanice and its architect continue to court the media, confirming their partnership as virtuosos of the stage.

EPILOGUE

FIGURE E.1 Paolo Portoghesi at the opening of the exhibition 'Paolo Portoghesi a via Giulia', Rome, 1986. With Renato Nicolini, on the right. © Paolo Portoghesi Archive.

In 1992, Paolo Portoghesi was at the peak of his career (Figure E.1). He was ending his second mandate as president of the Venice Biennale with a travelling exhibition on sacred space and the monotheist religions, organized at the Antichi Granai on the Giudecca in Venice.[1] At the show's opening party, Portoghesi was photographed holding hands with representatives of the religions on display – Judaism, Islam and Christianity – once more confirming his talent as a mediator able to bridge differences (Figure E.2).

FIGURE E.2 Paolo Portoghesi together with the representatives of the Israeli, Catholic and Islamic communities at the first opening of the itinerant exhibition *Lo spazio sacro nelle tre religioni monoteiste*, Venice, 1993. © Paolo Portoghesi Archive.

This exhibition was the natural outcome of Portoghesi's enduring historical research on sacred architecture, and anticipated the completion of the Mosque and Islamic Cultural Centre in Rome in 1995, one of the most controversial – and at the same time successful – realizations of Italian postmodern architecture. A crossroads of Western and Eastern cultures, the religious complex was at the centre of tense political dialogues and economic negotiations between Europe and Middle East (as discussed in Chapter 3), and it took two decades to finalize the works. During this period, Portoghesi's office signed off on a remarkable number of substantial built urban projects such as the residential complex for Enel workers (1981–88) in Tarquinia (Figure E.3) and the Residential Park Borsalino (1987–91) in Alessandria, the aesthetics of which reflected the opulence of the 1980s. By the start of the 1990s, Portoghesi and his sphere of action and influence had achieved an almost unparalleled momentum and reputation in Italy. Nevertheless, Portoghesi's career experienced a sudden setback provoked by external political circumstances.

By 1992, the postmodern wave had also reached its apex and was now ebbing in national and international contexts. Already in 1988, the *Deconstructivist Architecture* exhibition, curated by Philp Johnson and Mark Wigley at the Museum of Modern Art in New York, had attempted a conscious turn away from the postmodern path. As Mary McLeod diagnosed in her seminal essay 'Architecture and Politics in the Reagan Era', by this time,

FIGURE E.3 Paolo Portoghesi with Giovanna Massobrio, Residential complex for ENEL workers, 1981–88, Tarquinia. Photograph by Paolo Portoghesi. © Paolo Portoghesi Archive.

A new architectural tendency, associated both with post-structuralist theory and constructivist forms (in school jargon, the slash-crash projects and the Russian train wrecks), is in part a vehement reaction against postmodernism and what are perceived as its conservative dimensions: its historicist imagery, its complacent contextualism, its conciliatory and affirmative properties, its humanism, its rejection of technological imagery, and its repression of the new.[2]

In parallel, an epochal change of direction of political and economic nature were taking place, with the recent fall of the Berlin Wall and the end of Reagan and Thatcher's reign. At this very moment, too, Fredric Jameson published *Postmodernism, or, the Cultural Logic of Late Capitalism*, which, using a Marxist critique, stressed the link between contemporary culture and recent economic history, signalling a reflection on postmodernity as a temporal unit.

1992 *Annus horribilis*

In Italy, the end of the postmodern period was as emphatic as it was dramatic. There was a general awareness of pervasive, endemic wrongdoing associated with the country's institutions. It was 1988, and Roman singer Antonello Venditti, with his song 'In questo mondo di ladri'[3] ('In This World of Thieves'), voiced a sort of collective exorcism, a general perception that would soon materialize. In Italy, the political and cultural deregulation experienced in the 1980s, based on continuous scandals and huge national debt, was underpinned by an active yet silent system of bribery that burst in 1992, with the Tangentopoli (Bribeville) scandal.[4] The event triggered the investigation known as Mani Pulite (Clean Hands), a nationwide inquest into political corruption that implicated many members of the Italian political class.[5]

In 1990s Italy, the number of corrupt politicians was so extensive that the national newspapers reported on briberies every day for several years, and the escalation of events culminated in a series of suicides. The leader of the PSI, Bettino Craxi, made his public *mea culpa* in a memorable address to the House of Representatives, sharing his views on the involvement of the political class in the system of briberies, concluding: 'I do not think there is anybody in this room, responsible for important political organisations, who can stand up and swear an oath contrary to what I say, as sooner or later, the facts will make evident that it is perjury.'[6] Everybody stayed still and silent. Nobody in the room stood and, in a single moment, Craxi became the scapegoat of the entire political class. On 30 April 1993, while exiting the Hotel Raphael in Rome, Craxi was attacked by an angry crowd throwing coins and demanding his exit from politics and an ethical change in the management of the overall system. Tangentopoli thus resulted in the dissolution of the PSI and the progressive disappearance of other Italian political parties, such as the PCI and the Christian Democrats. The so-called 'First Republic' had come to an end.

Inevitably, these events reverberated across Italian postmodern culture and life. The exuberant habits of excess that had characterized the intoxicating 1980s – the bright colours and voluptuous forms, erudite quotes and the paradoxical ambitions to spread a democratic luxury – all of a sudden turned into the aesthetics of exaggeration, traceable in the grand character of the buildings. In particular, the earthquake that was Mani Pulite and the need to reform the political system meant that the building sector – and consequently the profession of architecture – endured a mortifying nationwide process of revision.[7] Subsequently, Italy's architectural culture went through a phase of stagnation, where every instance of cultural turmoil seemed to be restrained.[8] The Merloni Law, passed in 1994, was an urgent attempt to file away the experience of Tangentopoli and redeem the field of architecture by relaunching a system of public tenders on new ethical premises and in line with European regulations.[9] However, in order to inject rigour back into the construction sector, the quality of the architectural project became a secondary goal of the design process. Instead, the focus was on fostering a new and more transparent operational attitude.[10]

While Portoghesi witnessed the collapse of the PSI, the tumultuous events indirectly triggered the reshaping of his postmodern project. The spotlight on his presidential stage at the Venice Biennale was switched off as his mandate came to its natural conclusion; he lost the ideological support of his political party; and, concerning architectural design, there was now a need for a new aesthetic and ideals that reflected the changes enforced by the courts. A new ethical order was grabbing the attention of architects who were progressively becoming more engaged with a pragmatic approach to the discipline. The diaspora of Italian postmodern architects corresponded to a period of profound self-reflection and reformulation of design trajectories.[11]

The change of direction that occurred in 1992 Italy marked a substantial adjustment to Portoghesi's life and work organization. Back in Rome in 1993, after his escapade at the Venice Biennale, everything had radically changed.[12] For example, Zevi, now disenchanted by the academic world, had retired from the university and was working as an architectural writer, all while remaining a militant in the Partito Radicale Italiano (PRI). The new mayor of Rome, the centre-left coalition representative Francesco Rutelli, was about to launch a campaign for urban projects involving foreign architects – with no connection whatsoever with Tangentopoli – who included Richard Meier for the Museum of Ara Pacis (1995–2006) and Zaha Hadid for the MAXXI Museum (1998–2010).[13] These commissions came to the detriment of local architects who were left out of significant opportunities to build in the capital city.

Retreat to Calcata

The year 1992 was also the last that the Portoghesis could enjoy their memorable house in via Gregoriana, to where they had moved in 1972 after a short stopover in the Torrino in via di Porta Pinciana. With its large spaces and panoramic terrace, the house of via Gregoriana had soon been converted into a sophisticated residence that embraced the exuberance of the 1980s and played host to a long list of VIP guests.[14] But, for Portoghesi, the beginning of the 1990s brought a shift informed as much by conceptual terms as geographical decisions. And, by the end of the decade, Portoghesi and Massobrio had completed their definitive move to the medieval hill town of Calcata.[15]

Located on the outskirts of Rome and nestled in the Treja Valley, the small town of Calcata had attracted artists and bohemians, becoming a vital creative centre in the 1970s, when Portoghesi and Massobrio bought the first building of the 'house of the seven barns', as it became known.[16] The couple's decision to retreat to the countryside was motivated by two specific reasons: on the one hand, they wished to escape the tiring life of the city, with its endless commitments, relentless jet set and political turmoil; on the other, they could eventually set up a place that would reflect their shared world according to the aesthetic principles of the Art Nouveau.

The 'house of the seven barns' was probably the most successful project that Portoghesi and Massobrio carried out together. The couple initially refurbished the property purchased in 1973, and, with their sympathetic additions the house grew significantly over time: from weekend refuge to first house,[17] to an office and library formed by sequential rooms, each dedicated to a specific historical period, to a sanctuary of ideas and contemplation of nature. They also designed a majestic garden with a zoo populated by exotic species – a place marked by presences, memories, allusions and described as a singular 'gallery of ancestors', where history and nature merged. The grounds represented a meeting point and dialogue between Eastern and Western cultures, as well as a continuous game of atmospheres, colours and scents to recompose the harmony between humankind and nature.[18]

Inspired by the poetry of Rainer Maria Rilke and the architectural precedent of Villa Adriana in Tivoli, the house in Calcata became a postmodern *Gesamtkunstwerk*, where Portoghesi and Massobrio could realize the perfect blending of their personal and professional paths while finding a unique dimension untouched by external circumstances (Figure E.4). Indeed, the overarching ideas behind the house were based on the integration of art, architecture and nature – all directly inspired by those very tables, lamps and prints of the Art Nouveau tradition. And Calcata is where they based all of their activities: from running the architectural office to their private and social lives. When the Galleria Apollodoro closed in 1995, its furniture and collection were relocated to Calcata – the house's spatial generosity allowed for the display of the many furniture pieces collected over the years or designed by Portoghesi himself. The house was also designed as a

FIGURE E.4 Residence in Calcata designed by Paolo Portoghesi and Giovanna Massobrio, c. late 1970s. © Paolo Portoghesi Archive.

venue to host art events, cultural shows and society parties – such as those staged in the property's open-air theatre, attended by celebrities including Italian television presenter Pippo Baudo and actress and model Elsa Martinelli.[19]

After 1992, in the process of making Calcata his primary residence and field for design experimentation, Portoghesi took an environmental turn. He reinforced his role as an advocate of what, referring to Le Corbusier, he called *geoarchitettura* (geoarchitecture), a programme articulated through eight points[20] that are based on the relationship between nature and architecture and on a sense of responsibility and duty to respect the land.[21] According to geoarchitecture, if action is not taken on a global level, the dangers of future technological development cannot be fought.[22] Portoghesi's forward-looking turn to nature – almost prophetic in relation to the most recent campaigns for mitigation of climate change – was arguably the continuation, on different premises, of his postmodern modus operandi and line of research. In his book *Natura e Architettura*,[23] he considers nature as a precedent for architecture and uses the lap dissolve technique to compare natural shapes to architectural forms. In this respect, nature, as the architecture of the past, is instrumentalized to show continuity through the passage of time and to convey the idea that each architecture comes from one or more precedents.

Calcata was a retreat and a meditative and contemplative oasis, detached from the hustle and bustle of Rome. At a time of rethinking, Calcata became 'a choice'.[24] Its remoteness from the city allowed for the recovery of a calmer and more focused dimension, where the three components of Portoghesi's postmodern project (history, politics and media) could be reframed on new premises. It is here that Portoghesi was able to gather his historical collection, made of books, furniture and design; carry out his new and personal political programme based on the notion of geoarchitecture; and construct the theoretical framework to later launch his next magazine *Abitare la terra*. As such, for Portoghesi, Calcata turned out to be a deliberate step towards fully accomplishing his postmodern project, which, by the end of 1992, was entering a novel cultural phase.

FIGURE E.5 Paolo Portoghesi in his house in Calcata, July 2023. © Lea-Catherine Szacka.

CODA

Ceci, cher Phèdre, est le plus important: Pas de géométrie sans la parole. Sans elle, les figures sont d'accidents; et ne manifestant, ni ne servent, la puissance de l'esprit.[1]

Paolo Portoghesi exemplifies a professional and intellectual life lived to the fullest, intensely, ad hoc with his beloved baroque maestros. The authors address some of its highlights in an unexpected book that adopts a novel critical approach focusing on the dialogue between architecture and the cultural geometries that are intertwined in history, as in the Eupalinos dialogue, whose search for the 'taste of the eternal' inspired Portoghesi the architect.

Among the folds of a biography full of a thousand facets, I have carved out space to voice two or three things I know about him, dating back to a handful of years (*c.* 1975–79), during which I was able to observe his work as a historian and as an architect.

Even before I began to spend time in his office in Palazzo Pallavicini Rospigliosi and at the home of Portoghesi and his wife Giovanna Massobrio in via Gregoriana, the magazine *Controspazio* had introduced me to the man who had been its director since the years of its founding in Milan.

Claudio D'Amato, one of Portoghesi's closest collaborators, wrote in 2010: '*Controspazio*'s gestation period was essentially "Roman", and it came of age in the cultural climate of the student and worker protests of 1963–68, which had a strong following at the Faculty of Architecture in Rome ... [where at the time Paolo Portoghesi was teaching art and architecture literature].' But given the rather violent socio-political atmosphere of Rome, 'Portoghesi decided that the editorial office would be "Milanese". In Milan [at the Polytechnic] in fact, since 1967 he had held the chair of History of Architecture and had been elected Dean'.[2]

The conclusion of the Milanese period, which ended academically for Portoghesi in November of 1971, and for the magazine in 1973 with the untimely death of its first editor-in-chief, Ezio Bonfanti, brought the publication back to Rome, where

Renato Nicolini took Bonfanti's place. The editorial staff grew to include many young architects who at the time gravitated around Professor Ludovico Quaroni's Chair at the Instituto di Architettura in Viale Mazzini. Not far from there, a group of students and recent graduates of Quaroni's (including myself), worked side by side with some of the magazine's assistants and editors, including D'Amato. In the studio in via Germanico (where we would gather), Claudio had reserved the little kitchen for himself, turning it into an incubator for any and all intellectual contributions to *Controspazio*. New graduates were eager to discuss and challenge disparate conceptions of architecture. Interminable, challenging conversations and brainstorming sessions followed, with architecture as the discipline and philosophy as the method. Seminars on the writing of Galvano della Volpe, mixing Marxist ideas and enlightened humanism, were particularly unforgettable.

I graduated in 1974, and went to visit Portoghesi after spending a year working at the Dutch Architecture Archive in Amsterdam. I had not been his student, since my years at Valle Giulia did not coincide with his time teaching in Rome. But we had met on several occasions, albeit briefly, at the offices of Aldo Quinti's publishing house, Officina.[3]

At the time, I wanted to dig further into research on public housing and the Amsterdam School I had just begun, and Portoghesi was one of the few scholars who knew and appreciated the subject. I asked him for a letter of recommendation, which allowed me to retain my scholarship. More than ten years later, I was thrilled to read his review of my book, *La scuola di Amsterdam*, which had been published by Zanichelli.

In that autumn of 1975, my passion for archival work interested him, and he suggested that, under his supervision, I could begin a curatorial apprenticeship by ordering some of his extraordinary collection of photographs of Italian baroque architecture, which he had moved from via di Porta Pinciana to Palazzo Pallavicini Rospigliosi. And so, when my research in Holland allowed, I began to spend days organizing negatives, preparing selections requested for publications, and running down from the area of the Quirinale to Via Crispi to deliver orders to the Nannini photographic studio for black-and-white prints. Those images fascinated me, and I was captivated. Whenever he could, Paolo would take a bit of time to tell me something about them, or he would put them into groups and ask me to study the associations between them. In just a few years, I learned a great deal – it was a real education for me. I often worked with Paolo's secretary, Carla, who I knew from the years at the university; and who was also Giovanna Massobrio's assistant.

The Portoghesis lived in an apartment on the top floor of a palazzo in via Gregoriana, right across from Palazzo Zuccari, which hosted the Biblioteca Hertziana. I got my first card for the library then, thanks to a letter Paolo wrote for me. I have always been very proud of it. I would spend entire afternoons amid the stacks of books, perhaps after having been up to the Portoghesis' apartment, where Giovanna had put together a library of magazines and rare books on subjects ranging from the early twentieth century – the Vienna of Musil and Hoffmann, Art Deco, Liberty – to the 1950s.

The decor of the apartment was the magical universe in which those collections lived. There, I could leaf through the magazines *Ver Sacrum* and *Wendingen* and browse publications from 1920s Berlin and books on German expressionism. Beginning in the early 1970s, those collections gave rise to a series of books published by Laterza, written by Giovanna Massobrio and Paolo Portoghesi, all with the common denominator of the word 'album' in the title: *Album del Liberty* (1975), *Album degli anni Venti* (1976), *Album degli anni Cinquanta* (1977), *Album degli anni Trenta* (1978) and many others.

The second half of the 1970s was also the period of the project for the Mosque in Rome, which was being designed in the studio in Palazzo Pallavicini Rospigliosi. I remember collaborators coming and going, as well as innumerable meetings with consultants on structural aspects and on the elements intrinsic to the Islamic religious space. What about the height of the minaret? *L'Osservatore Romano* published a piece declaring that the height must not surpass that of the lantern of the cupola of St Peter's. Giulio Carlo Argan, mayor of Rome from 1976 to 1979, had immediately come out in favour of Portoghesi's design, although he spent hours arguing with Paolo about the height, which finally did not exceed the permitted height.

My last period in Portoghesi's studio coincided with the preparation of designs for the project 'Roma/amoR' (1979). It was a palindromic project: 'While *Roma*, sublime artifice, is surrounded by countryside ... *Amor* (love) has nature at its heart.'[4] It was an urban model that started from the relationship between interior and exterior, intended to make the 'interior landscape' a model of aggregation and growth for a new urban fabric featuring pre-existing environmental elements. The designs were large panels, plans for a 'daughter-city' with a star-shaped layout, immersed in nature. Much more recently, when I had the opportunity to study Lebbeus Woods's drawings for 'A-City' (*c.* 1982), I found in them the same sense of mourning for the loss of identity of the modern city.

The next decade marked the beginning of Portoghesi's period as a mediator, a 'smooth operator', which the authors' book has so efficaciously analysed.

MARISTELLA CASCIATO
Los Angeles, November 2022

NOTES

Acknowledgements

1 This book is the result of international research started in 2012. It has been written jointly in its entirety. The arguments, vision, structure and critical line of the book have all been discussed and fully shared by the authors. All the translations from the Italian and French have been executed by the authors.
2 Marco Biraghi, Gabriella Lo Ricco, Silvia Micheli, and Mario Viganò eds., *Italia 60/70. Una stagione dell'architettura* (Milano: Il Poligrafo, 2010).
3 Léa-Catherine Szacka, *Exhibiting the Postmodern: 1980 Venice Architecture Biennale* (Venice: Marsilio, 2016).
4 Silvia Micheli, 'Between History and Design: The Baroque Legacy in the Work of Paolo Portoghesi', in *The Baroque in Architectural Culture 1880-1980*, eds. Andrew Leach, John Macarthur and Maarten Delbeke (Surrey–Burlington: Ashgate, 2015), 195–210.
5 Silvia Micheli and Léa-Catherine Szacka, 'Paolo Portoghesi and the Postmodern Project', in *East, West, Central, Re-Framing Identities: Architecture's Turn to History, 1970-1990*, Akos Moravanszky and Torsten Lange, eds. (Basel: Birkhäuser, 2017), 179–91.
6 In 2016, Silvia and Léa-Catherine met in Rome to conduct archival work and Lea-Catherine visited Brisbane to develop the research.
7 Silvia Micheli and Léa-Catherine Szacka, 'Paolo's Triangolo', *AA Files* 72 (2016): 98–106.

Introduction

1 Paolo Portoghesi, 'Architecture and Revolution: Paolo Portoghesi in conversation with Nicolò Ornaghi and Guido Tesio', *San Rocco* 66, no. 14 (Spring 2018): 77.
2 Paolo Portoghesi, 'Le Luci del Paradiso Perduto', in *I nuovi Architetti Italiani*, ed. Giovanna Massobrio (Rome-Bari: Laterza, 1985), ix–xiv.
3 Richard Pommer, 'Bernardo Vittone, un architetto tra illuminismo e rococò by Paolo Portoghesi', *The Art Bulletin* 53, no. 1 (March 1971): 124–25.
4 Roberto Roscani, 'I teatri della discordia', *L'Unità*, 3 July 1984, 9. Tafuri also nicknamed Portoghesi *suonatore di clarinetto* (a clarinet player), insinuating that his foundational ideas were frivolous.

5   Oreste Pivetta, 'Architetti senza case', *L'Unità*, 4 August 1985, 15.
6   Pierluigi Nicolin, *Notizie sullo stato dell'architettura italiana* (Turin: Bollati Boringhieri, 1994), 64.
7   In the 1950s and 1960s, Rome was often referred to as the 'Hollywood on the Tiber', the Italian capital then emerging as a major location for international filmmaking, attracting many foreign productions to the Cinecittà studios. See Eugenia Paulicelli, 'Fashioning Rome: Cinema, Fashion, and the Media in the Postwar Years', *Annali d'Italianistica* 28 (2010): 257–78.
8   Paolo Portoghesi, *Guarino Guarini: 1624–1683* (Milan: Electa, 1956).
9   Eva Branscome, *Hans Hollein and Postmodernism: Art and Architecture in Austria, 1958–1985* (London: Routledge, 2016), 6.
10 Ibid.
11 From the description of the 'Bloomsbury Studies in Modern Architecture' series edited by Tom Avermaete and Janina Gosseye.
12 Tom Avermaete, Véronique Patteeuw and Christophe Van Gerrewey, eds., 'Action and Reaction in Architecture', *OASE* 97 (October 2016): 3.
13 Charles Jencks, *The Language of Post-Modern Architecture* (3rd revised and enlarged edition) (London: Academy Editions, 1981), 6. Originally published in 1977.
14 Fredric Jameson, *Postmodernism, or, the Cultural Logic of Late Capitalism* (Durham, NC: Duke University Press, 1991), introduction.
15 Branscome, *Hans Hollein and Postmodernism*, 7.
16 Marco Biraghi, Gabriella Lo Ricco, Silvia Micheli and Mario Viganò, eds., *Italia 60/70: Una stagione dell'architettura* (Padua: Il Poligrafo, 2010), 11.
17 Maria Letizia Conforto, Gabriele De Giorgi, Alessandra Muntoni and Marcello Pazzaglini, eds., *Il dibattito architettonico in italia 1945–1975* (Rome: Bulzoni 1977).
18 Manfredo Tafuri, *History of Italian Architecture, 1944–1985* (Cambridge, MA: The MIT Press, 1991); Amedeo Belluzzi and Claudia Conforti, *Architettura italiana 1944–1994* (Rome-Bari: Laterza, 1994).
19 Jean-Louis Cohen, *La coupure entre architectes et intellectuels, ou les enseignements de l'italophilie* (Paris: Edition Mardaga, 2015). Originally published in 1984.
20 Biraghi et al., eds., *Italia 60/70*.
21 Marco Biraghi and Silvia Micheli, *Storia dell'architettura italiana 1985–2015* (Turin: Einaudi, 2013).
22 Valerio Paolo Mosco, *Architettura italiana: Dal postmoderno ad oggi* (Milan: Skira, 2017). Mosco followed this volume with *Viaggio in Italia: Architetture e città* (Santarcangelo di Romagna: Maggioli, 2021), an anthology of Italian architecture and writing.
23 Diane Ghirardo, *Italy: Modern Architectures in History* (London: Reaktion Books, 2013).
24 Mark Jarzombek, '*Italy: Modern Architectures in History* by Diane Ghirardo', *Journal of the Society of Architectural Historians* 73, no. 3 (September 2014): 421–23.
25 Frédéric Migayrou ed., *La Tendenza: Italian architectures 1965–1985*, Paris, Éditions du Centre Pompidou, 2012.
26 Silvia Micheli and John Macarthur, eds., *Italy/Australia: Postmodern Architecture in Translation* (Melbourne: URO, 2018). See also the book's introduction by Léa-Catherine Szacka.

27 Giancarlo Priori, ed., *Paolo Portoghesi* (Milan: Zanichelli, 1985); Mario Pisani, *Paolo Portoghesi: Opere e progetti* (Milan: Electa, 1992).

28 Pisani, *Paolo Portoghesi: Opere e progetti*.

29 Giovanna Massobrio, Maria Ercadi and Stefania Tuzi, *Paolo Portoghesi: Architetto* (Milan: Skira, 2001).

30 Francesca Gottardo, ed., *Paolo Portoghesi, Architect* (Rome: Gangemi 2008). English edition available.

31 Petra Bernitsa, ed., *Paolo Portoghesi: The Architecture of Listening* (Rome: Gangemi, 2014). Italian edition available.

32 Benjamin Chavardès, *Italie post-moderne: Paolo Portoghesi, architecte, théoricien, historien* (Rennes: Presses Universitaires Rennes, 2022). See also Chavardès, 'From Neoliberty to Postmodernism', in *Post-war Architecture between Italy and the UK: Exchanges and Transcultural Influences*, eds. Lorenzo Ciccarelli and Clare Melhuish (London: UCL Press, 2021), 57–69.

33 See Portoghesi, 'Architeture and Revolution: Paolo Portoghesi in Conversation with Nicolò Ornaghi and Guido Tesio'.

34 Nicolò Ornaghi and Francesco Zorzi, 'Filippo Panseca, l'architetto del PSI', *Gizmo Architectural Review*, 14 April 2015, accessed 8 March 2022, http://www.gizmoweb.org/2015/04/filippo-panseca-larchitetto-del-psi/.

35 Manuel Orazi and Marco Vannucci, 'Architecture and Math', *Vesper* 5 (Fall–Winter 2021): 24–38.

36 Marco Vanucci, 'Paolo Portoghesi: The Field Theory', Drawing Matter, 9 November 2020, accessed 27 January 2022, https://drawingmatter.org/paolo-portoghesi-the-field-theory/.

37 In 2019, Portoghesi published his autobiography: Paolo Portoghesi, *Roma/amoR: Memoria, racconto, speranza* (Venice: Masilio, 2019). The title comes from his project and exhibition *Roma/amoR* held in Rome in 1979.

38 Francesco Moschini, *Paolo Portoghesi: Progetti e disegni 1949–1979 / Paolo Portoghesi: Projects and Drawings 1949–1979* (Rome: Rizzoli, 1979).

39 Mario Pisani ed., *Il punto su . . . Paolo Portoghesi* (Rome: Gangemi, 1993).

40 These sources are accessible through the historical archives of Italian national newspapers such as *Corriere della Sera*, *La Repubblica* and *L'Unità*.

41 On Portoghesi as a photographer, see Deborah Fausch, 'Robert Venturi's and Paolo Portoghesi's photographs of Rome', *Daidalos* 66 (1997): 76–83; and Benjamin Chavardès, 'La photographie critique au service d'une critique opératoire dans l'œuvre de Paolo Portoghesi', *Livraisons de l'histoire de l'architecture* 31 (2016): 23–37.

42 Pommer, 'Bernardo Vittone, un architetto tra illuminismo e rococò by Paolo Portoghesi'.

43 For the sketches of Paolo Portoghesi, we have also consulted Fabrizio Dal Col, *Paolo Portoghesi: Disegni 1949–2003* (Milan: Motta Editore, 2003).

44 Some of these materials are published in *A colloquio con Paolo Portoghesi*, ed. Petra Bernitsa and Enrico Valeriani (Rome: Gangemi, 2014).

45 See Szacka, *Exhibiting the Postmodern*.

46 Mary McLeod, 'Architecture and Politics in the Reagan Era: From Postmodernism to Deconstructivism', *Assemblage* 8 (February 1989): 22–59.

47 Paolo Portoghesi, *Le inibizioni dell'architettura moderna* (Rome-Bari: Laterza, 1974), 62.

48 Paolo Portoghesi, in Biraghi et al., eds., *Italia 60/70*, 261.

49 Paolo Portoghesi, in conversation with the authors, 8 September 2020.

50 Ibid.

51 Portoghesi, *Le inibizioni dell'architettura moderna*, 33.

52 Paolo Portoghesi, *Paolo Portoghesi: Di Francesco Borromini*, limited edition, kept in Portoghesi's personal archive, Calcata, Rome. Translation by the authors.

53 Ibid.

54 Portoghesi, *Le inibizioni dell'architettura moderna*, 40.

55 Telemaco Portoghesi Tuzi and Grazia Tuzi, *Quando si faceva la Costituzione* (Milan: Il Saggiatore, 2011).

56 Portoghesi, *Roma/amoR*, 38.

57 The Circolo Romano del Cinema was established in 1944, immediately after the liberation of Rome, first as the Associazione Culturale Cinematografica Italiana. Opened in 1930 in Piazza Barberini, the Cinema Barberini near the Triton fountain by Bernini was designed by architect Marcello Piacentini.

58 Paolo Portoghesi, in coversation with the authors, 2 October 2020.

59 The Facoltà di Architettura della Sapienza – Università di Rome was founded in 1919, the same year as the Bauhaus in Weimar.

60 Paolo Portoghesi in conversation with Silvia Micheli, February 25, 2011.

61 Portoghesi, *Roma/amoR*, 44.

62 See Enrico Valeriani, 'Il futuro dell'architettura a un cuore antico', in Bernitsa and Valeriani, eds., *A Colloquio con Paolo Portoghesi*, 7.

63 The magazine was published bi-monthly, ceased publication in 1979 but resumed in 2019.

64 Paolo Portoghesi, *L'opera del Borromini per l'altare maggiore della Chiesa di San Paolo a Bologna*, Rome, Istituto Poligrafico dello Stato – Libreria dello Stato, 1954.

65 For a survey of Portoghesi's early career design work see, *Paolo Portoghesi*, ed. Giancarlo Priori (Bologna: Zanichelli, 1985).

Chapter 1

1 In January 1980 Mendini initiated 'a progressive transformation of [the magazine's] content and graphics' which included a change in the design of its covers. During the first phase (1980–82; issues 602–23), the *Domus* covers featured 'protagonists', shifting the reader's interest from buildings to their authors. The second phase (from 1982) included a series of covers showing fashion models, architects, artists and intellectuals 'wearing branded dresses in settings furnished with contemporary objects'. On the role of 1980s *Domus* covers in the making of postmodern architecture, see Silvia Micheli, 'Alessandro Mendini, *Domus* and the Postmodern Vision (1979–1985)', in *Mediated Messages: Periodicals, Exhibitions and the Shaping of Postmodern Architecture*, eds. Véronique Patteeuw and Léa-Catherine Szacka (New York: Bloomsbury, 2018), 121–40.

2   The inspiration for this photograph might have been one of the posters for the film *Cabaret*, starring Liza Minnelli, directed by Bob Fosse and released in 1972.
3   Micheli, 'Alessandro Mendini, *Domus* and the Postmodern Vision', 121–40.
4   See Silvia Micheli and Léa-Catherine Szacka, 'Paolo Portoghesi and the Postmodern Project', in *Re-Framing Identities: Architecture's Turn to History, 1970–1990*, ed. Ákos Moravánszky and Torsten Lange (Basel: Birkäuser, 2017), 209–19.
5   Pippo Ciorra in conversation with the authors, videoconference, 2 November 2020.
6   Alessandro Mendini, 'Colloquio con Paolo Portoghesi', *Domus* 652 (July 1984): 1.
7   Charles Jencks, *The Story of Postmodernism* (London: Wiley, 2011), 75.
8   Paolo Portoghesi, *I nuovi architetti italiani*, ed. Giovanna Massobrio (Rome-Bari: Laterza, 1985).
9   Paolo Portoghesi and Bruno Zevi. 'Is Postmodern Architecture Serious? Paolo Portoghesi and Bruno Zevi in Conversation', *Architectural Design* 52, nos. 1–2 (1982): 20–21.
10 Mary McLeod, 'Frampton in Frame', *Architecture Today*, accessed 24 January 2023, https://architecturetoday.co.uk/frampton-in-frame/.
11 Mendini, 'Colloquio con Paolo Portoghesi'.
12 'Is Postmodern Architecture Serious?', *Architectural Design*.
13 Paolo Portoghesi, 'La moda del Postmodern', *Corriere della Sera*, 26 June 1983, 11.
14 As clarified by Jencks, 'The responsibility for coining this sinful term goes to Joseph Hudnut. . . . Except for an occasional slip here and there, by Philip Johnson or Nicolaus Pevsner, it was not used until my own writing on the subject, which started in 1975': Charles Jencks, 'Postmodern and Late Modern: The Essential Definitions', *Chicago Review* 35, no. 4 (1987): 31–58, here 33.
15 Gillo Dorfles, 'Nel design italiano molti anticipatori', *Corriere della Sera*, 26 June 1983, 12. During the 1980s Dorfles often defended postmodern architecture and design in the pages of *Corriere della Sera*.
16 Jameson, *Postmodernism: Or, the Cultural Logic of Late Capitalism*.
17 Paolo Portoghesi, 'Dopo l'architettura postmoderna', in *Dopo l'architettura postmoderna*, conference proceedings, Bissano 4–5 September 1981, ed. L. Ferrario (Rome: Kappa, 1983), 17–23.
18 Robert Dombroski and Ross Miller, 'Postmodern Rhetoric: Calvino's "Le città invisibili" and Architecture', in 'Italy 1991: The Modern and the Postmodern', special issue, *Annali d'Italianistica* 9 (1991): 230–41.
19 Jean-François Lyotard, *The Postmodern Condition* (Minneapolis: University of Minnesota Press, 1984), 15. First published in French in 1979.
20 Paolo Portoghesi, interview with the Léa-Catherine Szacka, Portoghesi's studio, Calcata, 27 March 2008.
21 Paolo Portoghesi, 'Il lievito della memoria', in *Dal Futurismo al futuro possibile dell'architettura contemporanea* (Milan: Skira, 2002), 70–81.
22 Marco Biraghi, *Project of Crisis: Manfredo Tafuri and Contemporary Architecture* (Cambridge, MA: The MIT Press, 2013), xi.
23 See, *La critica operativa e l'architettura*, ed. Luca Monica (Milan: Unicopli, 2002).
24 Manfredo Tafuri, *Teorie e storia dell'architettura* (Bari: Laterza, 1968), 161.

25 Andrew Leach, *Manfredo Tafuri: Choosing History* (Ghent: A&S Books, 2007), 250.
26 Manfredo Tafuri, *The Sphere and the Labyrinth: Avant-gardes and Architecture from Piranesi to the 1970s* (Cambridge, MA: MIT Press, 1987), 13. The book was first released in Italian in 1980.
27 Aldo Rossi, *A Scientific Autobiography*,(Cambridge, Mass.: MIT Press, 1981): 41.
28 Ibidem, 54.
29 Pier Vittorio Aureli, *The Project of Autonomy: Politics and Architecture Within and Against Capitalism* (Princeton, NJ: Princeton Architectural Press, 2008).
30 Antonio Monestiroli, *L'Architettura della realtà* (Milan: CLUP, 1979).
31 Luciano Patetta in discussion with the authors, Patetta's studio, Milan, 23 February 2015.
32 Paolo Portoghesi, 'Discorso preliminare', *Dizionario enciclopedico di architettura e urbanismo*, ed. Paolo Portoghesi, 6 vols. (Rome: Istituto Editoriale Romano, 1968), ix.
33 Ibid.
34 Portoghesi, ed., *Dizionario enciclopedico di architettura e urbanismo*.
35 Pisani ed., *Il punto su . . . Paolo Portoghesi*, 73.
36 Paolo Portoghesi in discussion with the authors, Piazza della Piscinula, 25 February 2015.
37 Ibid.
38 See Rossella Farina, ed., 'Indice generale delle annate 1969–1976', special issue, *Controspazio* 5–6, 1978.
39 Paolo Portoghesi in discussion with the authors, Piazza della Piscinula, 25 February 2015.
40 On Rossi's use of the concept of analogy see Léa-Catherine Szacka, 'Città Analoga: Aldo Rossi's Visual Theory on Display', in *Terms of Appropriation: Modern Architecture and Global Exchange*, ed. Ana Miljački and Amanda Reeser Lawrence (London: Routledge: 263–77).
41 Ezio Bonfanti graduated in 1963 at the Politecnico di Milano. He was a tutor in courses led by Ernesto Nathan Rogers and Paolo Portoghesi. He worked as an editor and author, first for *Casabella-continuità* and then for *Controspazio*.
42 Aldo Rossi's letter to Ezio Bonfanti written on 3 January 1971, published in Ezio Bonfanti, *Nuovo e moderno in architettura*, Marco Biraghi and Michelangelo Sabatini eds., (Milan: Bruno Mondadori, 2001), 367–69. See also, Paolo Portoghesi, 'La possibilità del passato', *Casabella* 694 (2001): 91–92.
43 Ibid.
44 Manfredo Tafuri, *Storia dell'architettura italiana* (Turin: Einaudi, 1986): 166–171.
45 Micha Bandini, 'Aldo Rossi', *AA Files* 1 (Winter 1981–82): 105–11.
46 See Sebastiano Fabbrini, *The State of Architecture: Aldo Rossi and the Tools of Internationalization* (Padua: Il Poligrafo, 2020).
47 Rafael Moneo, 'Aldo Rossi: The Idea of Architecture and the Modena Cemetery', *Oppositions* 5 (1976): 1–21.
48 Biraghi and Micheli, *Storia dell'architettura italiana*, 93–94.

49 Paolo Portoghesi, 'Concorso per il Cimitero di San Cataldo a Modena: La città dei vivi e la città dei morti', *Controspazio* 10 (1972): 2–3.
50 The jury included Carlo Melograni, Glauco Gresleri and Pier Luigi Cervellati too.
51 The exhibition was open from 6 October to 4 November 1979.
52 Silvia Micheli, 'Rossi between Portoghesi and Tafuri', in *Aldo Rossi: The Architecture and Art of the Analogous City*, Daniel Sherer ed., Princeton: Princeton University Press, 2021, Section 4.2.
53 Paolo Portoghesi, in coversation with the authors, 8 September 2020.
54 As Scaparro himself remarked in an interview recorded during the opening of the exhibition *La Biennale di Venezia 1979–1980. The Theatre of the World 'singular building'. Tribute to Aldo Rossi*, curated by Maurizio Scaparro, 10 February–31 July 2010, Ca' Giustinian, Venice, accessed 8 March 2022, https://www.youtube.com/watch?v=-JfPYSEAHbI.
55 Aaron Levy and William Menking, *Architecture on Display: On the History of the Venice Biennale of Architecture* (London: AA Publications, 2010), 40.
56 Portoghesi, *Roma/amoR*, 90.
57 Szacka, *Exhibiting the Postmodern*, 114.
58 Rossi underlined this conceptual difference in the presentation of his Teatro in the exhibition catalogue Venezia e lo Spazio scenico, La Biennale, Venezia 6 ottobre–4 novembre 1979, Mostra a Palazzo Grassi (Venice: La Biennale), 110.
59 Biraghi and Micheli, *Storia dell'architettura italiana*, 94.
60 Barbara Radice, ed., *Elogio del banale/Praise of the banal* (Turin–Milan: Lo studio forma-Alchimia, 1980), 6.
61 Paolo Portoghesi, in coversation with the authors, 8 September 2020.
62 Alessandro Mendini, 'Manifesto di Alchimia' (1984), Atelier Mendini Online Digital Archive.
63 Alessandro Mendini in conversation with Silvia Micheli, Via Sannio 24, Milan, February 2015.
64 Micheli, 'Alessandro Mendini, *Domus* and the Postmodern Vision', 123.
65 See 'L'oggetto banale', accessed 11 November 2022, francoraggi.com/project/biennale-venezia-loggetto-banale/.
66 Paolo Portoghesi, in conversation with the authors, 8 September 2020.
67 Radice, ed., *Elogio del Banale*, 14.
68 Silvia Micheli and Lorenzo Ciccarelli, 'The International Call: Italian Design Culture, Politics and Economics at the 1972 MoMA Exhibition and beyond', in *Italian Imprints* eds. Denise Costanzo and Andrew Leach (London: Bloomsbury, 2022), 522–53.
69 Alessandro Mendini, 'Per un'architettura banale' (1979), Atelier Mendini Online Digital Archive.
70 Established in New York in 1978, Max Protetch Gallery was renowned for showing and promoting architectural drawings. Since that time, Protetch has been an advocate of Italian design, introducing a crucial topic for our argument: the agency of art galleries and showrooms in the dissemination of postmodern Italian design and architecture.
71 Leach, *Manfredo Tafuri: Choosing History*, 4.

72 Ibid., 7.
73 Manfredo Tafuri, *L'architettura del Manierismo nel Cinquecento europeo* (Rome: Officina, 1966).
74 Paolo Portoghesi, *Roma barocca* (Rome: Bestetti, 1966). Tafuri's review of Portoghesi's *Roma barocca* appeared in *Paese Sera*, 20 January 1967.
75 Portoghesi, *Roma/amoR*, 73.
76 Leach, *Manfredo Tafuri: Choosing History*, 11.
77 The PSIUP (Italian Socialist Proletariat Unity Party) was formed on 12 January 1964 by a leftist section of the Italian Socialist Party (PSI). It was composed of people who felt that the PSI should make alliance with the Partito communista Italiano (PCI) rather than with the Democrazia Christiana (DC). See Leach, *Manfredo Tafuri: Choosing History*, 13.
78 Ibid., 15.
79 Micheli, Silvia and Léa-Catherine Szacka, 'Paolo's Triangolo', *AA Files 72* (2016): 98–106.
80 Bruno Zevi, letter to Paolo Portoghesi, 10 July 1978, Fondazione Bruno Zevi.
81 Paolo Portoghesi in conversation with the authors, 8 September 2020.
82 James S. Ackerman, 'In memoriam: Manfredo Tafuri, 1935–1994', *Journal of the Society of Architectural Historians* 53 (June 1994): 137–38.
83 Ibid.
84 Manfredo Tafuri, 'Per una critica dell'ideologia architettonica', *Contropiano* 1 (1969): 31–79. The essay was translated as 'Towards a Critique of Architectural Ideology', in *Architecture Theory Since 1968*, ed. K. Michael Hays (Cambridge, MA: The MIT Press, 1998), 6–35. Tafuri's original article later formed the basis of his book *Progetto e Utopia* (Rome-Bari: Laterza, 1973), which itself was translated as *Architecture and Utopia: Design and Capitalist Development* (Cambridge, MA: The MIT Press, 1976).
85 Tafuri, 'Per una critica dell'ideologia architettonica', 31–79.
86 Paolo Portoghesi, 'Editoriale', *Controspazio* 1 (1969): 7.
87 Paolo Portoghesi, 'Autopsia o vivisezione dell'architettura?', *Controspazio* 6 (1969): 5–7.
88 See Paolo Portoghesi in Biraghi et al., eds., *Italia 60/70*, 267.
89 Ibid.
90 Paolo Portoghesi, *Roma/amoR*, 73.
91 Ibid.
92 Ibid.
93 Manfredo Tafuri, 'L'éphémère est éternel. Aldo Rossi a Venezia', *Domus* 602 (1980): 7–11.
94 Manfredo Tafuri, *History of Italian Architecture*, 59, 79.
95 Ibid., 187.
96 Ibid., 186.
97 Ibid.
98 See Bruno Zevi, *Zevi su Zevi: Architettura come profezia* (Venice: Marsilio, 1993), 176–79; see also Roberto Dulio, *Introduzione a Bruno Zevi* (Rome: Laterza 2008), 127–28.

99 See Andrew Leach, *Manfredo Tafuri: Choosing History* (Ghent: A&S/Books, 2007), 33–39.
100 Paolo Portoghesi, in conversation with the authors, Piazza della Piscinula, Rome, 25 February 2015.
101 See Jean-Louis Cohen, *La coupure entre architectes et intellectuels, ou les enseignements de l'Italophilie* (Paris: Éditions Ardaga, 1984).
102 *L'Architecture d'Aujourd'hui*, 181, September–October 1975, curated by Manfredo Tafuri, Carlo Aymonino, Vittorio De Feo, Mario Manieri Elia, Francesco Dal Co etc.
103 On this topic, see Denise R. Costanzo, '"I Will Try My Best to Make It Worth It": Robert Venturi's Road to Rome', *Journal of Architectural Education* 70, no. 2 (2016): 269–83.
104 For more on this exhibition see, for example, Felicity Scott, *Architecture or Techno-Utopia: Politics after Modernism* (Cambridge, MA: The MIT Press, 2010); or Ingrid Halland-Rashidi, '(Re)working the Past, (Dis)playing the Future. Italy: New Domestic Landscape at MoMA, 1972', in *Proceedings of DRS2016 International Conference: Future–Focused Thinking*, 27–30 June, Brighton, United Kingdom, Design Research Society.
105 Paolo Fossati, *Il design in Italia, 1945–1972* (Turin: Einaudi, 1972).
106 Micheli and Ciccarelli, 'The International Call'.
107 Christian Norberg-Schulz became professor at Yale University in 1965 and served as dean of the Oslo School of Architecture from 1966 to 1992. In 1974 he was also a visiting professor at MIT. In 1979 he published his influential book, *Genius Loci: Towards a Phenomenology of Architecture*.
108 Jorge Otero-Pailos, *Architecture's Historical Turn: Phenomenology and the Rise of the Postmodern* (Minneapolis: University of Minnesota Press, 2010), 146.
109 Christian Norberg-Schulz, 'Casa Baldi, Rome', *ByggeKunst* 8 (1963): 205–11. See also Beata Labuhn, 'Dientzenhofer as an Untimely Teacher of Norberg-Schulz and his Students. Norberg-Schulz´s Research and Teachings on Bohemian Baroque, ca. 1960-1980', paper presented at the Seventh International Conference EAHN, Madrid, 23 June 2022.
110 In the 1970s, Norberg-Schulz wrote two books on the baroque: *Architettura Barocca* (Milan: Electa, 1971; in English: Baroque *Architecture (History of World Architecture)*, New York: Harry N. Abrams, 1971) and *Architettura Tardobarroca* (Milan: Electa, 1972).
111 Anna Ulrikke Andersen, *Following Norberg-Schulz* (London: Bloomsbury, 2021).
112 Ibid., 114.
113 Beata Labuhn, lecture 'Dientzenhofer as Untimely Teacher: Revisiting Christian Norberg-Schulz´s Research on- and Teaching of Bohemian Baroque, ca. 1960–1980', session S17 – Untimely Teachers. Recovering Postmodernism´s Anachronic Pedagogies, Seventh International Conference of the European Architectural History Network (Madrid, June 18, 2022).
114 In 1974, Norberg-Schulz even visited Jordan with Portoghesi and Vittorio Gigliotti.
115 For more on *Roma Interrotta* see Gabriele Mastrigli, 'The Cage of Imagination: Notes on "Roma Interrotta"', *Log* 32 (Fall 2014): 140–47. See also, Léa-Catherine Szacka, 'Roma Interrotta: Postmodern Rome as the Source of Fragmented Narratives', in

Rome, Postmodern Narratives of a Cityscape, ed. Dominic Holdaway and Filippo Trentin (London: Pickering and Chatto, 2013), 155–69.

116 The twelve architects were: Piero Sartogo (Italy), Costantino Dardi (Italy), Antoine Grumbach (France), James Stirling (UK), Paolo Portoghesi (Italy), Romaldo Giurgola (Italy/Australia), Robert Venturi (US), Colin Rowe (UK), Michael Graves (US), Rob Krier (LX), Aldo Rossi (Italy) and Leon Krier (UK). The *Roma Interrotta* exhibition then travelled to New York (Cooper Hewitt Museum); Mexico City; London (the Architectural Association); Toronto (Istituto Italiano di Cultura); Zurich (Institut für Geschichte und Theorie der Architektur); Bilbao (Collegio Official de Arcuitectos Vasco-Navarro); São Paulo (São Paulo Art Biennial); Paris (Centre Georges Pompidou) and Barcelona (Centro de Cultura Contemporanea).

117 *Roma Interrotta* (Rome: Incontri Internazionali d'Arte/Officina edizioni, 1978): 98–117.

118 This opposition towards the biennale's curatorial team would lead Frampton to develop his version of 'critical regionalism'. See Léa-Catherine Szacka, 'Criticism from Within: Kenneth Frampton and the Retreat from Postmodernism' in *OASE 97*: 109–20.

119 Letter from Paolo Portoghesi to Charles Jencks, 20 March 1979, found in Jencks's personal archive, Jencks Foundation. The letter followed Portoghesi's visit to London where he was hosted by Jencks.

120 Charles Jencks, 'The Rise of Post-Modern Architecture', *Architectural Association Quarterly* 7, no. 4 (October/December 1975): 3–14.

121 For more on this, See Léa-Catherine Szacka, 'Writing "from the Battlefield": Charles Jencks and The Language of Post-Modern Architecture', Jencks Foundation, accessed 26 January 2022, https://www.jencksfoundation.org/explore/text/writing-from-the-battlefield-charles-jencks-and-the-language-of-post-modern-architecture.

122 Casa Baldi was published in Part Three called 'Post-Modern Architecture', under the subsection 'Historicism, the beginning of PM' and on the same page as Lubetkin and Tecton's Highpoint II in Highgate (1938) as well as Franco Albini and Franca Helg's Rinascente Department Store in Rome (1957–62). See Charles Jencks, *The Language of Post-Modern Architecture*, 2nd ed. (London: Academy Editions, 1978), 81.

123 Paolo Portoghesi in discussion with the authors, 8 September 2020.

124 Beatriz Colomina, 'With, or without you: The ghosts of modern architecture', in *Modern Women*, ed. Cornelia Butler, Alexandra Schwartz (New York: The Museum of Modern Art, 2010), 218.

125 Portoghesi, *Roma/amoR*, 80.

126 See the professional CV of Giovanna Massobrio, kept at MAXXI, Rome. Collezione MAXXI Architettura/Fondo Paolo Portoghesi, which contains around forty projects between 1971 and 2006.

127 As an example, journalist Natalia Aspesi, when reporting from the opening of the 42nd edition of the Venice Film Festival in 1985, described Massobrio as: 'the beautiful wife of the President of the Biennale', wearing 'a Chanel dress embroidered with columns, in honour of her husband'. Natalia Aspesi, 'Il Lido si accende comincia la festa', *La Repubblica*, 27 August 1985.

128 Petra Berintsa and Enrico Valeriani, *A colloquio con Paolo Portoghesi* (Rome: Gangemi, 2014), 16.

129 The first book released by the couple was *La seggiola di Vienna: Storia dei mobili in legno curvato* (Turin: Martano, 1975). This was followed by *Album del Liberty* (1975), a richly illustrated book that articulates the phenomenon of Liberty through images (many unpublished). Then, they co-edited three albums about Liberty, respectively: *Album degli anni Venti* (1976), *Album degli anni Cinquanta* (1977) and *Album degli anni Trenta* (1978), books in which, as observed in *Roma/amoR*, 'the illustrations form a continuous story, and the texts suggest possible interpretations and connections with society and the events of the time',
101. In 1980, they published a book on Casa Thonet, and finally *La donna Liberty* (1983). All books, except for the first, were published by Rome- and Bari-based Laterza.

130 Paolo Portoghesi, 'Apollodoro', *Eupalino* 8 (1987): 30.

131 Ibid., 31.

132 *Lo Studiolo di Francesco I dei Medici e il suo doppio*, Giovanna Massobrio ed. (Rome: Apollodoro Edizioni, 1986).

133 Irene Bignardi, 'Un cocomero tricolore', *La Repubblica*, 2 December 1987.

134 See letter written by Massobrio to Aldo Rossi, Aldo Rossi Papers, Getty Research Institute, Special Collections.

135 Both women were close friends of Massobrio. See the video of the opening of the gallery edited by Furio Moretti and released by the private TV channel GBR, accessed 25 January 2022, https://www.youtube.com/watch?v=Y8X2PVDmzzc. During the 1980s, GBR was closely associated with the PSI.

136 Vincent Scully, 'How things got to be the way they are now', Portoghesi, Paolo, Vincent Scully, Charles Jencks, and Christian Norberg-Schulz. *The Presence of the Past: First International Exhibition of Architecture – Venice Biennale 80*. London: Academy Edition, 1981. Scully's perception of change in the cultural relationships between Europe and America had been anticipated by Peter Eisenman during the debate 'Quale Movimento Moderno' at the 1976 Venice Biennale. See Léa-Catherine Szacka, 'Debates on Display: Europa-America at the 1976 Biennale', in *Place and Displacement: Exhibiting Architecture*, ed. Thordis Arrhenius, Mari Lending, Wallis Miller and Jérémie Michael McGowan (Zurich: Lars Müller), 106.

Chapter 2

1 Portoghesi, *Roma/amoR*, 97. Also, Paolo Portoghesi in conversation with the authors, December 2020.

2 The portrait is the engraving in Giannini, Opera… of 1972 and in the *Opus Architectonicum* of 1725. See Paolo Portoghesi, 'An Unknown Portrait of Borromini', *The Burlington Magazine* 109, no. 777 (1967): 709–18.

3 Paolo Portoghesi, *After Modern Architecture* (New York: Rizzoli, 1982), 90.

4 Portoghesi, *Le inibizioni dell'architettura moderna*, 49.

5 Portoghesi, *Roma/amoR*, 49–50.

6   Portoghesi, *Le inibizioni dell'architettura moderna*, 49. As then Portoghesi specified: 'Ridolfi did not teach in the Faculty of Architecture, but in a professional school. When I was in the Faculty of Architecture, I greatly despised the professors before Quaroni arrived. Almost all of them were exponents of fascist architecture. My love for Ridolfi was born as a protest against these professors who did not teach anything. The only one I loved very much was Vincenzo Fasolo, who was the professor of the history of architecture. At one point I called Ridolfi, who had his studio in what is called the "Palazzo delle Streghe", a building built by him. I remember meeting him with Wolfgang Frankl; it was an exciting meeting. I also offered to go and work at his studio, but he said no. He didn't need collaborators. He was a great teacher.' Paolo Portoghesi, videoconference with the authors, 8 September 2020.

7   Portoghesi, *Roma/amoR*, 50.

8   In the catalogue of the exhibition, it is specified that: 'The organizers intended to complete the section with a show of Carlo Scarpa's drawings, but a hurried and reductive effort was discouraged for reasons of organization, and also because a large retrospective of Scarpa's work would be held in 1982.' Paolo Portoghesi, 'The End of Prohibitionism' in *The Presence of the Past: First International Exhibition of Architecture – Venice Biennale 80*, eds. Paolo Portoghesi, Vincent Scully, Charles Jencks and Christian Norberg-Schulz (London: Academy Editions, 1981), 12.

9   Portoghesi et al., eds., *The Presence of the Past*, 11.

10 Ibid, 12.

11 This educational approach was typical of the working group at the Milan-based office of *Casabella-continuità*, directed between 1953 and 1964 by Rogers. Between the end of the 1950s and mid-1960s, *Casabella-continuità* edited some monographic issues dedicated to the recovery of the lessons of the Modern Movement. See, for example, the issues on Frank Lloyd Wright (227, 1959); Adolf Loos (233, 1959); Henry van de Velde (237, 1960); Peter Behrens (240, 1960). Also, see specific articles published in the same journal by Rogers's pupils on subjects including Aldo Rossi on German architecture (235, 1960), Peter Behrens and the problem of modern dwelling (240, 1960) and Le Corbusier and the Tourette convent (246, 1960); Giorgio Grassi on Hendrik Petrus Berlage (249, 1961); Guido Canella on Soviet architecture (262, 1962) and Silvano Tintori on Tony Garnier as technician and politician of the city (255, 1961), to mention the most renowned.

12 Portoghesi began teaching in 1958 as assistant professor in the Scuola Superiore per il Restauro dei Monumenti, Università degli Studi di Roma La Sapienza until 1962, and as assistant professor of Italian Literature until 1967. He then took the role of full professor of the history of architecture at the Faculty of Architecture of the Politecnico di Milano from 1967 to 1977, where he also served as dean between 1968 and 1976 (with a short interruption due to the years of the protests). From 1977 to 1994 Portoghesi was full professor of the history of Architecture in the Faculty of Architecture at La Sapienza.

13 'I disegni tecnici di Leonardo', *Civiltà delle macchine* 1 (1955): 6–24.

14 Leon Battista Alberti, *De re aedificatoria*, ed. Giovanni Orlandi and Paolo Portoghesi (Milan: Il Polifilo, 1966).

15 Paolo Portoghesi and Bruno Zevi, eds., *Michelangiolo architetto* (Turin: Einaudi, 1964).

16 Paolo Portoghesi and Franco Borsi, *Victor Horta*, with a preface by Jean Delhaye (Rome: Edizioni del Tritone, 1969).

17 See Paolo Portoghesi, 'La ricerca continua', in *Controspazio* (December 1975): 78. For a complete presentation of the office work, see Christian Norberg-Schulz, ed., *Architetture di Paolo Portoghesi e Vittorio Gigliotti* (Rome: Officina Edizioni, 1982). Vittorio Gigliotti received his degree in engineering in Naples in 1947. In 1960, he founded an office with Bruno Zevi and in 1964 he started his collaboration with Portoghesi.

18 Jorge Otero-Pailos, 'Photo[historio]graphy: Christian Norberg-Schulz's Demotion of Textual History', *Journal of the Society of Architectural Historians* 66, no. 2 (2007): 220–41.

19 Paolo Portoghesi, *Borromini nella cultura europea* (Milan: Officina edizioni, 1964), vii.

20 Portoghesi stated his interest in Argan's interpretative thesis on baroque architecture and Borromini in 'Intervento di P. Portoghesi sulla relazione di B. Zevi', 536.

21 American art historian and educator Joseph Connors served as director of the American Academy in Rome between 1988 and 1992.

22 Robert Venturi, *Complexity and Contradiction in Architecture* (New York: The Museum of Modern Art, 1966).

23 At the time of writing *Guarino Guarini*, Portoghesi was also preparing significant articles on Borromini, Massobrio et al., *Paolo Portoghesi architetto*, 293.

24 On Vittone, see Paolo Portoghesi, *Bernardo Vittone. Un architetto tra illuminismo e Rococò* (Rome: Edizioni dell'Elefante, 1966).

25 Published with Electa, in the series Astra-Arengarium directed by Genoa-based architect Mario Labò.

26 Portoghesi, *Le inibizioni dell'architettura moderna*, 85.

27 Paolo Portoghesi, in conversation with the authors, videoconference in December 2020.

28 Portoghesi, *Le inibizioni dell'architettura moderna*, 74–75.

29 See Argan's endorsement on the back cover of *Roma barocca*.

30 Franco Borsi and Paolo Portoghesi, *Victor Horta*, 333.

31 *Casabella-continuità*, 215, 1957, 3–4.

32 Ibid.

33 From 1953 to 1964, the Milanese architect Ernesto Nathan Rogers edited the architectural journal *Casabella-continuità*. The first series of his impassioned editorials, published between 1953 and 1958, were collected in his book *Esperienza dell'architettura* (Turin: Einaudi, 1958). The third section of the book, 'Tradizione e architettura moderna', deals with the problem of the relationship between new architecture and the pre-existing context, theorizing a revolutionary design method, which Rogers names as the principle of the *preesistenze ambientali*. This idea had a deep influence on generations of Italian architects.

34 Moschini, *Paolo Portoghesi. Progetti e disegni*, 9.

35 *Comunità* was a cultural journal founded by Adriano Olivetti and was in circulation between 1946 and 1960, the year he died.

36 Paolo Portoghesi, 'Dal Neorealismo al Neoliberty', *Comunità* 65 (1958): 67.

37 For the quarrel with Banham, see also Maurizio Sabini, *Ernesto Nathan Rogers: The Modern Architect as Public Intellectual* (London: Bloomsbury, 2021), 141–45, and

Benjamin Chavardès in 'From Neoliberty to Postmodernism', in *Post-war Architecture between Italy and the UK*.

38 Reyner Banham, 'Neoliberty. The Italian Retreat from Modern Architecture', *The Architectural Review* 747 (April 1959): 231–35.

39 Ibid.

40 Paolo Portoghesi, 'Uno studioso inglese giudica l'architettura italiana', *Comunitá* 72 (1959): 68.

41 Ibid.

42 Ernesto Nathan Rogers, 'L'evoluzione dell'architettura. Risposta al custode dei frigidaires', *Casabella-continuità* 228 (June 1959): 2–4.

43 Portoghesi, *Le inibizioni dell'architettura moderna*, 27.

44 Manfredo Tafuri, *Theories and History of Architecture* (London: Granada, 1980), 51.

45 Portoghesi, 'Il lievito della memoria', in Franco Purini and Livio Sacchi, eds. *Dal futurismo al futuro possibile nell'architettura italiana contemporanea* [From Futurism to the Possible Future in Contemporary Italian Architecture] (Milan: Skira, 2002), 70–81.

46 See the debate triggered by the report 'Architettura italiana. 6 domande', *Casabella-continuità* 251 (1961): 3–32.

47 Monica, ed., *La critica operativa e l'architettura*.

48 Dulio, *Introduzione a Bruno Zevi*, 78.

49 Andrew Leach, 'Modern Architecture and the Actualisation of History: Bruno Zevi and Michelangiolo Architetto', in *History in Practice*, 25th International Conference of the Society of Architectural Historians Australia and New Zealand, Geelong, 2008, 6.

50 Alberto Franchini, 'L'Istituto Universitario di Architettura di Venezia come università produttiva', in *Bruno Zevi e la didattica dell'architettura*, ed. Piero Ostilio Rossi, with Francesca Romana Castelli, Luca Porqueddu, Gianpaola Spirito (Macerata: Quodlibet, 2019), 143–54.

51 Letter from Zevi to Portoghesi, Fondazione Bruno Zevi.

52 Piero Ostilio Rossi, 'Le proposte di riforma del Biennio 1964–1965', in *Bruno Zevi e la didattica dell'architettura*, 189–207.

53 Paolo Portoghesi, *Roma/amoR*, 56.

54 It was a significant show in a long list of other cultural initiatives dedicated to the anniversary. 'Da oggi le celebrazioni del 400° di Michelangiolo', *L'Unità*, 18 February 1964, 3.

55 Leach, 'Modern Architecture and the Actualisation of History', 9.

56 Bruno Zevi, 'Introduzione', in *Michelangiolo architetto*, ed. Paolo Portoghesi and Bruno Zevi (Turin: Einaudi 1964), 15.

57 For a detailed description of the design of the exhibition, see Benjamin Chavardès, *L'Italie post-moderne: Paolo Portoghesi, architecte, théoricien, historien* (Rennes: Presses Universitaires de Rennes, 2022), 49–50.

58 Carmen Andriani, 'Bruno Zevi. Pensiero e Azione', in *Bruno Zevi e la didattica dell'architettura*, 17–24.

59 Ibid.

60 The models are documented in the Fondazione Bruno Zevi.

61 Massobrio et al., *Paolo Portoghesi architetto*, 37.

62 Roberto Dulio, 'Le affinità elettive. Moretti e Zevi', in *Luigi Moretti, razionalismo e trasgressività tra barocco e informale*, ed. Bruno Reichlin, Leitizia Tedeschi (Electa: Milano, 2010), 437–41. On the influence of Moretti on Zevi regarding the production of interpretative models, see Caterina Padoa Schioppa, 'I diagrammi spaziali su Michelangelo', in *Bruno Zevi e la didattica dell'architettura*, 155–65.

63 Tiffany Lynn Hunt, 'Michelangelo in 1964: The Critical Model as Dialectical Image in Bruno Zevi's Renaissance Architecture', *Architectural Theory Review* 24, no. 2 (2020): 144–63.

64 Andriani, 'Bruno Zevi. Pensiero e Azione', in *Bruno Zevi e la didattica dell'architettura*, 17–24.

65 Paolo Portoghesi, *Roma/amoR*, 58.

66 Ibid.

67 Ibid.

68 Paolo Portoghesi ed., *Disegni di Francesco Borromini* (Rome: De Luca Editori d'arte, 1967).

69 See the discussion between Zevi and Portoghesi in *Studi sul Borromini*, vol. 1 (Rome: Accademia nazionale di San Luca, 1967), 507–42. See also Massobrio et al., *Paolo Portoghesi: architetto*, 37–39.

70 Portoghesi, 'Intervento di P. Portoghesi sulla relazione di B. Zevi', 531.

71 Portoghesi, *Le inibizioni dell'architettura moderna*, 76–80.

72 Massobrio et al., *Paolo Portoghesi architetto*, 38.

73 See the discussion between Zevi and Portoghesi in *Studi sul Borromini*, vol. 1 (Rome: Accademia nazionale di San Luca, 1967), 507–42. See also Massobrio et al., *Paolo Portoghesi architetto*, 37–39.

74 Massobrio et al., *Paolo Portoghesi architetto*, 38.

75 Ibid., 38.

76 Paolo Portoghesi, *Borromini: Architettura come linguaggio* (Milan: Electa, 1967).

77 For the review of the exhibition, see Corrado Verga, 'La mostra critica delle opere Borrominiane', *Arte Lombarda* 13, no. 1 (Spring, 1968): 137–39.

78 See letter written by Zevi to Portoghesi, 1978, Fondazione Bruno Zevi.

79 Maristella Casciato, 'The Italian Mosaic: The Architect as Historian', *Journal of the Society of Architectural Historians* 62, no. 1 (March 2003): 92–101.

80 Frédéric Migayrou, ed., *La Tendenza: Architectures Italiennes 1965-1985* (Paris: Centre Pompidou, 2012), see introduction, 11–23.

81 Moschini, *Paolo Portoghesi: Progetti e disegni*, 15.

82 Ibid., 18.

83 Pommer, 'Bernardo Vittone, un architetto tra illuminismo e rococò by Paolo Portoghesi'.

84 Portoghesi, *Bernardo Vittone. Un architetto tra illuminismo e Rococò*, cover.

85 Moschini, *Paolo Portoghesi. Progetti e disegni*, 23.

86 Otero-Pailos, 'Photo[historio]graphy: Christian Norberg-Schulz's Demotion of Textual History'.

87 Priori, ed., *Paolo Portoghesi*, 16.

88 Tafuri, *Theories and History of Architecture* (London: Granada, 1980), 157.
89 Paolo Portoghesi et al., 'The End of Prohibitionism', in *The Presence of the Past*, 9–14.
90 See Micheli 'Between History and Design'.
91 Portoghesi, 'Intervento di P. Portoghesi sulla relazione di B. Zevi', 534.
92 Portoghesi, *Guarino Guarini* (unpaginated).
93 Portoghesi, *Borromini nella cultura europea*, introductory note.
94 Ibid.
95 Ribichini, Luca and Elena Tinacci, eds., *The Modernity of Borromini: A Lesson by Paolo Portoghesi* (Rome: ARE/MAXXI, 2021), 81.
96 Portoghesi, 'Intervento di P. Portoghesi sulla relazione di B. Zevi', 532–33.
97 Argan, 'Nella crisi del mondo moderno', *Il punto su . . . Paolo Portoghesi*, Pisani ed., 13.
98 Zevi, 'Attualità del Borromini', in *Studi sul Borromini*, 509.
99 Paolo Portoghesi, 'Sulla metodologia della storia dell'architettura', in *Architektur weiterdenken* (Zurich: Institute für Geschichte und Teorie der Architektur, 2004), 12–17. In this didactic essay, Portoghesi articulates his historical method of reading and interpreting the historical documents related to a building.
100 Dal Col, 'Presto o Tardi', in *Paolo Portoghesi* (Milan: Federico Motta, 2003), 11–16.
101 Portoghesi, *Le inibizioni dell'architettura moderna*, 85.
102 Paolo Portoghesi, *Disegni di Francesco Borromini* (Rome: De Luca, 1967).
103 Ibid., 3.
104 Drawing kept in the Architecture Collection at the Albertina Museum, Vienna.
105 Paolo Portoghesi, *Disegni di Francesco Borromini*, 11.
106 Ibid., 19.
107 Portoghesi, 'Intervento di P. Portoghesi sulla relazione di B. Zevi', 533–34. This moment of the project has already been suggested by Rudolf Wittkower in *Arte e Architettura in Italia, 1600–1750* (Turin: Einaudi, 1972), 170–71.
108 Paolo Portoghesi, 'L'angelo della storia', in *La storia dell'architettura. Problemi di metodo e di didattica*, conference proceedings (Istituto di storia dell'architettura, Università di Firenze, 1976), 33–47.
109 Portoghesi, *Borromini nella cultura europea*, 15.
110 Ribichini and Tinacci, eds., *The Modernity of Borromini*, 38.
111 Portoghesi, 'Sulla metodologia della storia dell'architettura', in *Architektur weiterdenken*, 12–17.
112 Portoghesi, *Borromini nella cultura europea*, xi.
113 Ibid., ix–xxiv.
114 Micheli 'Between History and Design', 102.
115 Giulio Carlo Argan, *Borromini* (Milan: Mondadori, 1952), 71–72; Wittkower, *Arte e architettura in Italia*, 173.
116 Wittkower, *Arte e architettura in Italia*, 170.
117 Portoghesi, *Borromini nella cultura europea*, xi.

118 Ibid., xvi–xvii.
119 Bruno Zevi, 'Borromini today. In the 400th anniversary of his birth, 1599', *L'Architettura: Cronache e Storia*, 519 (1999): 55.
120 This interview is published in Paolo Portoghesi, *Leggere l'architettura* (Rome: Newton Compton, 1981), 110–22.
121 The show was promoted and organized by a team led by Lidia Motta. See Donatella Boni, *Discorsi dell'altro mondo. Nascita e metamorfosi del colloquio fantastic postumo* (Verona: Ombre Corte, 2019), 77, 135.
122 Gian Lorenzo Bernini was played by actor Eros Pagni, interviewed by Portoghesi with a script by Vittorio Sermonti.
123 For the original audio of the interview with Borromini, accessed 26 January 2022, see https://www.raiplaysound.it/audio/2020/06/Le-interviste-impossibili--Paolo-Portoghesi-incontra-Francesco-Borromini--1b77e0cd-d2e2-4bec-8032-2551759e5508.html.
124 This was a technique, as discussed in Boni, *Discorsi dell'altro mondo*, 21.
125 Baldi made his debut as a director of short documentaries, and in 1958 he received the Golden Lion for best short film at the Venice film festival with *Il pianto delle zitelle* (The Crying of Spinsters). He directed several independent films, which are characterized by his social critiques. Baldi also worked as a producer for feature films by Pier Paolo Pasolini, Robert Bresson, Nelo Risi, Jean-Marie Straub and Dacia Maraini, among others.
126 *Automi e macchine* (1957), filmmaker Gian Vittorio Baldi and subject by Paolo Portoghesi, accessed 4 April 2023, https://youtu.be/69FgjPG0GdM.
127 Casa Baldi was the last work built by Portoghesi's father.
128 Paolo Portoghesi, *Poesia della curva* (Rome: Gangemi, 2021), 11.
129 See 'Un edificio problematico: Casa Baldi sull'ansa della Flaminia, a Roma, *architetto Paolo Portoghesi*, polemica con l'autore', *L'architettura: Cronache e storia* 86, no. 8 (December 1962): 510–21.
130 Portoghesi, *Le inibizioni dell'architettura moderna*, 59.
131 Christian Norberg-Shulz, 'La "visione" di Paolo Portoghesi', in *Il punto su . . . Paolo Portoghesi*, ed. Pisani, 53–59.
132 As exemplified in the drawings included in the exhibition catalogue *Paola Levi Montalcini, Paolo Portoghesi & Vittorio Gigliotti* (Rome: Studio Farnese, 1969), unpaginated.
133 Portoghesi, *Poesia della curva*, 10.
134 Portoghesi, *Le inibizioni dell'architettura moderna*, 41.
135 Moschini, *Paolo Portoghesi. Progetti e disegni*, 92–93.
136 Thomas W. Ennis, 'Geometry scholars designs villas that stirs up architectural debate', *New York Times*, August 30 (1964). Casa Baldi was also included in the exhibition *Transformation in modern architecture* curated by Arthur Drexler at MoMA in 1979.
137 Charles Jencks, *The Language of Post-Modern Architecture*, 3rd ed. (London: Academy Editions, 1981), 81–82.
138 Moschini, *Paolo Portoghesi: Progetti e disegni*, 7.

139 See 'Un edificio problematico: Casa Baldi sull'ansa della Flaminia, a Roma, *architetto Paolo Portoghesi*, polemica con l'autore'.

140 Moschini, *Paolo Portoghesi: Progetti e disegni*, 9.

141 Centre Pompidou Drawings Archive/AM 2009-2-856.

142 Portoghesi, 'Casa Baldi sull'ansa della Flaminia, a Roma', *L'architettura cronache e storia*, 512.

143 Massobrio et al., *Paolo Portoghesi: Architetto*, 38.

144 Marco Vanucci, 'Paolo Portoghesi: The Field Theory', in *Drawing Matter*, 9 November 2020, accessed 22 February 2022, https://drawingmatter.org/paolo-portoghesi-the-field-theory/.

145 Ibid.

146 Ibid.

147 Paolo Portoghesi, 'Casa Andreis a Scandriglia, Rieti', *L'Architettura: Cronache e Storia*, no. 137 (1967): 706–19, 713.

148 Christian Norberg-Shulz, 'La "visione" di Paolo Portoghesi', 55.

149 Priori, ed., *Paolo Portoghesi*, 54.

150 Massobrio et al., *Paolo Portoghesi: Architetto*, 60.

151 Ibid.

152 See photograph kept at the Paolo Portoghesi Archive, and published in Ribichini and Tinacci, eds., *The Modernity of Borromini*, 172.

153 Manfredo Tafuri, *Il concorso per i nuovi uffici della Camera dei Deputati* (Rome: Edizioni universitarie italiane, 1968), 42.

154 Calvesi was director of the art sector in 1984 and 1986.

155 Natalia Aspesi, 'Brontolando Brontolando', *La Repubblica*, 9 June 1984.

Chapter 3

1 Pippo Ciorra in conversation with the authors, 2 November 2020.

2 McLeod, 'Architecture and Politics in the Reagan Era: From Postmodernism to Deconstructivism', 29.

3 Ibid.

4 Mario Viganò, 'Architecture: Political Involvement Versus Disciplinary Autonomy', in *La Tendenza: Italian Architectures 1965–1985*, 91.

5 Gae Aulenti left the Communist Party in 1952, when learning of Stalin's anti-semitism.

6 Letizia Caruzzo, 'La rivolta di Aldo Rossi e Guido Canella', accessed 9 September 2021, https://www.doppiozero.com/materiali/la-rivolta-di-aldo-rossi-e-guido-canella.

7 Guido Canella, 'Motivi di un'antologia', in *SA Sovremmennaja Arkhitektura 1926–1930*, ed. Guido Canella and Maurizio Meriggi (Bari: Dedalo, 2007), 7.

8 Pier Vittorio Aureli, 'The Difficult Whole', *Log* 9 (Winter/Spring 2007): 39–61.

9 Nicolini launched one of the most successful summer festivals of its time, the Estate Romana. See Federica Fava, *Estate Romana: Tempi e pratiche della città effimera*

(Macerata: Quodlibet, 2017). See also Manuel López Segura, 'Seeking to Salvage Italian Democracy: Architectural Inflections of Political Compromise at the Estate Romana, 1977–1985', in *Architecture and Democracy 1965–1989: Urban Renewal, Populism and the Welfare State*, proceedings of the Sixth Annual Conference of the Jaap Bakema Study Centre, November 2019, 31–40.

10 Biraghi, Marco, *L'architetto come intellettuale* (Turin: Einaudi, 2020), 47.

11 Raphael Zariski, 'The Italian Socialist Party: A Case Study in Factional Conflict', *The American Political Science Review* 56, no. 2 (June 1962): 372–90.

12 Aureli, *The Project of Autonomy*, 18.

13 Antonio Labalestra, 'La cultura comunista e la formazione del nuovo architetto negli anni Sessanta', *Quaderni di Architettura e Design* 2 (2019): 53–74.

14 Alberto Cavallari, 'Milano non riesce a trovare il suo vero volto culturale', *Corriere della Sera*, 27 July 1964, 3.

15 Nicolò Ornaghi, 'Nuovi clienti', 25 October 2015, accessed 8 March 2022, http://www.gizmoweb.org/2015/10/nuovi-clienti/.

16 Michele Achilli, *L'Architetto Socialista* (Venice: Marsilio, 2018), 15.

17 Giorgio Ciucci and Francesco Dal Co, *Architettura italiana del Novecento* (Milan: Electa, 1990), 221.

18 Italian extra-parliamentary groups of the 1960s and 1970s were informal associations and movements (such as Lotta Continua, Potere Operaio, Il Manifesto and Avanguardia Operaia), with no rules or hierarchical subdivision of tasks, mainly joined by young people and students. Motivated by far-left revolutionary ideals, they often considered violence as a way to fulfil their political goals.

19 'Un documento del PCI sulla crisi di Architettura', *Corriere della Sera*, 5 November 1976, 15.

20 Portoghesi attended these meetings until 1994. Portoghesi, *Roma/amoR*.

21 On the *Sperimentazione*, see 'I documenti della sperimentazione' in the 'Milano-Architettura' special issue dedicated to the Faculty of Milan between 1967 and 1973 in *Controspazio* 1, 44–48. See also Marcello De Carli, '1967–1968: La strana sperimentazione della Facoltà di Architettura del Politecnico di Milano', 15 February 2014, accessed 22 June 2021, http://www.paisia.eu/wp-content/uploads/2014/07/La-strana-sperimentazione-140220.pdf.

22 Marco Biraghi, 'Universitá. La Facoltà di Architettura del Politecnico di Milano (1963–64)', in Biraghi et al., eds., *Italia 60/70*, 87–97.

23 'Si elegge il Preside', *Corriere della Sera*, 18 October 1968, 8.

24 Paolo Portoghesi in Biraghi et al., eds., *Italia 60/70*, 262.

25 Luca Goldoni, 'I Giacobini dietro la scrivania', *Corriere della Sera*, 3 February 1971, 8.

26 Paolo Portoghesi and Virgilio Vercelloni, *La Storia dell'Architettura nell'epoca della 'sperimentazione': Corso al Politecnico di Milano (1970–1971)*, ed. Marco Biraghi (Milan: Franco Angeli, 2021), 8.

27 Gabriella Lo Ricco and Silvia Micheli, '1963–74: Cronologia', in *La Rivoluzione Culturale: La Facoltà di Architettura del Politecnico di Milano 1963–64*, Milano, Facoltà Di Architettura Civile, 23 November–16 December 2009, 6–18, accessed 22 November 2022, http://www.gizmoweb.org/wp-content/uploads/2009/10/la-rivoluzione-culturale-catalogo-bassa-protetto.pdf.

28 Paul Ginsborg, *Storia dell'Italia dal dopoguerra ad oggi* (Turin: Einaudi, 2006), 405.
29 Ginsborg, *Storia dell'Italia dal dopoguerra ad oggi*, 416.
30 'Braccio di ferro al Politecnico', *Corriere della Sera*, 4 June 1969, 8.
31 Portoghesi, *Le inibizioni dell'architettura moderna*, 239.
32 Ibid., 240.
33 Ibid.
34 Portoghesi in Biraghi et al., eds., *Italia 60/70*, 263.
35 Ginsborg, *Storia dell'Italia dal dopoguerra ad oggi*, 438.
36 'Aperta un'istruttoria per i fatti di via Tibaldi', *Corrierei della Sera*, 7 August 1971, 9.
37 Ibid., 407.
38 Paolo Portoghesi, in conversation with the authors, Rome, 25 February 2015.
39 Umberto Eco, 'Le mie prigioni', *L'Espresso*, 20 June 1973, 10.
40 Paolo Portoghesi, in conversation with the authors, 25 February 2015.
41 'Battaglia alla facoltà di architettura. Feriti venti agenti della polizia', *Corriere della Sera*, 7 June 1971, 4 and attachment.
42 Guglielmo (Billi) Bilancioni in discussion with the authors, 21 April 2021.
43 Portoghesi, *Le inibizioni dell'architettura moderna*, 229.
44 Anton Virgilio Savona, 'La Ballata di via Tibaldi', 1973, accessed 15 June 2021, https://www.antiwarsongs.org/canzone.php?id=15843&lang=en.
45 Portoghesi, *Le inibizioni dell'architettura moderna*, 228.
46 Franco Albini, Lodovico Barbiano di Belgiojoso, Piero Bottoni, Guido Canella, Carlo De Carli, Aldo Rossi and Vittoriano Viganò were suspended together with Portoghesi.
47 Massimo Cavallini, 'Il magistero della speculazione', *L'Unità*, 29 December 1972, 3.
48 'La facoltà negli ultimi vent'anni', *Corriere della Sera*, 11 November 1976, 13.
49 Fertilio Dario, 'Portoghesi se ne va', *Corriere della Sera*, 23 October 1976, 8.
50 Giovanni Belingardi, 'Il professore di barocco che scelse le contestazioni', *Corriere della Sera*, 24 October 1976, 19.
51 Portoghesi in Biraghi et al., eds., *Italia 60/70*, 263.
52 Aureli, *The Project of Autonomy*, 80.
53 Antonio Padellaro, 'Che cosa cambia in queste elezioni: Le facce nuove del 20 Giugno', *Corriere della Sera*, 21 May 1976, 2.
54 Ferruccio De Bortoli, 'I nuovi milanesi che contano nel PSI', *Corriere della Sera*, 12 April 1978, 4.
55 Portoghesi, *Roma/amoR*, 105.
56 See 'The Economic Miracle' in the Encyclopaedia Britannica, accessed 24 September 2017, https://www.britannica.com/place/Italy/The-economic-miracle.
57 Alberto Volpi, 'Craxismo', *Doppiozero*, accessed 26 September 2017, https://www.doppiozero.com/craxismo.
58 Bettino Craxi, 'Per l'avvio del governo della "non sfiducia"', in *Discorsi parlamentari*, ed. Gennaro Acquaviva (Rome-Bari: Laterza, 2007), from 'L'impossibile intesa', 122.

59 Paul Ginsborg, *L'Italia del tempo presente: Famiglia, società civile, Stato 1980–1996* (Turin: Einaudi, 1998), 281.

60 Paolo Bagnoli, 'Il Vangelo socialista', *Nuova Antologia* 619, (October–December 2018): 124–34.

61 Extract from the original article published on 27 August 1978 in *L'Espresso*. Written by PSI sociologist Luciano Pellicani, it was commissioned by Craxi.

62 Giovanni Fasanella, 'Quei nemici per la pelle', *L'Unità*, 3 May 1987, 12.

63 Paolo Portoghesi, 'The End of Prohibitionism' in *The Presence of the Past*, 9–13.

64 Antonio Piva, Francesca Bonicalzi and Pierfranco Galliani, eds., *Architettura e politica / Architecture and Politics* (Rome: Gangemi, 2007), 62.

65 *Questione di feeling* was written by Cocciante and Mogol.

66 Portoghesi, *Roma/amoR*, 105.

67 Paola Desideri, *Il potere della parola. Il linguaggio politico di Bettino Craxi* (Venice: Marsilio, 1987), 15.

68 Philip Willan, 'Bettino Craxi', *The Guardian*, 20 January 2000, accessed 26 September 2017, https://www.theguardian.com/news/2000/jan/20/guardianobituaries.philipwillan.

69 Micheli, 'Alessandro Mendini, *Domus* and the Postmodern Vision', 115–33.

70 See video of the advertisement, accessed 26 May 2021, https://www.youtube.com/watch?v=k8jZb-Lj3GQ.

71 McLeod, 'Architecture and Politics in the Reagan Era: From Postmodernism to Deconstructivism', 25.

72 Italo Calvino, *Le città invisibili* (Turin: Einaudi, 1972).

73 Deyan Sudjic, *Edifice Complex: The Architecture of Power* (London: Penguin Books, 2011).

74 See Fava, *Estate Romana*.

75 See Léa-Catherine Szacka, 'Le populisme de l'éphémère: Postmodernisme et scénographies urbaines en France et en Italie (1976–1989)', in *La fabrique des images: L'architecture à l'ère postmoderne*, ed. Federico Ferrari (Geneva: In Folio, 2018), 63–86. See also Jean-Claude Daufresne, *Fête à Paris au XXe siècle: Architectures éphémères de 1919 à 1989* (Paris: Mardaga, 2001).

76 Sara Colarizi, 'La trasformazione della leadership. Il PSI di Craxi (1976–1981)', in *Gli anni ottanta come storia*, ed. Simona Colarizi, Piero Craveri, Silvio Pons and Gaetano Quagliarello (Soveria Mannelli: Rubettino, 2004), 44.

77 The PSI had used the hammer and sickle (superimposed on a book and a rising sun) as its symbol since 1919. However, in 1978 Craxi commissioned artist Filippo Panseca to redesign the party logo and he proposed using a red carnation for its symbolic relation to Labour Day. See Tano Gullo, 'Filippo Panseca: Così inventai il garofano per il mio amico Bettino Craxi', *La Repubblica*, 1 June 2015.

78 Gennaro Acquaviva and Luigi Covatta, eds., *Decisione e processo politico: La lezione del governo Craxi (1983–1987)* (Padua: Marsilio, 2014, 86–87).

79 Ginsborg, *L'Italia del tempo presente*, 283.

80 Portoghesi, *Roma/amoR*, 91.

81 Szacka, *Exhibiting the Postmodern*.

82 Paolo Belardi, ed., *NAU Novecento Architettura Umbria* (Foligno: Il Formichiere, 2014). The linearity of the overall result – each gate at the one end of the inflated space – was a metaphor for Portoghesi's relationship with Aymonino, two cultural trajectories respectively running in parallel but hardly intersecting.

83 See Paolo Portoghesi, 'Apparati per la Festa de l'Unità', *Epoca* 1173 (28 September 1984). Also, Costantino Dardi, Sergio Petruccioli and Franco Purini and Laura Thermes designed small structures for the event.

84 After leaving the PCI, Ripa di Meana enrolled in the PSI at the beginning of 1960s, like Portoghesi, and was one of the intellectually freer and bolder representatives of the socialist area. His role in the Biennale del dissenso is well described in Fabio Martini, *Controvento. La vera storia di Bettino Craxi* (Soveria Mannelli: Rubbettino, 2020), 49–55. See also Léa-Catherine Szacka and Luca Guido, 'The Biennale as Agent Provocateur for Democracy', *Volume #41: How to Build a Nation*, 2014: 22–28.

85 Carlo Ripa di Meana and Gabriella Mecucci, *L'ordine di Mosca. Fermate la Biennale del dissenso* (Rome: Liberal, 2007).

86 Roddolo, *La Biennale*, 104.

87 Luca Guido, 'The Biennale of Dissent 1977', *Art + Media Journal* 12 (2017): 17–28, here 22.

88 Roddolo, *La Biennale*, 105.

89 Guido, 'The Biennale of Dissent 1977', 24.

90 Dario Micacchi, 'Aperta la Biennale', *L'Unità*, 16 November 1977, 3.

91 Ferruccio De Bortoli, 'No alla dittatura della parola, si alla letteratura del dissenso', *Corriere della Sera*, 4 March 1978, 5.

92 Ibid.

93 Bernitsa and Valeriani, eds., *A colloquio con Paolo Portoghesi*, 20.

94 Paolo Portoghesi, in conversation with the authors, 2 October 2020.

95 Léa-Catherine Szacka and Vittorio Gregotti, 'A Conversation with Vittorio Gregotti', *Log* 20 (Fall 2010): 39–43, here 41.

96 Natalia Aspesi, 'Il Lido si accende, comincia la festa', *La Repubblica*, 25 August 1985.

97 The song was released in 1978 in the album *Che cosa vuoi che sia una canzone*, https://www.vascorossi.net/it/discografia/ma-cosa-vuoi-che-sia unacanzone/522-31600.html. Accessed 28 June 2023.

98 Ricky Burdett, 'Italian Style: Latin Lesson', *Building Design*, 3 June 1983, 24–28.

99 'Biennale: Il PSI candida Portoghesi alla presidenza', *Corriere della Sera*, 11 March 1983, 4.

100 Toni Iop, 'Paolo Portoghesi nuovo presidente della Biennale', *L'Unità*, 12 March 1983, 6.

101 Maria Teresa Meli, 'Martelli: "Io e De Michelis in competizione. Ma lui era sempre più preparato degli esperti"', *Corriere della Sera*, 11 May 2019. Interview with Claudio Martelli published on the occasion of the death of Gianni De Michelis.

102 Bernitsa and Valeriani, eds., *A colloquio con Paolo Portoghesi*.

103 See letter written in 1988, part of the correspondence between Giovanni Spadolini (president of the Senate) and Paolo Portoghesi (president of the Biennale). Giovanni

Spadolini, 1.12.12.626, Archivio Storico, Senato della Repubblica, accessed 28 October 2021, https://patrimonio.archivio.senato.it/inventario/scheda/giovanni-spadolini/IT-AFS-066-003703/biennale-venezia-43-esposizione-internazionale-d-arte.

104 For instance, in 1988 a screening of Martin Scorsese's *The Last Temptation of Christ* was almost cancelled due to objections by the Christian Democrats who considered the movie offensive. 'La DC: "Togliete il film di Scorsese"', *Corriere della Sera*, 30 July 1988, 14.

105 'Per la Biennale incontro del PCI con il presidente', *L'Unità*, 23 July 1975, 7.

106 'Polemiche alla Biennale', *Corriere della Sera*, 11 November 1984, 21.

107 Gino Fantin, 'La Biennale rischia il naufragio', *Corriere della Sera*, 16 December 1984, 8.

108 Cesare de Seta, 'Tanti bei progetti fuori dalla realtà', *Corriere della Sera*, 7 August 1985, 3.

109 Portoghesi, *Roma/amoR*, 102.

110 Ibid.

111 Manfredo Tafuri, 'L'éphémère est éternel. Aldo Rossi a Venezia', *Domus* 602, 1980, 7–11.

112 See, for instance, Tafuri's observations in his *Storia dell'architettura italiana*, 227–229.

113 'Biennale, il PSI fa incetta di poltrone', *La Repubblica*, 16 October 1987.

114 Sandro Scabello, 'I programmi formulati dai direttori della Biennale', *Corriere della Sera*, 18 February 1979, 6.

115 A recent publication has for the first time documented this rather forgotten exhibition, see Helen Thomas (ed.) *Architecture in Islamic Countries: Selections from the Catalogue for the Second International Exhibition of Architecture Venice 1982/83*, Zurich: gta Verlag, 2022.

116 *Architettura nei paesi Islamici. Seconda mostra internazionale di architettura* (Venice: La Biennale, 1982), 12.

117 Viola Bertini, 'Hassan Fathy (1900–1989)', *The Architectural Review*, 1468, February 2020, accessed 30 January 2023, https://www.architectural-review.com/essays/reputations/hassan-fathy-1900-1989.

118 Fiorella Minervino, 'E l'Islam ritorna a imporsi a Venezia', *Corriere della Sera*, 21 November 1982, 12.

119 Francesco Perego, 'L'architettura islamica in mostra alla Biennale', *Corriere della Sera*, 14 November 1982, 7.

120 Ibid.

121 Vittorio Ianari, 'L'Italia e il Medio Oriente: Dal "neoatlantismo" al *peace-keeping*', in *L'Italia Repubblicana nella crisi degli anni settanta. Tra guerra fredda e distensione*, eds. Agostino Giovagnoli and Silvio Pons (Soveria Mannelli: Rubbettino Editore), 2003, 383–95, 392.

122 On the story ENI-Petromin, see Donato Speroni, *L'intrigo saudita. La strana storia della maxitangente Eni-Petromin* (Castelvecchi: Cooper, 2009).

123 Portoghesi, *Roma/amoR*, 148.

124 *La Civiltà Cattolica* 145, no. 1, journal 3451 (2 April 1994): 283.

125 Vittorio Ianari, 'L'Italia e il Medio Oriente', 383.

126 M. Pet., 'Portoghesi "La mia moschea"', *Corriere della Sera*, 5 July 1985, 29.

127 'Sette milioni di dollari per la moschea di Roma', *Corriere della Sera*, 13 December 1974, 3.

128 'Quattro possibili moschee. Quale si farà?', *Corriere della Sera*, 27 February 1976, 12.

129 The team led by Sergio Bianconcini; the team including Paolo Portoghesi and Gigliotti; the Manchester-based Iraqi architect Sami Mousawi and Tommaso and Gilberto Valle.

130 For the issues regarding the authorship of the Grande Moschea, see the correspondence between Portoghesi, Gigliotti and Mousawi, MAXXI Museo Nazionale delle Arti del XXI Secolo, Rome. Collezione MAXXI Architettura/Archivio Portoghesi. The problematic aspect of the mosque's authorship was that, in the press, the design was often mistakenly attributed solely to Portoghesi. From the many letters exchanged between Portoghesi, Gigliotti and Mousawi, and sent to the media, it appears that the confusion was due to Portoghesi's international reputation, which unintentionally led to him overshadowing the two other authors of the project.

131 One project was part of the Airport for Khartum; the other was designed for the residence of King Hussein.

132 Paolo Conti, 'Ho ricevuto minacce di morte per la Moschea di Roma', *Corriere della Sera*, 17 February 2018. See also, Alberto Sposito, ed., 'Stupor Mundi', in *La moschea di Roma* (Palermo: Alloro Editrice, 1993), 12.

133 Sposito, ed., 'Giulio Carlo Argan', *La moschea di Roma*, 21 (from an interview released in 1992).

134 Mario Pisani, 'Dialogo con Portoghesi', in *La moschea di Roma*, 25.

135 Paolo Portoghesi, 'L'architettura dell'ascolto', in *Paolo Portoghesi. Opere e progetti*, 86–93.

136 M. Pet., 'Portoghesi "La mia Moschea"'.

137 Bernitsa and Valeriani, eds., *A colloquio con Paolo Portoghesi*, 64.

138 Livio Sacchi, *Architettura e identità islamica* (Milano: Franco Angeli, 2015), 81.

139 Bernitsa and Valeriani, eds., *A colloquio con Paolo Portoghesi*, 64.

140 Portoghesi, 'L'architettura dell'ascolto', in *Paolo Portoghesi: Opere e progetti*, 86–93.

141 Ibid.

142 Pisani, 'Dialogo con Portoghesi', in *La moschea di Roma*, 25.

143 'Polemico dibattito sulla Moschea a Monte Antenne', *Corriere della Sera,* 8 May 1979.

144 Professor and engineer, respectively Guido Guy and Aldo Spirito, oversaw the structural engineering of the mosque and cultural centre.

145 From the MAXXI bulletin 136. Collezione MAXXI Architettura/Archivio Portoghesi.

146 'Cominciati i lavori per la Moschea. Finanziamenti dal mondo arabo', *Corriere della Sera*, 28 June 1984: 27.

147 From the MAXXI bulletin 136. Collezione MAXXI Architettura/Archivio Portoghesi.

148 Portoghesi, *Roma/amoR*, 148.

149 Ibid.

150 Giulio Carlo Argan, handwritten letter to Paolo Portoghesi, 1995, published in the Festschrift produced for Portoghesi's sixtieth birthday, Pisani, *Paolo Portoghesi*, 73.

Chapter 4

1. Casa Papanice appeared in *Casa Vogue* 8, 1971.
2. The trip was supported by the Biennale with the Italian Ministries of Foreign Affairs and Tourism and Spectacle, as well as the Venice City Council. See leaflet of the initiative 'Il viaggio del Teatro del Mondo da Venezia a Dubrovnik', https://www.moltenimotta.it/teatro-del-mondo/.
3. The Adriatic trip took place from 10 to 22 August 1980.
4. *Casa Vogue*, January 1980.
5. Maurizio Scaparro, accessed 26 January 2022, https://www.moltenimotta.it/teatro-del-mondo/.
6. The event was recorded in a short movie, *Saving Lieb House* (2009), starring Frederic Schwartz, Denise Scott Brown, Robert Venturi and Jim Venturi, directed by John Halpern and Jim Venturi.
7. 'It is actually the emerging systems of communication that came to define the twentieth-century culture the mass media that are the true site within which modern architecture is produced and with which it directly engages. In fact, one could argue (this is the main argument of this book) that modern architecture only became modern with its engagement with the media.' Beatriz Colomina, *Privacy and Publicity: Modern Architecture as Mass Media* (Cambridge: The MIT Press, 1996), 14.
8. Ibid., 13–14.
9. David Robey, 'Umberto Eco: Theory and Practice in the Analysis of the Media', in *Culture and Conflict in Post-war Italy: Essays on Mass and Popular Culture*, ed. Zygmunt G. Baranski and Robert Lumley (London: Macmillan, 1990), 160–77, here 160.
10. Andreas Huyssen, 'Mapping the Postmodern', *New German Critique* 33 (Autumn, 1984): 5–52, here 22.
11. Ibid.
12. Massobrio et al., *Paolo Portoghesi: Architetto*, 17.
13. The Mosque of Rome featured shortly in the movie *Stanno tutti bene* by Giuseppe Tornatore released in 1990, starring Marcello Mastroianni.
14. See Adrian Forty, *Words and Buildings: A Vocabulary of Modern Architecture* (London: Thames and Hudson, 2000), 11.
15. Benjamin Blankenbehler, 'Post-Modernism of Venturi and Philip Johnson: Engaging the Image of Culture', *Architecture Revived*, 4 September 2015, accessed 3 April 2022, http://architecturerevived.com/post-modernism-of-venturi-and-philip-johnson-engaging-the-image-of-culture/.
16. See the photographic section of Bernitsa and Valeriani, eds., *A colloquio con Paolo Portoghesi*, 49–124.
17. See Bruno Zevi, *Zevi su Zevi: Architettura come Profezia* (Venezia: Marsilio, 1993); Andrea Oppenheimer Dean, *Bruno Zevi on Modern Architecture Paperback* (New York: Rizzoli, 1983); and Dulio, *Introduzione a Bruno Zevi*.
18. Oppenheimer Dean, *Bruno Zevi on Modern Architecture*, 11.
19. *L'Espresso* is one of Italy's most prominent weekly news magazines, founded in 1955 by the publishing house of Carlo Caracciolo and the progressive industrialist Adriano

Olivetti. During Zevi's tenure, *L'Espresso* was the only weekly magazine in Italy to have a section exclusively dedicated to architecture. Zevi's collaboration with *L'Espresso* started in 1955 and continued to 2000. There was only one break in his collaboration with the magazine: from 18 June to 19 November 1967, when, according to Zevi, *L'Espresso* assumed an anti-Israeli position.

20 Zevi was an impassioned advocate of modern architecture in Italy. Zevi launched and edited the magazine *Metron* from 1945, and then *L'Architettura: cronache e storia*. Oppenheimer Dean, *Bruno Zevi on Modern Architecture: cronache e storia*, 11.

21 Bruno Zevi, *Saper vedere l'architettura* (Torino: Einaudi, 1948). Translated in 1957 by Milton Gendel for Horizon Press.

22 Founded by Bruno Zevi in 1959 in Rome, the IN/ARCH (National Institute of Architecture) aimed to bring together the professional and cultural side of architecture, as well as to support the promotion and coordination of disciplinary studies and initiatives in Italy.

23 See, for example, the roundtable on Monday 23 October 1978 dedicated to 'La Biennale – Architettura', involving Portoghesi, Enrico Crispolti, Vittorio Gregotti, Paolo Portoghesi e Lara Vinca Masini. A poster of the event is held at the Fondo Francesco Moschini AAM. Architettura Arte Moderna, Rome.

24 Conceived and conducted by the journalist Maurizio Costanzo, the *Maurizio Costanzo Show* ran, with some interruptions, between 1982 and 2022.

25 Episode available at https://www.youtube.com/watch?v=lBoYobZPjTU, accessed 2 November 2021.

26 *Paolo Portoghesi racconta Francesco Borromini*, directed by Stefano Roncoroni, featured on RSI Radiotelevisione svizzera di lingua italiana on 2 October 1967. See https://lanostrastoria.ch/entries/0OYn1ldBXbK, accessed 2 November 2021.

27 Massobrio et al., *Paolo Portoghesi: architetto* (Rome: Gangemi, 2001), 17.

28 *La presenza del passato*, directed by Maurizio Cascavilla, 32 min. (RAI, 1980).

29 *Viaggio nella Biennale: Architettura*, directed by Marcello Ugolini, 52 min. (RAI, 1980).

30 Paolo Portoghesi, 'Il formato delle riviste di architettura', *Domus* 635 (1983): 2–11.

31 For an overview of the major Italian magazines of the 1960s and 1970s, see Micheli, 'Le riviste italiane d'architettura degli anni '60 e '70', in *Italia 60/70*, 124–38.

32 Between 1953 and 1956, Portoghesi wrote eleven articles for *Civiltà delle macchine*.

33 The magazine was financially supported by Finmeccanica – the company of the Istituto per la Ricostruzione Industriale (IRI).

34 He once wrote 'my adored Leonardo-Virgilio'. See Paolo Portoghesi, 'Per Leonardo Sinisgalli' in *Leonardo Sinisgalli: Promenades architecturales* (Bergamo: Pierluigi Lubrica, 1987), 5–12.

35 With some of his works awarded at the Venice Film Festival.

36 Paolo Portoghesi, 'Borromini in ferro', *Civiltà delle machine* 2 (1953): 50–53.

37 *Marcatrè* was founded in Genoa in 1963.

38 Eugenio Battisti, 'La Tavolata e il Fumuoir', *Marcatré* 1 (1963): 2.

39 The last issue of *Casabella-continuità* was that of 1963–64.

40 Dedalo was headed by the figure of Raimondo Coga, who at that time qualified himself as one of the leading publishers of non-parliamentary nature.

41 Paolo Portoghesi, 'Editoriale', *Controspazio* 1 (June 1969): 7.

42 Paolo Scrivano, 'Where Praxis and Theory Clash with Reality: *Controspazio* and the Italian Debate over Design, History and Ideology, 1969–1973,' in *Revues d'architecture dans les années 1960 et 1970. Fragments d'une histoire événementielle, intellectuelle et matérielle /Architectural Periodicals in the 1960s and 1970s: Towards a Factual, Intellectual and Material History*, ed. Alexis Sornin, Hélène Jannière and France Vanlaethem (Montreal: Institut de Recherche en Histoire de l'architecture, 2008), 246.

43 Scrivano, 'Where Praxis and Theory Clash with Reality', 249.

44 Over the years, the editorial board of *Controspazio* included Ezio Bonfanti, Massimo Scolari, Luciano Patetta, Virgilio Vercelloni, Maria Grazia Messina, Benigno Cuccuru, Renato Nicolini, Gianni Accasto, Giampaolo Ercolani, Vanna Fraticelli, Giorgio Muratore, Antonio Monroy, Maurizio Ascani, Alessandro Anselmi, Claudio D'Amato, Daniela Fonti, Guglielmo Monti, Livio Quaroni, Giuseppe Rebecchini, Duccio Staderini, Laura Thermes and Francesco Cellini.

45 Ezio Bonfanti, 'La cultura architettonica a Milano. Strumenti e Istituzioni', in *Ezio Bonfanti: Nuovo e Moderno in Architettura*, ed. Marco Biraghi and Michelangelo Sabatino (Milan: Bruno Mondadori, 2001), 339.

46 Claudio D'amato Guerrieri, '*Controspazio* as a "Little Magazine"', *Magazine del festival dell'architettura*, accessed 2 November 2021, https://www.famagazine.it/index.php/famagazine/article/view/84/676#_ftn5.

47 As explained by its former editorial board member Claudio D'Amato Guerrieri, *Contropsazio* grew in the cultural climate of student and workers' struggles which flourished in the School of Architecture of Rome from 1963 and continued until the point of radical break that was the so-called 'Battle of Valle Giulia' (March 1, 1968).

48 Carlo Gandolfi, 'Controspazio', in *Architettura del Novecento: Teorie, scuole, e eventi*, eds. Marco Biraghi and Alberto Ferlenga, vol. 1 (Turin: Einaudi, 2012: 246–50).

49 Massimo Scolari, 'The New Architecture and the Avant-Garde', in *Architecture Theory since 1968*, ed. K. Michael Hays (Cambridge: The MIT Press, 1998, 124–43). The article was first published in 1973 in *Architettura razionale*, ed. Ezio Bonfanti (Milan: Franco Angeli, 1973).

50 Scrivano, 'Where Praxis and Theory Clash with Reality', 249.

51 D'amato Guerrieri, '*Controspazio* as a "Little Magazine"'.

52 Paolo Portoghesi in conversation with the authors, Rome, 25 February 2015.

53 D'amato Guerrieri, '*Controspazio* as a "Little Magazine"'.

54 Subscription programme attached to each issue.

55 *Pan* was an art and literary magazine published between 1895 and 1900 in Berlin by Otto Julius Birebaum and Julius Meier-Graefe. The magazine played an important role in the development of Art Nouveau in Germany. *Ver Sacrum* was the official magazine of the Vienna Secession. It was founded in 1898 by Gustav Klimt and Max Kurzweil and was published until 1903.

56 See Catharine Rossi, 'Architecture Goes Disco', *AA Files* 69 (2014): 138–45.

57 Mateo Kries, Jochen Eisenbrand, Catharine Rossi and Nina Serulus, eds., *Night Fever: Designing Club Culture: 1960–Today* (Basel: Vitra Design Museum, 2018).

58 Gabriele Basilico and Bernardo Valli, *Dancing in Emilia* (Ivrea: Priuli & Verlucca, 1980).

59 'Appuntamenti', *Corriere della Sera*, 17 October 1987, 36.

60 'Il Piper 80 cambia ancora faccia', *L'Unità*, 11 January 1983, 10.
61 Giovanni Rebecchini, in conversation with the authors, 6 September 2022.
62 Ibid.
63 Giovanni Rebecchini, 'I Processi del Piper' in Pisani, ed., *Paolo Portoghesi*, 63–68.
64 Rossana Lampugnani, 'Vittoriano condannato, con la condizionale', *L'Unità*, 28 January 1986, 15.
65 See the proceedings of the trial, *Processo all'altare della Patria. Atti del Processo al monument Vittorio Emanuele II*, Rome – Milan: Mediocredito del Lazio, Libri Scheiwiller, 1987.
66 The event was called 'Serata al Piper 80'.
67 '*Domus*: Serata al Piper', *Domus* 652 (1984): 63.
68 'Nasce una rivista sulla citta e la casa', *Corriere della Sera*, 16 January 1984.
69 For example Portoghesi, but also Aldo Rossi and Guido Canella, were following closely Italian neorealist cinema. See Guido Canella and Aldo Rossi 'Architettura e realismo', unpublished, winter 1955, Aldo Rossi Papers, Getty Research Institute, box 9, folder 151.
70 David Escudero, 'Beyond Filmmaking: Searching for a Neorealist Architecture in Italy, 194X–195X', *The Journal of Architecture* 24, no. 4 (2019): 441–68.
71 For more on neorealism and architecture see David Escudero, *Neorealist Architecture Aesthetics of Dwelling in Postwar Italy* (London: Routledge, 2022).
72 Paolo Portoghesi interviewed by Renato Pallavicini, in 'La Mostra dei miei sogni', *L'Unità*, 17 September 1990, 21.
73 Paolo Portoghesi, in conversation with the authors, 2 October 2020.
74 Ibid.
75 The film was distributed only in 1967 after problems with censorship and distribution. Featuring Paolo Carlini, Luciano Morelli, Anna Bragaglia and Marco Guglielmi.
76 Portoghesi in Maurizio Cascavilla, *Utopia, utopia*, 1969.
77 Paolo Portoghesi, in conversation with the authors, 2 October 2020.
78 Ibid.
79 The other finalists were: Jean Nouvel, Aldo Rossi, Sverre Fehn, James Stirling, Carlo Aymonino, Mario Botta, Fumihiko Maki, Steven Holl/Marlies Hentrup/Norbert Heyers and Oswald Mathias Ungers. The jury included Francesco Dal Co, Manfredo Tafuri, Kurt Foster, Arata Isozaki, and Gianluigi Rondi.
80 Léa-Catherine Szacka, 'Massimo Scolari's Ali and the Institutional Reframing of the Venice Biennale', in Wouter Davidts, Susan Holden, Ashley Paine, eds., *Trading between Architecture and Art*, Valiz, 2019.
81 Franco Borsi and Paolo Porteghesi, *Victor Horta* (Roma-Bari: Laterza, 1982), 1. First edition was published in 1969 by Edizione del Tritone.
82 Paolo Portoghesi, in conversation with the authors, 2 October 2020.
83 Ibid.
84 Ibid.
85 Ibid.
86 Casa Papanice is well documented in the Archivio Casa Papanice, part of the Papanice Foundation. See also the book by Edmondo Papanice, *Casa Papanice*, Rome, 2023.

87 See Paolo Boccacci, 'Casa Papanice a Roma, arriva il vincolo per il capolavoro di Portoghesi', *La Repubblica*, 16 February, 2021.

Epilogue

1 Daniela Pasti, 'Canta architetto la Gloria di Dio', *La Repubblica*, 21 November 1992. The exhibition then travelled to Munich, London and Berlin.
2 McLeod, 'Architecture and Politics in the Reagan Era: From Postmodernism to Deconstructivism', 43.
3 Antonello Venditti, 'In questo mondo di ladri', from the eponymous album released in 1988.
4 For the impact of Mani Pulite and Tangentopoli on Italian architecture, see Biraghi and Micheli, *Storia dell'architettura italiana*, 120–33.
5 For the relationship of Mani Pulite and Milan, see John Foot, 'From Boomtown to Bribesville: The Images of the City, Milan, 1980–97', *Urban History* 26, no. 3 (December 1999): 393–412.
6 Acquaviva, ed., Bettino Craxi: *Discorsi parlamentari*, 473–84. See also the video, accessed 26 January 2022, https://www.youtube.com/watch?v=Jud08s96QfY.
7 On the history of Italian architecture during the early 1990s, see Biraghi and Micheli, *Storia dell'architettura italiana*, second part.
8 Pierluigi Nicolin, 'Looking at Tangentopoli', *Lotus* 82 (1994): 106.
9 On the process of revising the practices of construction sectors and the Merloni Law, see Biraghi and Micheli, *Storia dell'architettura italiana*, 115–33.
10 Vittorio Gregotti, 'Il disprezzo della qualità', *Casabella* 617 (1994): 2–5.
11 Biraghi and Micheli, *Storia dell'architettura italiana*, 120–33.
12 Portoghesi, *Roma/amoR*, 82.
13 On the involvement of foreign architects in Italy during the 1990s and 2000s, see Biraghi and Micheli, *Storia dell'architettura italiana*, 134–74.
14 For the long list of guests at house in via Gregoriana, see Massobrio et al., *Paolo Portoghesi: Architetto*, 14.
15 Portoghesi, *Roma/amoR*. In 1993, Portoghesi and Massobrio had to leave the house in via Gregoriana. They rented another apartment for four years, during which they would spend the weekends in Calcata, to where they gradually moved. Massobrio et al., *Paolo Portoghesi: Architetto*, 14.
16 Portoghesi first explored the Treja valley with his family in the mid-1950s, when he was still a young boy. Portoghesi and Massobrio bought the first house in 1973 and then expanded through the purchases of adjacent properties.
17 Portoghesi, *Roma/amoR*.
18 Massobrio et al., *Paolo Portoghesi: Architetto*, 236.
19 Ibid.; see also Bernitsa and Valeriani, eds., *A colloquio con Paolo Portoghesi*.
20 Bernitsa and Valeriani, eds., *A colloquio con Paolo Portoghesi*, 31.

21 Paolo Portoghesi, *Geoarchitettura: Verso un'architettura della responsabilità* (Milan: Skira, 2005).

22 In the wake of this turn to nature, since 2001 Portoghesi has published the magazine *Abitare la Terra*, which is characterized by the sensibility towards the natural environment.

23 Paolo Portoghesi, *Natura e Architettura* (Milan: Skira, 1999), translated into English in 2000. This book is based on an exhibition that Portoghesi organized in 1969 at Galleria Farnese in Rome and titled *Storia e natura come nutrimento*.

24 Portoghesi, *Roma/amoR*.

Coda

1 Paul Valéry, 'Eupalinos; ou, l'Architecte' (Paris: Gallimard, 1924), 143. [This, dear Phedre, is the most important: There is no geometry without speech. Without it, the figures are accidents; neither manifesting nor serving the power of the spirit.] Translation by Léa-Catherine Szacka.

2 Claudio D'Amato Guerrieri, 'Controspazio come "piccola rivista"', *Magazine del Festival dell'Architettura*, 2010, accessed 8 March 2022, https://www.famagazine.it/index.php/famagazine/article/view/84/643.

3 In 1964, Officina Edizioni debuted with two titles: *La Crisi semantica delle arti* by Emilio Garroni and *Borromini nella cultura europea* by Paolo Portoghesi. The next year, Portoghesi proposed a list of titles to Quinti, all linked to a wide-ranging historical approach, which led to the "Officina di Architettura" collection, under the guidance of Portoghesi himself. See Maristella Casciato, 'Quarante années de publications en architecture: Officina edizioni, un éditeur italien et ses auteurs', in *Le livre et l'architect* (Brussels: Mardaga, 2011).

4 Paolo Portoghesi, *Roma/amoR. Memoria, racconto, speranza* (Venice: Marsilio, 2019), 122.

BIBLIOGRAPHY

Accasto, Gianni. 'Gli avvenimenti: 1967–71', *Controspazio* 1 (1973): 40–41.
Achilli, Michele. *L'architetto Socialista*. Venice: Marsilio, 2018.
Ackerman, James S. 'In memoriam: Manfredo Tafuri, 1935–1994', *Journal of the Society of Architectural Historians* 53 (June 1994): 137–38.
Acquaviva, Gennaro and Luigi Covatta, eds. *Decisione e processo politico: La lezione del governo Craxi (1983–1987)*. Padua: Marsilio, 2014.
Andersen, Anna Ulrikke. *Following Norberg-Schulz*. London: Bloomsbury, 2021.
Andriani, Carmen. 'Bruno Zevi. Pensiero e Azione', in *Bruno Zevi e la didattica dell'architettura*. eds. Piero Ostilio Rossi, with Francesca Romana Castelli, Luca Porqueddu, Gianpaola Spirito. Macerata: Quodlibet, 2019: 17–24.
Argan, Giulio Carlo. *Borromini*. Milan: Mondadori, 1952.
Argan, Giulio Carlo. 'Nella crisi del mondo moderno', in *Paolo Portoghesi*, ed. Mario Pisani. Rome: Gangemi, 1993: 13–18.
Aspesi, Natalia, 'Brontolando Brontolando', *La Repubblica*, 9 June 1984.
Aspesi, Natalia. 'Il Lido si accende, comincia la festa', *La Repubblica*, 25 August 1985.
Aureli, Pier Vittorio. 'The Difficult Whole', *Log* 9 (Winter/Spring 2007): 39–61.
Aureli, Pier Vittorio. *The Project of Autonomy: Politics and Architecture within and against Capitalism*. New York: Buell Center – Princeton Architectural Press, 2008.
Avermaete, Tom, Véronique Patteeuw and Christophe Van Gerrewey, eds. 'Action and Reaction in Architecture', *OASE* 97 (October 2016).
Bagnoli, Paolo. 'Il Vangelo socialista', *Nuova Antologia: Rivista di lettere, scienze e arti* 619 (October–December 2018): 124–34.
Ballabio, Fabrizio and Alessandro Conti. 'Sentimental Education', *AA Files* 73 (2016): 129–37.
Bandini, Micha. 'Aldo Rossi', *AA Files* 1 (Winter 1981–82): 105–11.
Banham, Reyner. 'Neoliberty: The Italian Retreat from Modern Architecture', *The Architectural Review* 747 (April 1959): 231–35.
Banham, Reyner. 'Industrial design e arte popolare', *Civiltà delle macchine* (1995): 12–15.
Baranski, Zygmunt G. and Robert Lumley, eds. *Culture and Conflict in Post-war Italy: Essays on Mass and Popular Culture*. London: Macmillan, 1990.
Basilico, Gabriele and Bernardo Valli, *Dancing in Emilia*. Ivrea: Priuli & Verlucca, 1980.
Battisti, Eugenio. 'La Tavolata e il Fumuoir', *Marcatré* 1 (1963): 2.
Belardi, Paolo, ed. *NAU Novecento Architettura Umbria*. Foligno: Il Formichiere, 2014.
Belingardi, Giovanni. 'Il professore di barocco che scelse le contestazioni', *Corriere della Sera*, 24 October 1976.
Belluzzi, Amedeo and Claudia Conforti, *Architettura italiana 1944–1994*. Rome–Bari: Laterza, 1994.

Bernitsa, Petra, ed., *Paolo Portoghesi: The Architecture of Listening Rome*, exhibition catalogue. Rome: Gangemi, 2014.
Bernitsa, Petra and Maria Ercadi, eds. *Paolo Portoghesi*. Milan: Skira, 2006.
Bernitsa, Petra and Enrico Valeriani, eds. *A colloquio con Paolo Portoghesi*. Rome: Gangemi, 2014.
Bertini, Viola. 'Hassan Fathy (1900–1989)', *The Architectural Review* 1468, February 2020, accessed 30 January 2022, https://www.architectural-review.com/essays/reputations/hassan-fathy-1900-1989
Bignardi, Irene. 'Un cocomero tricolore', *La Repubblica*, 2 December 1987.
Biraghi, Marco. *Project of Crisis: Manfredo Tafuri and Contemporary Architecture*. Cambridge, MA: The MIT Press, 2013.
Biraghi, Marco. *L'architetto come intellettuale*. Turin: Einaudi, 2020.
Biraghi, Marco, ed. *Paolo Portoghesi, Virgilio Vercelloni. La Storia dell'Architettura nell'epoca della 'sperimentazione': Corso al Politecnico di Milano (1970–1971)*. Milan: Franco Angeli, 2021.
Biraghi, Marco and Alberto Ferlenga, eds. *Architettura del Novecento: Teorie, scuole, e eventi*, vol. 1. Turin: Einaudi, 2012.
Biraghi, Marco and Silvia Micheli. *Storia dell'architettura italiana 1985–2015*. Milan: Einaudi, 2013.
Biraghi, Marco and Michelangelo Sabatino, eds. *Ezio Bonfanti: Nuovo e Moderno in Architettura*. Milan: Bruno Mondadori, 2001.
Biraghi, Marco, Gabriella Lo Ricco, Silvia Micheli and Mario Viganò, eds. *Italia 60/70. Una stagione dell'architettura*. Padua: Il Poligrafo, 2010.
Blankenbehler, Benjamin. 'Post-Modernism of Venturi and Philip Johnson: Engaging the Image of Culture', *Architecture Revived*, 4 September 2015, accessed 3 April 2022, http://architecturerevived.com/post-modernism-of-venturi-and-philip-johnson-engaging-the-image-of-culture/.
Boccacci, Paolo. 'Casa Papanice a Roma, arriva il vincolo per il capolavoro di Portoghesi', *La Repubblica*, 16 February, 2021.
Boccacci, Paolo. 'Paolo Portoghesi: Per i miei 90 anni regalatemi il restauro di Casa Papanice', *La Repubblica*, 1 November 2021.
Bonfanti, Ezio, ed. *Architettura razionale*. Milan: Franco Angeli, 1973.
Bonfanti, Ezio. 'La cultura architettonica a Milano. Strumenti e Istituzioni', in *Ezio Bonfanti: Nuovo e moderno in architettura*, eds. Marco Biraghi and Michelangelo Sabatino. Milan: Bruno Mondadori, 2001.
Boni, Donatella. *Discorsi dell'altro mondo: Nascita e metamorfosi del colloquio fantastico postumo*. Verona: Ombre Corte, 2019.
Branscome, Eva. *Hans Hollein and Postmodernism: Art and Architecture in Austria, 1958–1985*. London: Routledge, 2016.
Burdett, Richard. 'Italian Style: Latin Lesson', *Building Design*, 3 June 1983: 24–28.
Calvino, Italo. *Le città invisibili*. Turin: Einaudi, 1972.
Canella, Guido and Maurizio Meriggi, eds. *SA Sovremmennaja Arkhitektura 1926–1930*. Bari: Dedalo, 2007.
Canella, Guido and Aldo Rossi 'Architettura e realismo', unpublished, winter 1955, Aldo Rossi Papers, Getty Research Institute, box 9, folder 151.
Caruzzo, Letizia. 'La rivolta di Aldo Rossi e Guido Canella', accessed 9 September 2021, https://www.doppiozero.com/materiali/la-rivolta-di-aldo-rossi-e-guido-canella.
Casciato, Maristella. 'The Italian Mosaic: The Architect as Historian', *Journal of the Society of Architectural Historians* 62(1), (March 2003): 92–101.

Casciato, Maristella, 'Quarante années de publications en architecture: Officina edizioni, un éditeur italien et ses auteurs', in *Le livre et l'architect*. Brussels: Mardaga, 2011.
Cavallari, Alberto. 'Milano non riesce a trovare il suo vero volto culturale', *Corriere della Sera*, 27 July 1964.
Cavallini, Massimo. 'Il magistero della speculazione', *L'Unità*, 29 December 1972: 3.
Chavardès, Benjamin, 'La photographie critique au service d'une critique opératoire dans l'œuvre de Paolo Portoghesi', *Livraisons de l'histoire de l'architecture* 31 (2016): 23–37.
Chavardès, Benjamin, 'Bruno Zevi e Paolo Portoghesi: I "fratelli nemici" della critica operativa', in *Bruno Zevi e la didattica dell'architettura*, eds. Piero Ostilio Rossi, with Francesca Romana Castelli, Luca Porqueddu, Gianpaola Spirito. Macerata: Quodlibet, 2019: 241.
Chavardès, Benjamin, 'From Neoliberty to Postmodernism', in *Post-war Architecture between Italy and the UK: Exchanges and Transcultural Influences*, eds. Lorenzo Ciccarelli and Clare Melhuish. London: UCL Press, 2021: 57–69.
Chavardès, Benjamin, *L'Italie post-moderne: Paolo Portoghesi, architecte, théoricien, historien*. Rennes: Presses Universitaires Rennes, 2022.
Ciccarelli, Lorenzo and Clare Melhuish. *Post-war Architecture between Italy and the UK: Exchanges and Transcultural Influences*. London: UCL Press, 2021.
Ciucci, Giorgio and Francesco Dal Co. *Architettura italiana del '900*. Milan: Electa, 1990.
Cohen, Jean-Louis. *La coupure entre architectes et intellectuels, ou les enseignements de l'Italophilie*. Paris: Éditions Ardaga, 1984.
Colarizi, Sara. 'La trasformazione della leadership. Il PSI di Craxi (1976-1981)', in *Gli anni Ottanta come storia*, eds. Simona Colarizi, Piero Craveri, Silvio Pons and Gaetano Quagliarello. Soveria Mannelli: Rubettino, 2004.
Colomina, Beatriz. *Privacy and Publicity: Modern Architecture as Mass Media*. Cambridge: MIT Press, 1996.
Colomina, Beatriz. 'With, or Without You: The Ghosts of Modern Architecture', in *Modern Women*, eds. Cornelia Butler, Alexandra Schwartz. New York: The Museum of Modern Art, 2010.
Conforto, Cina, Gabriele De Giorgi, Alessandra Muntoni, Marcello Pazzaglini eds. *Il dibattito architettonico in italia 1945-1975*. Rome: Bulzoni 1977.
Conti, Paolo. 'Ho ricevuto minacce di morte per la Moschea di Roma', *Corriere della Sera*, 17 February 2018.
Conti, Paolo. 'L'architetto: Credo ancora nel Socialismo, ma Craxi sbagliò', *Corriere della Sera*, 18 February 2018.
Costanzo, Denise R. '"I Will Try My Best to Make It Worth It": Robert Venturi's Road to Rome', *Journal of Architectural Education* 70(2), (2016): 269–83.
Craxi, Bettino. 'Per l'avvio del governo della "non sfiducia"', in *Discorsi parlamentari: 1969-1993*, ed., Gennaro Acquaviva. Rome-Bari: Laterza, 2007, 11–24.
Crespi, Alberto. 'Il successo di un modo nuovo di fare politica', *L'Unità*, 18 September 1984.
Dal Col, Fabrizio. 'Presto o Tardi', in *Paolo Portoghesi: Disegni 1949-2003*. Milan: Federico Motta, 2003, 6–16.
D'amato Guerrieri, Claudio. *Controspazio* as a 'Little Magazine', accessed 2 November 2021, https://www.famagazine.it/index.php/famagazine/article/view/84/676#_ftn5.
Dario, Fertilio. 'Portoghesi se ne va', *Corriere della Sera*, 23 October 1976: 8.
Daufresne, Jean-Claude. *Fête à Paris au XXe siècle: Architectures éphémères de 1919 à 1989*. Paris: Mardaga, 2001.

De Bortoli, Ferruccio. 'No alla dittatura della parola, si alla letteratura del dissenso', *Corriere della Sera*, 4 March 1978: 5.

De Bortoli, Ferruccio. 'I nuovi milanesi che contano nel PSI', *Corriere della Sera*, 12 April 1978: 4.

De Carli, Marcello. '1967–1968: La strana sperimentazione della Facoltà di Architettura del Politecnico di Milano', 15 February 2014, accessed 22 June 2021 http://www.paisia.eu/wp-content/uploads/2014/07/La-strana-sperimentazione-140220.pdf.

De Seta, Cesare. 'Tanti bei progetti fuori dalla realtà', *Corriere della Sera*, 7 August 1985.

Desideri, Paola. *Il potere della parola: Il linguaggio politico di Bettino Craxi*. Venice: Marsilio, 1987.

Dombroski Robert and Ross Miller. 'Postmodern Rhetoric: Calvino's "Le città invisibili" and Architecture', in 'Italy 1991: The Modern and the Postmodern', special issue, *Annali d'Italianistica* 9 (1991): 230–41.

Dorazio, Piero. 'Se i partiti rinunciassero a lottizzare', *Corriere della Sera*, 6 September 1987.

Dorfles, Gillo. 'Nel design italiano molti anticipatori', *Corriere della Sera*, 26 June 1983: 12.

Drexler, Arthur. *Transformations in Modern Architecture*. New York: MoMA, 1979.

Dulio, Roberto. *Introduzione a Bruno Zevi*. Milan: Laterza, 2008.

Dulio, Roberto. 'Le affinità elettive. Moretti e Zevi', in Bruno Reichlin, L. Tedeschi eds. *Luigi Moretti, razionalismo e trasgressività tra barocco e informale*, Milan: Electa, 2010: 437–41.

Durbiano, Giovanni. *I Nuovi Maestri: Architettura tra politica e cultura nel dopoguerra*. Venice: Marsilio, 2000.

Eco, Umberto. 'Le mie prigioni', *L'Espresso*, 20 June 1973: 10.

Ennis, Thomas W. 'Geometry Scholar Designs Villas that Stirs Up Architectural Debate', *New York Times*, 30 August 1964.

Escudero, David. 'Beyond Filmmaking: Searching for a Neorealist Architecture in Italy, 194X–195X', *The Journal of Architecture* 24(4), (2019): 441–68.

Escudero, David. *Neorealist Architecture Aesthetics of Dwelling in Postwar Italy*. London: Routledge, 2022.

Fabbrini, Sebastiano. *The State of Architecture: Aldo Rossi and the Tools of Internationalization*. Padua: Il Poligrafo, 2020.

Fasanella, Giovanni. 'Quei nemici per la pelle', *L'Unità*, 3 May 1987: 12.

Fausch, Deborah. 'Robert Venturi's and Paolo Portoghesi's Photographs of Rome', *Daidalos* 66 (1997): 76–83.

Fava, Federica. *Estate Romana: Tempi e pratiche della città effimera*. Macerata: Quod Libet, 2017.

Foot, John. 'From Boomtown to Bribesville: The Images of the City, Milan, 1980–97', *Urban History* 26(3), (December 1999): 393–412.

Forty, Adrian. *Words and Buildings: A Vocabulary of Modern Architecture*. London: Thames and Hudson, 2000.

Fossati, Paolo. *Il design in Italia, 1945–1972*. Turin: Einaudi, 1972.

Franchini, Alberto. 'L'Istituto Universitario di Architettura di Venezia come università produttiva', eds. Piero Ostilio Rossi, with Francesca Romana Castelli, Luca Porqueddu, Gianpaola Spirito. *Bruno Zevi e la didattica dell'architettura*. Macerata: Quodlibet, 2019: 143–54.

Gandolfi, Carlo, 'Controspazio', in *Architettura del Novecento: Teorie, scuole, e eventi*, eds. Marco Biraghi and Alberto Ferlenga, vol. 1. Turin: Einaudi, 2012: 246–50.

Gervasoni, Marco. 'L'impossibile intesa: Craxi, Berlinguer e il PCI', in *Bettino Craxi: Il riformismo e la sinistra italiana*, ed. Andrea Spiri. Venice: Marsilio, 2014.

Ghirardo, Diane. *Italy: Modern Architectures in History*. London: Reaktion Books, 2013.
Ghirardo, Diane. *Aldo Rossi and the Spirit of Architecture*. New Haven/London: Yale University Press, 2019.
Ginsborg, Paul. *Storia dell'Italia dal dopoguerra ad oggi*. Turin: Einaudi, 1989.
Ginsborg, Paul. *L'Italia del tempo presente: Famiglia, società civile, Stato 1980–1996*. Turin: Einaudi, 1998.
Ginsborg, Paul. *Italy and its Discontents: Family, Civil Society, State 1980–2001*. London: Penguin Books, 2001.
Goldoni, Luca. 'I Giacobini dietro la scrivania', *Corriere della Sera*, 3 February 1971: 8.
Gottardo, Francesca ed. *Paolo Portoghesi Architect*. Rome: Gangemi 2008.
Gregotti, Vittorio. 'Il disprezzo della qualità', *Casabella* 617 (1994): 2–5.
Guido, Luca. 'The Biennale of Dissent 1977', *Art + Media Journal* 12 (2017): 17–28.
Gullo, Tano. 'Filippo Panseca: Così inventai il garofano per il mio amico Bettino Craxi', *La Repubblica*, 1 June 2015.
Halland-Rashidi, Ingrid. '(Re)working the Past, (Dis)playing the Future. Italy: New Domestic Landscape at MoMA, 1972', in *Proceedings of DRS2016 International Conference: Future-Focused Thinking*, 27–30 June, Brighton, UK, Design Research Society.
Hays, K. Michael, ed. *Architecture Theory Since 1968*. Cambridge, MA: The MIT Press, 1998.
Hunt, Tiffany Lyn. 'Michelangelo in 1964: The Critical Model as Dialectical Image in Bruno Zevi's Renaissance Architecture', *Architectural Theory Review*, 24 (2), (2020): 144–63.
Huyssen, Andreas. 'Mapping the Postmodern', *New German Critique* 33, Modernity and Postmodernity (Autumn, 1984): 5–52.
Ianari, Vittorio. 'L'Italia e il Medio Oriente: Dal "neoatlantismo" al *peace-keeping*', in *L'Italia Repubblicana nella crisi degli anni settanta: Tra guerra fredda e distensione*, eds. Agostino Giovagnoli and Silvio Pons. Soveria Mannelli: Rubbettino Editore, 2003, 383–95.
Iop, Toni. 'Paolo Portoghesi nuovo presidente della Biennale', *L'Unità*, 12 March 1983: 6.
Jameson, Fredric. *Postmodernism, or The Cultural Logic of Late Capitalism*. Durham, NC: Duke University Press, 1991.
Jarzombek, Mark. 'Italy: Modern Architectures in History by Diane Ghirardo', Review *Journal of the Society of Architectural Historians* 73(3), (September 2014): 421–23.
Jencks, Charles. 'The Rise of Postmodern Architectures', *Architectural Association Quarterly* 7(4), (October–December 1975): 3–14.
Jencks, Charles. *The Language of Post-Modern Architecture*. London: Academy Editions, 1977.
Jencks, Charles. 'Postmodern and Late Modern: The Essential Definitions', *Chicago Review* 35(4), (1987): 31–58.
Jencks, Charles. *The Story of Postmodernism*. London: Wiley, 2011.
Kries, Mateo, Jochen Eisenbrand, Catharine Rossi and Nina Serulus, eds. *Night Fever: Designing Club Culture: 1960–Today*. Basel: Vitra Design Museum, 2018.
Labalestra, Antonio. 'La cultura comunista e la formazione del nuovo architetto negli anni Sessanta', *Quaderni di Architettura e Design*, Politecnico di Bari, no. 2, 2019: 53–73.
Lampugnani, Rossana. 'Vittoriano condannato, con la condizionale', *L'Unità*, 28 January 1986: 15.
Laurenzi, Laura, 'Io Panseca l'artista orfano del garofano'. *La Repubblica*, 11 August 1993.
Leach, Andrew. *Manfredo Tafuri: Choosing History*. Ghent: A&S Books, 2007.

Leach, Andrew. 'Modern Architecture and the Actualisation of History: Bruno Zevi and Michelangiolo Architetto', in *History in Practice*, 25th International Conference of the Society of Architectural Historians Australia and New Zealand, Geelong, 2008: 1–19, accessed 22 June 2021, http://hdl.handle.net/10072/40066.

Levy, Aaron and William Menking. *Architecture on Display: On the History of the Venice Biennale of Architecture*. London: AA Publications, 2010.

Lo Ricco, Gabriella and Silvia Micheli, '1963–74: Cronologia', in *La Rivoluzione Culturale: La Facoltà di Architettura del Politecnico di Milano 1963–64*, Milan, Facoltà Di Architettura Civile, 23 November–16 December 2009, 6–18, accessed 22 November 2022, http://www.gizmoweb.org/wp-content/uploads/2009/10/la-rivoluzione-culturale-catalogo-bassa-protetto.pdf.

López Segura, Manuel. 'Seeking to Salvage Italian Democracy: Architectural Inflections of Political Compromise at the Estate Romana, 1977–1985', in *Architecture and Democracy 1965–1989: Urban Renewal, Populism and the Welfare State*, Proceeding, Sixth Annual Conference Jaap Bakema Center, November 2019: 31–40.

Luzi, Gianluca. 'La festa dell'Unità apre i battenti tornando a Roma dopo 10 anni'. *La Repubblica*, 26 August 1984.

Lyotard, Jean-François. *The Postmodern Condition*. Minneapolis: University of Minnesota Press, 1984 (1979).

Martini, Fabio. *Controvento. La vera storia di Bettino Craxi*. Soveria Mannelli: Rubettino, 2020.

Massobrio, Giovanna, ed. *Lo Studiolo di Francesco I dei Medici e il suo doppio*. Rome: Apollodoro Edizioni, 1986.

Massobrio, Giovanna and Paolo Portoghesi. *La seggiola di Vienna: Storia dei mobili in legno curvato*. Turin: Martano, 1975.

Massobrio, Giovanna and Paolo Portoghesi. *Album del Liberty*. Rome-Bari: Laterza, 1975.

Massobrio, Giovanna and Paolo Portoghesi. *Album degli anni Venti*. Rome-Bari: Laterza, 1976.

Massobrio, Giovanna and Paolo Portoghesi. *Album degli anni Cinquanta*. Rome-Bari: Laterza, 1977.

Massobrio, Giovanna and Paolo Portoghesi. *Album degli anni Trenta*. Rome-Bari: Laterza, 1978.

Massobrio, Giovanna and Paolo Portoghesi. *La donna Liberty*. Rome-Bari: Laterza, 1983.

Massobrio, Giovanna, Maria Ercadi, and Stefania Tuzi, eds. *Paolo Portoghesi Architetto*. Rome: Gangemi, 2001.

Mastrigli, Gabriele. 'The Cage of Imagination: Notes on "Roma Interrotta"', *Log* 32 (Fall 2014): 140–47.

McLeod, Mary. 'Architecture and Politics in the Reagan Era: From Postmodernism to Deconstructivism', *Assemblage* 8 (February 1989): 22–59.

McLeod, Mary. 'Frampton in Frame', *Architecture Today*, accessed 24 January 2022, https://architecturetoday.co.uk/frampton-in-frame/.

Meli, Maria Teresa. 'Martelli: "Io e De Michelis in competizione. Ma lui era sempre più preparato degli esperti"', *Corriere della Sera*, 11 May 2019.

Mendini, Alessandro. 'Colloquio con Paolo Portoghesi', *Domus* 652 (July 1984): 1.

Micacchi, Dario. 'Aperta la Biennale', *L'Unità*, 16 November 1977: 3.

Micheli, Silvia. 'Between History and Design: The Baroque Legacy in the Work of Paolo Portoghesi', in *The Baroque in Architectural Culture 1880–1980*, eds. Andrew Leach, John Macarthur and Maarten Delbeke (Surrey–Burlington: Ashgate, 2015): 195–210.

Micheli, Silvia. 'Alessandro Mendini, *Domus* and the Postmodern Vision (1979–1985)' in *Mediating Messages: On the Role of Exhibitions and Periodicals in Shaping Postmodern*

Architecture, eds. Véronique Patteeuw and Léa-Catherine Szacka. London: Bloomsbury, 2018: 115–33.
Micheli, Silvia and Lorenzo Ciccarelli, 'The International Call: Italian Design Culture, Politics and Economics at the 1972 MoMA Exhibition and Beyond', in *Italian Imprints*, eds. Denise Costanzo and Andrew Leach. London: Bloomsbury, 2022: 522–53.
Micheli, Silvia and John Macarthur, eds. *Italy/Australia: Postmodern Architecture in Translation*. Melbourne: URO, 2018.
Micheli, Silvia and Léa-Catherine Szacka, 'Paolo's Triangolo', *AA Files* 72 (2016): 98–106.
Micheli, Silvia and Léa-Catherine Szacka, 'Paolo Portoghesi and the Postmodern Project', in *Re-Framing Identities: Architecture's Turn to History, 1970–1990*, eds. Ákos Moravánszky and Torsten Lange. Basel: Birkäuser: 2017, 209–19.
Migayrou, Frédéric ed., *La Tendenza: Architectures Italiennes 1965–1985*. Paris, France: Centre Pompidou, 2012.
Minervino, Fiorella. 'E l'Islam ritorna a imporsi a Venezia', *Corriere della Sera*, 21 November 1982: 12.
Moneo, Rafael. 'Aldo Rossi: The Idea of Architecture and the Modena Cemetery', *Oppositions* 5 (1976): 1–21.
Monestiroli, Antonio. *L'architettura della realtà*. Milan: CLUP, 1979.
Monica, Luca, ed. *La critica operativa e l'architettura*. Milan: UNICOPLI, 2002.
Moschini, Francesco. *Paolo Portoghesi: Progetti e Disegni/Projects and Drawings 1949–1979*. New York: Rizzoli International Publications, 1979.
Mosco, Valerio Paolo. *Architettura italiana. Dal postmoderno ad oggi*. Milan: Skira, 2017.
Mosco, Valerio Paolo. *Viaggio in Italia. Architetture e città*. Santarcangelo di Romagna: Maggioli, 2021.
Nicolin, Pierluigi. *Notizie sullo stato dell'architettura italiana*. Turin: Bollati Boringhieri, 1994.
Nicolin, Pierluigi. 'Looking at Tangentopoli', *Lotus* 82 (1994): 106.
Norberg-Schulz, Christian. 'Casa Baldi, Rome', *ByggeKunst* 8 (1963): 205–11.
Norberg-Schulz, Christian. *Baroque Architecture (History of World Architecture)*. New York: Harry N. Abrams, 1971.
Norberg-Schulz, Christian. *Architettura Barocca*. Milan: Electa, 1971.
Norberg-Schulz, Christian. *Architettura Tardobarroca*. Milan, Electa, 1972.
Norberg-Schultz, Christian, ed. *Architetture di Paolo Portoghesi e Vittorio Gigliotti*. Rome: Officina Edizioni, 1982.
Norberg-Schulz, Christian. 'La "visione" di Paolo Portoghesi', in *Paolo Portoghesi*, ed., Mario Pisani. Rome: Gangemi, 1993: 53–59.
Nolan, Mary. *The Transatlantic Century: Europe and the United States 1890–2010*. Cambridge: Cambridge University Press, 2012.
Oppenheimer Dean, Andrea. *Bruno Zevi On Modern Architecture*. New York: Rizzoli, 1983.
Orazi, Manuel and Marco Vannucci, 'Architecture and Math', *Vesper* 5, Moby Dick: Adventures and Discoveries (Fall–Winter 2021): 24–38.
Orlandi, Giovanni and Paolo Portoghesi, eds. Leon Battista Alberti, *De re aedificatoria*. Milan: Il Polifilo, 1966.
Ornaghi, Nicolò and Francesco Zorzi, 'Filippo Panseca, l'architetto del PSI', accessed 8 March 2022, http://www.gizmoweb.org/2015/04/filippo-panseca-larchitetto-del-psi/.
Ornaghi, Nicolò. 'Nuovi clienti', 25 October 2015, accessed 8 March 2022, http://www.gizmoweb.org/2015/10/nuovi-clienti/.
Ostilio Rossi, Piero 'Le proposte di riforma del Biennio 1964–1965', in *Bruno Zevi e la didattica dell'architettura*, eds. Piero Ostilio Rossi, with Francesca Romana Castelli, Luca Porqueddu, Gianpaola Spirito. Macerata: Quodlibet, 2019: 189–207.

Otero-Pailos, Jorge. 'Photo[historio]graphy: Christian Norberg-Schulz's Demotion of Textual History', *Journal of the Society of Architectural Historians* 66(2), (2007): 220–41.

Otero-Pailos, Jorge. *Architecture's Historical Turn: Phenomenology and the Rise of the Postmodern*. Minneapolis: University of Minnesota Press, 2010.

Padellaro, Antonio. 'Che cosa cambia in queste elezioni: Le facce nuove del 20 Giugno', *Corriere della Sera*, 21 May 1976: 2.

Padoa Schioppa, Caterina. 'I diagrammi spaziali su Michelangelo', in *Bruno Zevi e la didattica dell'architettura*, eds. Piero Ostilio Rossi, with Francesca Romana Castelli, Luca Porqueddu, Gianpaola Spirito. Macerata: Quodlibet, 2019: 155–65.

Pasti, Daniela. 'Canta architetto la Gloria di Dio', *La Repubblica*, 21 November 1992.

Paulicelli, Eugenia. 'Fashioning Rome: Cinema, Fashion, and the Media in the Postwar Years.' *Annali d'Italianistica* 28 (2010): 257–78.

Perego, Francesco. 'L'architettura islamica in mostra alla Biennale', *Corriere della Sera*, 14 November 1982.

Pet, M. 'Portoghesi "La Mia Mosche"', *Corriere della Sera*, 5 July 1985.

Pettena, Gianni. *Effimero urbano e città: Le feste della Parigi rivoluzionari*. Venice: Marsilio, 1979.

Pigafetta, Giorgio. *Saverio Muratori, architetto: Teoria e progetti*. Venice: Marsilio, 1990.

Pisani, Mario. *Paolo Portoghesi: Opere e progetti*. Milan: Electa, 1992.

Piva, Antonio, Francesca Bonicalzi, Pierfranco Galliani, eds. *Architettura e Politica. Architecture and politics*. Rome: Gangemi, 2007.

Pivetta, Oreste. 'Architetti senza case', *L'Unità*, 4 August 1985: 15.

Pommer, Richard. 'Bernardo Vittone, un architetto tra illuminismo e rococò by Paolo Portoghesi', *The Art Bulletin* 53(1), (March 1971): 124–25.

Portoghesi, Paolo. 'Borromini in ferro', *Civiltà delle macchine* 2 (1953): 50–53

Portoghesi, Paolo. 'Dal mito allo standar', *Civiltà delle macchine* 4 (1953): 28–31.

Portoghesi, Paolo. *L'opera del Borromini per l'altare maggiore della Chiesa di San Paolo a Bologna*. Rome: Istituto Poligrafico dello Stato - Libreria dello Stato, 1954.

Portoghesi, Paolo. *Guarino Guarini: 1624–1683*. Milan: Electa, 1956.

Portoghesi, Paolo. 'Dal Neorealismo al Neoliberty', *Comunità* 65 (1958): 67.

Portoghesi, Paolo. 'Uno studioso inglese giudica l'architettura italiana', *Comunitá* 72, 1959.

Portoghesi, Paolo. *Borromini nella cultura europea*, Milan: Officina edizioni, 1964.

Portoghesi, Paolo, *Bernardo Vittone. Un architetto tra illuminismo e Rococò*. Rome: Edizioni dell'Elefante, 1966.

Portoghesi, Paolo. *Roma barocca*. Rome: estetti, 1966.

Portoghesi, Paolo. 'Casa Andreis a Scandriglia, Rieti', *L'Architettura: Cronache e Storia* 137 (1967): 706–19.

Portoghesi, Paolo. *Borromini: Architettura come linguaggio*. Milan: Electa, 1967.

Portoghesi, Paolo. 'An Unknown Portrait of Borromini.' *The Burlington Magazine* 109 (777), (1967): 709–708.

Portoghesi, Paolo, ed. *Dizionario enciclopedico di architettura e urbanismo*, 6 vols., Rome: Istituto Editoriale Romano, 1968.

Portoghesi, Paolo. 'Editoriale', *Controspazio* 1 (June 1969): 7.

Portoghesi, Paolo. 'Autopsia o vivisezione dell'architettura?', *Controspazio* 6 (1969): 5–7

Portoghesi, Paolo. 'Concorso per il Cimitero di San Cataldo a Modena: La città dei vivi e la città dei morti', *Controspazio* 10 (1972): 2–3.

Portoghesi, Paolo. *Le inibizioni dell'architettura moderna*. Rome-Bari: Laterza, 1974.

Portoghesi, Paolo. 'La Ricerca continua', *Controspazio* (December 1975): 7.

Portoghesi, Paolo. 'L'angelo della storia', *La storia dell'architettura. Problemi di metodo e di didattica*, conference proceedings, Istituto di storia dell'architettura. Università di Firenze, 1976: 33–47.
Portoghesi, Paolo. *Leggere l'architettura*. Rome: Newton Compton, 1981.
Portoghesi, Paolo. *After Modern Architecture*. New York: Rizzoli, 1982.
Portoghesi, Paolo. 'Dopo l'architettura postmoderna', in *Dopo l'architettura postmoderna*, conference proceedings, Bissano 4–5 September 1981, ed. L. Ferrario. Rome: Kappa, 1983: 17–23.
Portoghesi, Paolo. 'Il formato delle riviste di architettura', *Domus* 635, 1983: 2–11.
Portoghesi, Paolo. 'La moda del Postmodern', *Corriere della Sera*, 26 June 1983: 11.
Portoghesi, Paolo. 'Apparati per la Festa de l'Unità', *Epoca* 1173, 28 September 1984.
Portoghesi, Paolo. 'Le Luci del Paradiso Perduto', *I nuovi Architetti Italiani*, ed. Giovanna Massobrio. Rome-Bari: Laterza, 1985.
Portoghesi, Paolo. 'Per Leonardo Sinisgalli' in *Leonardo Sinisgalli. Promenades architecturales*, Bergamo: Pierluigi Lubrica, 1987: 5–12.
Portoghesi, Paolo. 'Apollodoro', *Eupalino* 8 (1987): 30.
Portoghesi, Paolo, interviewed by Renato Pallavicini, in 'La Mostra dei miei sogni', *L'Unità*, 17 September 1990: 21.
Portoghesi, Paolo. *Natura e Architettura*. Milan: Skira, 1999.
Portoghesi, Paolo. *Nature and Architecture*. Milan: Skira, 2000.
Portoghesi, Paolo. 'La possibilità del passato', *Casabella* 694 (2001): 91–92.
Portoghesi, Paolo. 'Il lievito della memoria', in *Dal Futurismo al futuro possibile dell'architettura contemporanea*, Milan: Skira, 2002, 70–81.
Portoghesi, Paolo. 'Sulla metodologia della storia dell'architettura', *Architektur weiterdenken*, Institute für Geschichte und Teorie der Architektur. Zurich, 2004: 12–17.
Portoghesi, Paolo. *Geoarchitettura: Verso un'architettura della responsabilità*. Milan: Skira, 2005.
Portoghesi, Paolo. 'Architecture and Revolution: Paolo Portoghesi in Conversation with Nicolo Ornaghi and Guido Tesio', *San Rocco* 66(14), (Spring 2018): 77.
Portoghesi, Paolo. *Roma/amoR: Memoria, Racconto, Speranza*. Venice: Marsilio, 2019.
Portoghesi, Paolo. *Poesia della Curva*, Rome: Gangemi, 2021.
Portoghesi, Paolo and Franco Borsi, *Victor Horta*, Rome: Edizioni del Tritone, 1969.
Portoghesi, Paolo and Giovanni Orlandi, eds. Leon Battista Alberti, *De Re Aedificatoria*. Milan: Il Polifilo, 1966.
Portoghesi, Paolo and Bruno Zevi, eds. *Michelangiolo architetto*. Turin: Einaudi, 1964.
Portoghesi, Paolo and Bruno Zevi. 'Is Postmodern Architecture Serious? Paolo Portoghesi and Bruno Zevi in Conversation', *Architectural Design* 52(1–2), (1982): 20–21.
Portoghesi, Paolo, Vincent Scully, Charles Jencks, and Christian Norberg-Schulz. *The Presence of the Past: First International Exhibition of Architecture – Venice Biennale 80*. London: Academy Edition, 1981.
Portoghesi Tuzi, Telemaco and Grazia Tuzi, *Quando si faceva la Costituzione*. Milan: Il Saggiatore, 2011.
Priori, Giancarlo ed. *Paolo Portoghesi*. Bologna: Zanichelli, 1985.
Purini, Franco. *La misura italiana dell'architettura*. Rome–Bari: Laterza, 2008.
Radice, Barbara, ed. *Elogio del banale/Praise of the Banal*. Turin–Milan: Lo studio forma-Alchimia, 1980.
Rebecchini, Giovanni. 'I Processi del Piper' in Mario Pisani ed., *Paolo Portoghesi*, Rome: Gangemi, 1993: 63–68.

Ribichini, Luca and Elena Tinacci, eds. *The Modernity of Borromini: A Lesson by Paolo Portoghesi*. Rome: ARE/MAXXI, 2021.
Ripa di Meana, Carlo and Gabriella Mecucci. *L'ordine di Mosca. Fermate la Biennale del dissenso*. Rome: Liberal, 2007.
Robey, David. 'Umberto Eco: Theory and Practice in the Analysis of the Media', in *Culture and Conflict in Post-war Italy: Essays on Mass and Popular Culture*, eds. Zygmunt G. Baranski and Robert Lumley. London: Macmillan, 1990: 160–177.
Roddolo, Enrica. *La Biennale: Arte, polemiche, scandali e storie in laguna*. Venice: Marsilio, 2003.
Rogers, Ernesto Nathan. *Esperienza dell'architettura*. Turin: Einaudi, 1958.
Rogers, Ernesto Nathan. 'L'evoluzione dell'architettura. Risposta al custode dei frigidaires', *Casabella-continuità* 228 (June 1959): 2–4.
Roscani, Roberto. 'I teatri della discordia', *L'Unità*, 3 July 1984: 9.
Rossi, Aldo. *Autobiografia scientifica*. Parma: Pratiche, 1990.
Rossi, Catharine. 'Architecture Goes Disco', *AA Files* 69 (2014): 138–45.
Sabini, Maurizio. *Ernesto Nathan Rogers: The Modern Architect as Public Intellectual*. London: Bloomsbury, 2021.
Sacchi, Livio. *Architettura e Identità Islamica*. Milan: Franco Angeli, 2015.
Savona, Anton Virgilio. *La Ballata di via Tibaldi*, 1973, accessed 15 June 2021, https://www.antiwarsongs.org/canzone.php?id=15843&lang=en.
Scabello, Sandro. 'I programmi formulati dai direttori della Biennale', *Corriere della Sera*, 18 February 1979.
Schulze, Franz. *Philip Johnson: Life and Work*. New York: A.A. Knopf, 1994.
Scolari, Massimo, 'The New Architecture and the Avant-Garde', in *Architecture Theory since 1968*, ed. K. Michael Hays. Cambridge: The MIT Press, 1998, 124–43.
Scott, Felicity. *Architecture or Techno-Utopia: Politics after Modernism*. Cambridge, MA: The MIT Press, 2010.
Scrivano, Paolo. 'Where Praxis and Theory Clash with Reality: *Controspazio* and the Italian Debate over Design, History and Ideology, 1969–1973' in *Revues d'architecture dans les années 1960 et 1970. Fragments d'une histoire événementielle, intellectuelle et matérielle/ Architectural Periodicals in the 1960s and 1970s: Towards a Factual, Intellectual and Material History*, eds. Alexis Sornin, Hélène Jannière and France Vanlaethem. Montréal: Institut de Recherche en Histoire de l'architecture, 2008.
Speroni, Donato. *L'intrigo saudita. La strana storia della maxitangente Eni-Petromin*. Castelvecchi: Cooper, 2009.
Sposito, Alberto ed, 'Stupor Mundi', in *La moschea di Roma*. Palermo: Alloro Editrice, 1993.
Sudjic, Deyan. *Edifice Complex: The Architecture of Power*. London: Penguin Books, 2011.
Szacka, Léa-Catherine. 'A Conversation with Vittorio Gregotti', *Log* 20 (Fall 2010): 39–43.
Szacka, Léa-Catherine. 'Roma Interrotta: Postmodern Rome as the Source of Fragmented Narratives', in *Rome, Postmodern Narratives of a Cityscape*, eds. Dominic Holdaway and Filippo Trentin. London: Pickering and Chatto, 2013: 155–69.
Szacka, Léa-Catherine. 'Debates on Display: Europa-America at the 1976 Biennale', in *Place and Displacement: Exhibiting Architecture*, eds. T. Arrhenius, M. Lending, W. Miller and J. McGowan. Zurich: Lars Müller, 2014: 97–112.
Szacka, Léa-Catherine. 'Criticism From Within: Kenneth Frampton and the Retreat from Postmodernism'. *OASE* 97 (2016): 109–20.
Szacka, Léa-Catherine. *Exhibiting the Postmodern: 1980 Venice Architecture Biennale*. Venice: Marsilio, 2016.

Szacka, Léa-Catherine. 'Città Analoga: Aldo Rossi's Visual Theory on Display', in *Terms of Appropriation: Modern Architecture and Global Exchange*, eds. Ana Miljački and Amanda Reeser Lawrence. London: Routledge, 2018: 263–77.
Szacka, Léa-Catherine. 'Le populisme de l'éphémère: Postmodernisme et scénographies urbaines en France et en Italie (1976–1989)' in *La fabrique des images: L'architecture à l'ère postmoderne*, ed. Federico Ferrari. Geneva: In Folio, 2018: 63–86.
Szacka, Léa-Catherine. 'Writing "from the Battlefield": Charles Jencks and The Language of Post-Modern Architecture', Jencks Foundation, accessed 26 January 2022, https://www.jencksfoundation.org/explore/text/writing-from-the-battlefield-charles-jencks-and-the-language-of-post-modern-architecture.
Szacka, Léa-Catherine and Luca Guido. 'The Biennale as Agent Provocateur for Democracy', vol. 41: *How to Build a Nation*, 2014: 22–28.
Tafuri, Manfredo, *L'architettura del Manierismo nel Cinquecento europeo*. Rome: Officina, 1966.
Tafuri, Manfredo. *Teorie e storia dell'architettura*. Bari: Laterza, 1968: 161.
Tafuri, Manfredo. *Il concorso per i nuovi uffici della Camera dei Deputati*. Rome: Edizioni universitarie italiane, 1968: 42.
Tafuri, Manfredo. 'Per una critica dell'ideologia architettonica', *Contropiano* 1 (1969): 31–79.
Tafuri, Manfredo. 'L'éphémère est éternel. Aldo Rossi a Venezia', *Domus* 602 (1980): 7–11.
Tafuri, Manfredo. *Storia delll'architettura italiana 1944–1985*. Turin: Einaudi, 1986.
Tafuri, Manfredo. *The Sphere and the Labyrinth: Avant-gardes and Architecture from Piranesi to the 1970s*. Cambridge, MA: MIT Press, 1987.
Tafuri, Manfredo. *History of Italian Architecture, 1944–1985*. Cambridge, MA: MIT Press, 1989.
Tafuri, Manfredo, P. Marconi and P. Portoghesi, et al., 'Il metodo di progettazione del Borromini', in *Studi sul Borromini. Atti del convegno promosso dall'Accademia nazionale di S. Luca*, eds. G. De Angelis d'Ossat. Rome: De Luca, 1967, vol. 2, 35–70.
Thomas, Helen, ed. *Architecture in Islamic Countries: Selections from the Catalogue for the Second International Exhibition of Architecture Venice 1982/83*, Zurich: gta Verlag, 2022.
Valéry, Paul, 'Eupalinos; ou, l'Architecte'. Paris: Gallimard, 1924.
Van Gerrewey, Christophe, Patteeuw, Véronique, & Avermaete, Tom. 'Action and Reaction in Architecture'. *Action and Reaction in Architecture*, OASE 97, 2016.
Vanucci, Marco. 'Paolo Portoghesi: The Field Theory', *Drawing Matter*, 9 November 2020, accessed 22 February 2022, https://drawingmatter.org/paolo-portoghesi-the-field-theory/.
Venturi, Robert. *Complexity and Contradiction in Architecture*. New York: The Museum of Modern Art, 1966.
Verga, Corrado. 'La mostra critica delle opere Borrominiane', *Arte Lombarda* 13(1), INDICI 1955–1967 (semester 1, 1968): 137–39.
Volpi, Alberto. 'Craxismo' in *Doppiozero*, accessed 26 September 2017, http://www.doppiozero.com/dossier/anniottanta/craxismo.
Willan, Philip. 'Bettino Craxi', *The Guardian*, 20 January 2000, accessed 26 September 2017, https://www.theguardian.com/news/2000/jan/20/guardianobituaries.philipwillan.
Wittkower, Rudolf, *Arte e architettura in Italia: 1600–1750*. Turin: Einaudi, 1972.
Zariski, Raphael. 'The Italian Socialist Party: A Case Study in Factional Conflict', *The American Political Science Review* 56(2), (June 1962): 372–90.

Zevi, Bruno. *Verso un'architettura organica*. Torino: Giulio Einaudi editore, 1945.
Zevi, Bruno. *Saper vedere l'architettura*. Torino: Einaudi, 1948.
Zevi, Bruno. *Storia dell'architettura moderna*. Torino: Einaudi, 1950.
Zevi, Bruno. *Towards an Organic Architecture*. London: Faber & Faber, 1950.
Zevi, Bruno. *Architecture as Space: How to Look at Architecture*. New York: Horizon Press, 1957.
Zevi, Bruno *Spazi dell'architettura moderna*. Torino: Einaudi, 1973.
Zevi, Bruno. *The Modern Language of Architecture*. Seattle: University of Washington Press, 1978.
Zevi, Bruno. *Zevi su Zevi: Architettura come profezia*. Venice: Marsilio, 1993.
Zevi, Bruno. *Erich Mendelsohn: The Complete Works*. Berlin: Birkhäuser Verlag, 1999.
Zevi, Bruno. 'Borromini today. In the 400th anniversary of his birth, 1599', *L'Architettura: Cronache e storia*, 519 (1999): 55.

* * *

'Aperta un'istruttoria per i fatti di via Tibaldi', *Corrierei della Sera*, 7 August 1971: 9.
'Appuntamenti', *Corriere della Sera*, 17 October 1987, 36.
Architettura nei paesi Islamici. Seconda mostra internazionale di architettura. Venice: La Biennale, 1982.
'Battaglia alla facoltà di architettura: Feriti venti agenti della polizia', *Corriere della Sera*, 7 June 1971: 4.
'Biennale: Il PSI candida Portoghesi alla presidenza', *Corriere della Sera*, 11 March 1993.
'Biennale, il PSI fa incetta di poltrone', *La Repubblica*, 16 October 1987.
'Braccio di ferro al Politecnico', *Corriere della Sera*, 4 June 1969: 8.
'Cominciati i lavori per la Moschea. Finanziamenti dal mondo arabo', *Corriere della Sera*, 28 June 1984: 27.
'Da oggi le celebrazioni del 400° di Michelangiolo', *L'Unità*, 18 February 1964: 3.
'Domus: Serata al Piper', *Domus* 652 (1984): 63.
'I disegni tecnici di Leonardo', *Civiltà delle macchine* 1 (1955): 6–24.
'I documenti della sperimentazione' in the 'Milano-Architettura' special issue dedicated to the Faculty of Milan between 1967 and 1973 in *Controspazio* 1: 44–48.
'Il lievito della memoria', in *Dal futurism al future possibile nell'architettura contemporanea*. Milan: Skira, 2002: 70–81.
'Il Piper 80 cambia ancora faccia', *L'Unità*, 11 January 1983: 10.
'La Biennale rischia il naufragio', *Corriere della Sera*, 16 December 1984.
'La DC: "Togliete il film di Scorsese"', *Corriere della Sera*, 30 July 1988.
La Civiltá Cattolica 145(1), journal 3451 (2 April 1994): 283.
'La facoltà negli ultimi vent'anni', *Corriere della Sera*, 11 November 1976: 13.
'Moschee. Quale si farà?', *Corriere della Sera*, 27 February 1976: 12.
'Nasce una rivista sulla città e la casa', *Corriere della Sera*, 16 January 1984.
'Per la Biennale incontro del PCI con il presidente', *L'Unità*, 23 July 1975: 7.
'Polemiche alla Biennale', *Corriere della Sera*, 11 November 1984.
'Polemico dibattito sulla Moschea a Monte Antenne', *Corriere della Sera*, 8 May 1979.
Processo all'altare della Patria. Atti del Processo al monument Vittorio Emanuele II. Rome – Milan: Mediocredito del Lazio, Libri Scheiwiller, 1987.
Roma Interrotta. Rome: Incontri Internazionali d'Arte/Officina edizioni, 1978.
'Sette milioni di dollari per la moschea di Roma', *Corriere della Sera*, 13 December 1974: 3.

'Si elegge il Preside', *Corriere della Sera*, 18 October 1968: 8.
'Un documento del PCI sulla crisi di Architettura', *Corriere della Sera*, 5 November 1976: 15.
'Un edificio problematico: Casa Baldi sull'ansa della Flaminia, a Roma, *architetto Paolo Portoghesi,* polemica con l'autore' *L'architettura cronache e storia* 86, Anno VIII, 8 December 1962: 510–21.

INDEX: PAOLO'S WORLD

Aalto, Hugo Alvar Henrik, 64, 67
Abbado, Claudio, 114
Accademia di San Luca, 24
Accasto, Gianni, 191
Achilli, Michele, xv, 10, 92
Ackerman, James Sloss, 40, 60
Al Abdullah, Rania, 149
Alberti, Leon Battista, 58
Albini, Franco, 56, 93, 94
Amato, Giuliano, 52
Ambasz, Emilio, 5, 37
Andreotti, Giulio, 120, 135, 137
Anselmi, Alessandro, 133
Apollodorus of Damascus, 50
Aragonne, 25
Architetti and Urbanisti Associati, (AUA) 39
Argan, Giulio Carlo, 26, 28, 49, 52, 60, 61, 65, 71, 73, 91, 118, 120, 163
Ascani, Maurizio, 133, 191
Asor Rosa, Alberto, 131
Aspesi, Natalia, 113
Assunto, Rosario 28
Aulenti, Gaetana 'Gae', 90, 91
Aymonino, Carlo, 31, 42, 90, 91, 110, 114, 115, 133

Baldi, Gian Vittorio, 76, 141
Banfi, Gianluigi, 61
Banham, Reyner, 62, 63, 80
Barbaro, Umberto, 17
Barbiano di Belgiojoso, Lodovico 93
Basilico, Gabriele, 135
Battisti, Cesare, 48
Battisti, Eugenio, 130

Baudo, Giuseppe 'Pippo', 157
Bauhaus, 41, 131, 168
Bazzoni, Luigi, 129
BBPR (office), 49, 61, 62
Bee Gees (music group), 135
Beeby, Thomas, H., 5
Beguinot, Corrado, 99
Behrens, Peter, 176
Benedetti, Sandro, 28
Benevolo, Leonardo, 39, 69
Benjamin, Walter Bendix Schönflies, 26
Berlage, Hendrik Petrus, 176
Berlusconi, Silvio, 7, 128
Bernasconi, Antonio, 130
Bernini, Gian Lorenzo, 75
Bertini, Aldo, 65
Bettini, Sergio, 65
Bilancioni, Guglielmo 'Billi', 10, 134, 137
Bofill, Ricardo, 116, 136, 138
Bonelli, Renato, 65
Bonfanti, Ezio, 29, 40, 95, 131, 161, 162
Bonito Oliva, Achille, 107, 136, 137
Bornigia, Giancarlo, 136
Borromini, Francesco, 4, 16, 17, 39, 48, 50, 55, 57, 60, 61, 63, 66, 67, 69, 70, 71, 72, 73, 74, 75, 76, 78, 80, 120, 128, 129, 130
Borsi, Franco, 28
Botta, Mario, 193
Bottoni, Piero, 92, 93, 94
Bouchet, Barbara, 146
Bramante, Donato, 50, 78
Bresson, Robert, 181
Brigidini, Daniele, 92
Bruschi, Arnaldo, 28
Buenos Aires, 134

Buonarroti, Michelangelo, 41, 58, 64, 65, 66, 72, 73
Burdett, Richard, 113

Cacciari, Massimo, 114, 131
Calcata, xiii, xv, 13, 45, 49, 156, 157, 158
Calvesi, Maurizio, 52, 86
Calvino, Italo, 74, 106
Camilleri, Andrea Calogero, 75
Canella, Guido, 29, 31, 90, 91, 92, 94, 97, 98
Cantafora, Arduino, 36
Capanna, Mario, 100
Caracciolo, Carlo, 190
Carassa, Francesco, 97
Casabella-continuità, 26, 29, 38, 57, 61, 62, 90, 91, 130, 170, 176
Cascavilla, Maurizio, 'Azio' 129, 141
Cavallari, Alberto, 91
Cellini, Francesco, 109, 115
Cervellati, Pier Luigi, 171
Cinecittà, 109, 126
Ciucci, Giorgio, 42
Civiltà delle macchine, 17, 64, 129, 130
Cocciante, Riccardo, 102
Coga, Raimondo, 191
Cohen, Jean-Louis, 6, 7, 42
Colomina, Beatriz, 48, 125
Conforti, Claudia, 137
Connors, Joseph James, 60
Contropiano. Materiali marxisti, 40, 131
Controspazio. Mensile di architettura e urbanistica, xii, xiii, 29, 30, 40, 57, 95, 129, 130, 131, 132, 133, 134, 135, 161, 162
Cortéz, Hércules, 123
Cossiga, Francesco, 53
Costanzo, Maurizio, 128
Craxi, Benedetto 'Bettino', xiii, 13, 42, 50, 89, 100, 101, 102, 104, 105, 106, 107, 109, 110, 111, 113, 115, 120, 135, 154
Crispolti, Enrico, 112
Crotti, Sergio, 48
Cuccuru, Benigno, 191

D'Amato Guerrieri, Claudio, 109, 133, 161, 162
D'Aronco, Raimondo, 194

Da Vinci, Leonardo, 58
Dal Co, Francesco, xv, 10, 42, 142
Dardi, Costantino, 136
DC (Democrazia Cristiana), 91, 113
De Bonis, Antonio, 134
De Carli, Carlo, 93, 94, 97
De Chirico, Giorgio, 87
De Feo, Vittorio, 173
De Mendoza, Alberto, 146, 147
De Michelis, Cesare, 113
De Michelis, Giovanni 'Gianni', 187
De Michelis, Marco, 42
De Pisis, Filippo, 87
De Seta, Cesare, 114
De Sica, Vittorio, 140
Deluigi, Mario, 64
Domus, 22, 24, 34, 35, 37, 129, 130, 135, 137, 168
Dorfles, Angelo Eugenio 'Gillo', 25, 60, 130
Dossetti, Giuseppe, 16
Drugman, Alfredo 'Fredi', 97
Duchamp, Henri-Robert-Marcel, 87

Eco, Umberto, 28, 74, 99, 126, 130
Eisenman, Peter, 31, 42
Ennis, Thomas, W., 80
Ercadi, Maria, 8
Epoca, xiii, 13
Ercolani, Gianpaolo, 191
Eronico, Egidio, 134
Estate Romana, 106, 185
Eupalino. Cultura della città e della casa, xii, xiii, 129, 134, 135, 137

Fanfani, Amintore, 16
Fasolo, Vincenzo, 38, 176
Fathy, Hassan, 116
Fehn, Sverre, 193
Fenech, Edwige, 146
Finzi, Bruno, 94
Fontana, Lucio, 64
Fonti, Daniela, 133, 191
Foster, Kurt, 193
Frampton, Kenneth, 46, 174
Franceschini, Dario, 149
Francesco I dei Medici, 52
Frankl, Wolfgang, 176
Fraticelli, Vanna, 191

Gabetti & Isola (office), 22
Gabetti, Roberto, 62
Garnier, Tony, 176
Gaudì, Antoni, 67, 78, 115
Galasso, Giuseppe, 112, 113
Galleria Apollodoro, 12, 48, 50, 128, 156
Gambetti, Giacomo, 111
Gardella, Ignazio, 22, 31, 56, 57, 63
Garnier, Tony, 176
Gassman, Vittorio, 107
Gehry, Frank Owen, 78
Gelmetti, Vittorio, 65
Genesis (music group), 136
Giancaro, Pia, 146
Giannini, Giancarlo, 123
Giedion, Sigfried, 43, 44, 60, 69
Gigliotti, Vittorio, xii, 45, 58, 64, 67, 81, 86, 118, 120, 123, 143, 145, 173, 188
Ginsborg, Paul, 101
Gioseffi, Decio, 65
Giurgola, Romaldo, 174
Goude, Jean-Paul, 106
Goya, Francisco José de, 87
Gramsci, Antonio Francesco, 91
Grassi, Giorgio, 26, 133, 176
GRAU (Gruppo Romano Architetti Urbanisti), 70
Graves, Michael, 37, 174
Gregotti, Vittorio, xv, 6, 10, 90, 111, 112, 113, 114, 117, 130, 190
Gresleri, Glauco, 171
Grumbach, Antoine, 174
Gruppo 63 (literary movement), 75, 126, 130
Guarini, Guarino, 4, 17, 60, 69, 70, 120
Guidoni, Enrico, 28

Hadid, Zaha, 155
Heidegger, Martin, 38, 43
Helg, Franca, 56, 174
Hentrup, Marlies, 193
Herlitzka, Roberto, 75
Heyers, Norbert, 193
Hoffmann, Josef, 52, 163
Holl, Steven, 193
Hollein, Hans, 6, 37, 116
Hong Kong, 134
Horta, Victor Pierre, 61, 71, 142, 143
Hudnut, Joseph F., 169

Il Marcatrè. Rivista di cultura contemporanea, 130, 191
Insolera, Italo, 28
Isola, Aimaro, 22, 62
Isozaki, Arata, 193
IUAV (Istituto Universitario Architettura Venezia), 31, 39, 42, 63, 64, 114, 115

Jameson, Fredric, 5, 154
Johnson, Philip Cortelyou, 5, 24, 57, 127, 152, 169, 190, 196

Kahn, Louis Isadore, 24, 78, 115, 131
King Faysal of Saudi Arabia, 117
Klotz, Heinrich, 5
Koening, Klaus, 137
Krier, Leon, 174
Krier, Robert, 174

L'Espresso, 128, 190
La Pira, Giorgio, 16
La Sapienza, xii, 17, 38, 39, 58, 64, 168, 176
Las Vegas, 135
La Tendenza (architecture group), 7, 29, 67, 132, 133
La voce comunista, 91
Labò, Mario, 177
Latour, Alessandra, 134
Le Corbusier, *pseudonym of* Charles Édouard Jeanneret, 48, 78, 80, 81, 115, 157, 176
Lenin, *pseudonym of* Vladimir Ilyich Ulyanov, 101
Leopardi, Giacomo, 38
Levi Montalcini, Paola, 81
Lonardi Buontempo, Graziella, 45
London, 46, 48, 193
Longo, Pietro, 89
Loos, Adolf, 176
Lotta Continua (extra-parliamentary organization), 98, 183
Luzi, Mario, 15
Lyotard, Jean-François, 25

Macleod, Mary, 105
Maki, Fumihiko, 193
Maldonado, Tomás, 112
Malgeri, Francesco, 28
Manzoni, Piero, 136

Maraini, Dacia, 181
Marcialis, Giuseppina, 90, 91
Martelli, Claudio, 113
Martino, Sergio, 145
Martinelli, Elisa Tia 'Elsa', 157
Masotti, Arnaldo, 94
Massobrio, Giovanna, xiii, xv, 8, 10, 13, 45, 48, 49, 50, 52, 53, 55, 89, 141, 156, 161, 162, 163, 174, 175, 193
Mastroianni, Marcello, 123, 190
Matia Bazar (music group), 137
Max Protetch Gallery, 37, 171
McLuhan, Herbert Marshall, 126
Meier, Richard, 155
Melograni, Carlo, 171
Memphis-Milano (office), 26, 105
Mendini, Alessandro, xv, 2, 6, 10, 22, 24, 26, 34, 35, 36, 37, 67, 135, 137, 168
Messina, Maria Grazia, 191
Michelucci, Giovanni, 56
Milan, 2, 22, 23, 24, 26, 29, 31, 35, 42, 43, 48, 58, 61, 92, 93, 98, 100, 102, 105, 107, 111, 113, 127, 130, 131, 133, 135, 161, 176, 193
Milo, Sandra, *pseudonym of* Salvatrice Elena Greco, 136
Mina, *pseudonym of* Anna Mazzini, 102
Minnelli, Liza, 169
Miraglia, Emilio, 145, 146
Misasi, Riccardo, 99
Mitterrand, François, 106
Modo, 135
Moneo, Rafael, 31, 142
Monestiroli, Antonio, 27, 31
Monroy, Antonio, 191
Monti, Guglielmo, 191
Moravia, Alberto, 45
Moretti, Furio, 175
Moretti, Luigi, 17, 57, 65, 130,
Morris, William, 52, 55
Moschini, Francesco, xv, 9, 10, 62, 67, 78
Motta, Lidia, 181
Mousawi, Sami, 118, 120, 188
Movimento studentesco (student group), 95
Muratori, Saverio, 17, 26, 62, 63

Nasseef, Abdallah Omar, 120
Navone, Paola, 35

Negri, Antonio, 131
Nervi, Pier Luigi, 120, 133
Nietzsche, Friedrich Wilhelm, 26
New York 31, 37, 43, 64, 134, 135, 152, 171, 174
Nicolin, Pierluigi, 2
Nicolini, Renato, 28, 91, 106, 127, 133, 141, 162, 183, 185, 191
Nolli, Giovanni Battista 'Giambattista', 45
Nono, Luigi, 114
Norberg-Schulz, Christian, xiii, 8, 28, 43, 44, 45, 46, 58, 69, 76, 81, 173, 175
Nouvel, Jean, 193

Oechslin, Werner, 28
Olbrich, Joseph Maria, 115
Olivetti, Adriano, 177, 190
Ontani, Luigi, 137

Pagliai, Ugo, 148
Pagni, Eros, 181
Pallottino, Massimo, 28
Pan, 134
Pane, Roberto, 65
Panseca, Filippo, 9, 106, 107, 109, 135, 186
Papadakis, Andreas, 48
Papanice, Edmondo, 149
Papanice, Pasquale, 143
Paris 106
Pasolini, Pier Paolo, 181
Patetta, Luciano, xv, 10, 27, 95, 131, 191
PCI (Partito Comunista Italiano), 90, 91, 92, 93, 95, 100, 101, 111, 113, 114, 155, 172, 186
Pellicani, Luciano, 185
Peressutti, Enrico, 61
Pertini, Alessandro 'Sandro', 101, 120
Petruccioli, Attilio, 115
Petruccioli, Sergio, 186
Pettena, Giovanni 'Gianni', 106
Pevsner, Nikolaus, 169
Piacentini, Marcello, 168
Piano, Renzo, 114
Picasso, Pablo Ruiz, 87
Pietilä, Raili, 116
Pietilä, Reima, 116
Pink Floyd (music group), 136
Piper (discotheque), 136, 137, 192

Piranesi, Giovanni Battista, 131
Polesello, Gianugo, 131
Politecnico di Milano, 1, 2, 7, 8, 10, 29, 30, 35, 39, 48, 92, 93, 94, 95, 97, 99, 100, 102, 111, 113, 127, 129, 130, 131, 133, 141, 170, 176
Ponti, Giovanni 'Gio', 34, 130, 133
Portoghesi, Bianca, 13
Portoghesi, Franco, 14
Portoghesi, Laura, 16
Portoghesi, Lucia, 14
Portoghesi, Pia, 16
Portoghesi, Virgilio, 13
Pouillon, Fernand, 115
PRI (Partito Radicale Italiano), 42, 155
Priori, Giancarlo, xv, 110, 134
Proudhon, Pierre-Joseph, 101
PSI (Partito Socialista Italiano), 2, 39, 42, 43, 50, 89, 90, 91, 92, 93, 94, 100, 101, 102, 104, 105, 106, 107, 109, 111, 112, 113, 115, 117, 129, 135, 154, 155, 172, 175, 185, 186
PSIUP (Partito Socialista Italiano di Unità Proletaria), 39
Puppa, Daniela, 35
Purini, Franco, xv, 102, 136, 186

Quaroni, Livio, 191
Quaroni, Ludovico, 17, 28, 38, 56, 62, 63, 162, 176
Quasimodo, Salvatore, 15
Quilici, Folco, 129
Quinti, Aldo, 38, 162, 194

Radice, Barbara, 34,
Raggi, Franco, xv, 10, 35
Rauschenberg, Robert, 136
Reagan, Ronald Wilson, 152, 154
Rebecchini, Giovanni, xv, 10, 136, 137,
Rebecchini, Giuseppe, 191
Reinhart, Fabio, 31
Restany, Pierre, 137
Ridolfi, Mario, 22, 56, 57, 62, 63, 78, 131, 176
Rietveld, Gerrit, 78,
Rigo, Mario, 90
Rilke, Rainer Maria, 44, 156
Rimbaud, Jean Nicolas Arthur, 38

Ripa di Meana, Carlo, 110, 111, 112, 113, 186
Ripa di Meana, Marina, 52
Risi, Nelo, 181
Rogers, Nathan Ernesto, 6, 22, 57, 61, 62, 63, 76, 90, 93, 131, 170, 176, 177
Roma Interrotta, 7, 45, 174
Rome xii, xiii, xv, 2, 3, 8, 9, 10, 12, 13, 14, 16, 17, 18, 23, 24, 26, 28, 38, 39, 41, 42, 43, 44, 45, 49, 50, 53, 55, 56, 58, 63, 64, 66, 76, 80, 86, 91, 94, 100, 102, 105, 106, 110, 111, 114, 116, 117, 118, 119, 120, 122, 123, 126, 127, 128, 133, 134, 136, 141, 143, 145, 146, 152, 154, 155, 156, 158, 161, 162, 163, 165, 166, 168, 174, 175, 185, 190, 194
Ronconi, Luca, 111
Roncoroni, Stefano, 128
Rondi, Gianluigi, 193
Rossi, Aldo, xii, xiii, 2, 6, 26, 28, 29, 30, 31, 32, 33, 34, 37, 41, 67, 90, 113, 114, 115, 124, 131, 133, 148, 149, 174, 176, 184, 192
Rossi, Vasco, 113
Rotterdam, 134
Rowe, Colin, 174
Rutelli, Francesco, 155

Sanguineti, Edoardo, 75, 130
Saragat, Giuseppe 28
Savio, Oscar, 64
Savona, Anton Virgilio, 99
Sartogo, Piero, 45, 174
Sartre, Jean-Paul Charles, 38
Scaparro, Maurizio, 31, 32, 41, 124
Scarpa, Carlo, 176
Schifano, Mario, 136
Schröder-Schräder, Truus, 78
Scola, Ettore, 123, 145
Scolari, Massimo, 95, 131, 132, 142, 191
Scorsese, Martin, 187
Scott Brown, Denise, 6, 46, 189
Scully, Vincent Joseph, 2, 24, 31, 46, 53, 175
Sedlmayr, Hans, 60
Sermonti, Vittorio, 181
Sinan, Mimar, 115, 120
Sinisgalli, Leonardo, 15, 17, 64, 129
Società, 91
Sottsass, Ettore, 26
Spadolini, Giovanni, 137, 187

Staderini, Duccio, 191
Steinberg, Leo, 60
Stern, Robert A. M., 3, 6, 46
Stirling, James, 142, 174, 193.
Strada Novissima, 4, 22, 33, 34, 35, 38, 41, 43, 45, 57, 64, 109, 115, 129, 141
Straub, Jean-Marie, 181
Strehler, Giorgio, 107
Studio Alchimia (design collective), 26, 34, 35, 67, 105

Tafuri, Manfredo, xii, xiii, 2, 6, 7, 24, 26, 28, 31, 37, 38, 39, 40, 41, 42, 58, 63, 69, 86, 90, 114, 115, 165, 192
Tassel, Émile, 142, 143
Thatcher, Margaret Hilda, 154
Terragni, Giuseppe, 78
The Grays (architecture group), 24
Thermes, Laura, 133, 186, 191
Tigerman, Stanley, 37
Tintori, Silvano, 176
Tornatore, Giuseppe, 141, 189
Trussardi, Nicola, 107
Tuzi, Stefania, 134

Ugolini, Marcello, 129
Ungaretti, Giuseppe, 15
Ungers, Oswald Mathias, 31, 193

Valéry, Paul, 134
Van de Velde, Henry, 176
Van der Rohe, Ludwig Mies, 56, 78
Valle, Gino, 31

Vanoni, Ornella, 107
Velázquez, Diego Rodríguez de Silva, 87
Venditti, Antonio 'Antonello', 154
Venice, 2, 23, 24, 26, 34, 35, 39, 41, 42, 50, 63, 89, 109, 114, 115, 140, 141, 142, 151
Venice Biennale, xii, xv, 2, 4, 11, 13, 19, 22, 34, 35, 41, 43, 45, 50, 56, 58, 86, 87, 89, 102, 109, 110, 111, 112, 113, 114, 115, 124, 127, 129, 133, 140, 141, 142, 151, 155
Venturi, Robert Charles, 6, 24, 37, 43, 46, 60, 80, 125, 174, 189
Ver Sacrum, 134, 163, 192
Vercelloni, Virgilio, 95, 131, 191
Viganò, Vittoriano, 48, 184
Vinca Masini, Lara, 190
Vitti, Monica, *pseudonym of* Maria Luisa Ceciarelli, 52, 123, 124, 145
Vittone, Bernardo, 60, 69, 120
Vogue, xiii, 13, 124

Warburg, Aby Moritz, 69
Warhol, Andy, 136
Watteau, Jean-Antoine, 87
Wigley, Mark, 152
Willan, Philip, 105
Wittkower, Rudolf, 60, 73
Wright, Frank Lloyd, 63, 67, 176

Zevi, Bruno, xiii, 2, 17, 22, 24, 26, 39, 41, 42, 57, 63, 64, 65, 66, 67, 69, 74, 81, 104, 116, 128, 129, 137, 155, 177, 190

www.ingramcontent.com/pod-product-compliance
Lightning Source LLC
Chambersburg PA
CBHW052107300426
44116CB00010B/1559